CRIMINAL THAT I AM

A Memoir

JENNIFER RIDHA

SCRIBNER

New York   London   Toronto   Sydney   New Delhi

Scribner
An Imprint of Simon & Schuster, Inc.
1230 Avenue of the Americas
New York, NY 10020

First Scribner hardcover edition May 2015

SCRIBNER and design are registered trademarks of The Gale Group, Inc.,
used under license by Simon & Schuster, Inc., the publisher of this work.

For information about special discounts for bulk purchases, please contact Simon &
Schuster Special Sales at 1-866-506-1949 or business@simonandschuster.com.

The Simon & Schuster Speakers Bureau can bring authors to your live event.
For more information or to book an event, contact the Simon & Schuster Speakers
Bureau at 1-866-248-3049 or visit our website at www.simonspeakers.com.

Manufactured in the United States of America

10 9 8 7 6 5 4 3 2 1

ISBN 978-1-4767-8572-1
ISBN 978-1-4767-8574-5 (ebook)

For my mother and my father: thank you for loving me anyway

"Alexei Alexandrovich," she said, looking up at him and not lowering her eyes under his gaze, directed at her hair, "I am a criminal woman, I am a bad woman, but I am the same as I said I was then, and I've come to tell you that I cannot change anything."

TOLSTOY, *ANNA KARENINA*

To know your own illness is the proper remedy.

RUMI

CONTENTS

AUTHOR'S NOTE

This book has been created from court filings, transcripts and dockets, e-mails, text messages, journals, notes, newspaper articles, and, more than anything else, my individual and necessarily imperfect recollections. Many of the names have been changed. I have omitted people and events where they are not integral to the story. With the sole exception of my co-conspirator, none of the people included or omitted had any knowledge or involvement in the illegal acts described in this book. No one I've known would ever do something so stupid.

CRIMINAL
THAT I AM

CHAPTER 1

Busted

I can fall asleep anywhere. Airports, movie theaters, bathroom stalls. Once during law school, seated in the gallery of an overcrowded courtroom during a murder trial I was supposed to be observing, I managed to curl into the fetal position, legs pulled to my chest, head pressed against the pew. I awoke only when I felt a crude poke to the shoulder and opened my eyes to see a court guard who had but six words for me: "Wake your ass up or leave."

I take my aptitude for sleep seriously, not only because of the pleasures it offers but also because of sleep's unparalleled ability to provide refuge from all waking hells. It therefore strikes me as odd in the wee hours of July 26, 2010, that I suddenly sit upright in bed, as though someone has just doused me with water. I look around my bedroom for the cause. There doesn't seem to be one: the clock indicates that the time is just shy of five in the morning, and even through my groggy disposition I can see that everything is accounted for, nothing is out of place. I am in a brief period between two jobs— one has concluded the week before, and the other does not begin for several more. Lacking obligations, I issue a personal sleep decree and go back to sleep.

An hour later, I hear my doorbell ring. Having already determined that there is no reason to be awake, I ignore it. Probably the mailman, I tell myself.

I suppose only moments pass before I hear the doorbell ring again. I don't stir. The doorbell rings again. And then again. Soon, the doorbell is being pressed in such rapid succession that its wail is now an uninterrupted siren from the front door.

Confused, and not a little annoyed, I slink out of bed and make my way to the living room. Once there, I realize that the cry of the doorbell is accompanied by a heavy pounding, one that causes the door to shake with each blow. This is not the mailman, I think.

No, even in my half-slumber, I know that this is clearly something much more ominous. I ask through the door, "Who is it, please?"

The pounding and ringing stop.

"It's the Department of Justice."

I wish I could say that I'm baffled as to the reason why the Department of Justice is at my doorstep. But I will venture that most people who are visited at an unconventional hour by law enforcement have a decent idea of why they are there. I do, at least. And so, when I hear these words through the door, I feel a heavy dread run through me.

I close my eyes and press my forehead against the door in the hopes I can possibly will their presence away. This doesn't work. After a moment I clear my throat and say, "Yes?"

"Open the door."

The man's request seems easy enough. I move my hand toward the knob, but before I turn it, a lawyerly thought passes through my brain.

"Why?" I ask.

There is a pause on the other side of the door. From the agent's silence, I deduce that this visit is not accompanied by a warrant, not one for my arrest nor one for the search of my home. This means that I don't have to open the door. I don't have to do anything at all.

The agent seems to follow my thought process. "Just open the door. I'm starting to wake up your neighbors."

Sure enough, I hear the chain and latch of the door of my elderly neighbor, Patrick, a sweet man in precarious health who always stops to ask me how I am doing. Even after today, he will not discuss what he sees this morning. When I run into him in the hallway, he will only ask me how I am doing. "I'm fine," I will tell him. "I'm just fine."

Now that poor Patrick is awake, and the agents are not going anywhere, the options are few. I take a deep breath. This is it, I think. This is where it all begins.

I open the door. I see the first of two federal agents, a burly white man in his late forties. He doesn't seem happy that I have made him wait at my door. Next to him is a black woman, whose age I will not guess, in a pantsuit and glasses. I later learn that she is not on my case but has accompanied Burly Man because of a Department of Justice policy requiring male agents to visit female suspects at home with a female agent in tow. This is a good policy. The expression on Burly Man's face frightens me. Lady Agent softens things up a bit.

Even though I know why they're here, I'm still in shock. I have stepped out of my body and am watching this exchange happen to someone else. The active part of my brain has been switched off; I have only at my disposal its default settings. I'm processing everything matter-of-factly, as though Burly Man is here to fix my cable, not to advise me of a criminal investigation that is being conducted in my honor.

Burly Man shows me his badge. I look at it in the hopes it provides some loophole about why he should not be standing in my foyer. I find no loophole. He places the badge back in a black leather case and then pulls from the inside pocket of his jacket a white envelope.

"I'm here to give you this letter," he says. "And I want you to read it right now."

I take the letter from his hand. My default settings are in charge. I don't have to read this right now, I think. And I don't want to read a letter whose contents I already know, especially not in front of Burly Man, who will probably be able to detect that I already know. I stare at the envelope, wondering if there is some way I can get out of this.

I look up at Burly Man. Read it, his eyes insist. Now.

I open the letter. It is a target letter. As I read, I imagine a faint bull's-eye appearing on my forehead.

The letter is written on stationery for the United States Attorney's Office for the Southern District of New York. The letter, addressed to me, states its method of delivery as "By Hand." The letter also says that I am a target of a federal investigation, that I should be aware that the

Office plans on presenting this investigation to a grand jury. Would I like to come in to meet with the prosecutor's office and say something for myself? Or would I prefer to be indicted? Sincerely, Some Prosecutor.

As I read the letter, I do not react to its contents. I am mindful that Burly Man is watching me closely. Lady Agent, on the other hand, appears to be somewhat disinterested. I see her looking around my apartment as though she is hoping something better will grab her attention.

I hand the letter back to Burly Man. "It's for you," he says, as though bestowing a gift. "Keep it."

"Okay," I say.

"Do you have anything you'd like to say about the letter?" he asks.

"If it's all right," I say, knowing full well that it is, "I'd prefer to speak to an attorney before I say anything."

Burly Man's face falls. I suspect that he's hoping that in my rude awakening I don't recall this most basic precept of criminal procedure, that I've never seen an episode of *Law & Order*. But I do, and I have.

"Well, now that you've said the word 'attorney' I can't ask you anything else about this." He is disappointed.

Yes, I think. That's why I said it.

"Can we still come in?" he asks.

Shit, I think. Shit, shit, shit. I've already mustered all of the energy I have for this encounter and can feel my shock beginning to fade into crude awareness. I want Burly Man and Lady Agent to go away so I can fall apart in peace. But I also don't think it would serve me well to push them away.

"Yes, of course," I hear myself say.

Burly Man takes a seat on the sofa in the living room. As he sits down, I notice a large diet root beer stain near his feet on the cream-colored rug. The stain has been there for quite some time, only addressed in previous weeks by my stepping over it. For a fleeting moment I hear my mother's voice admonishing me to always have my home ready for company. But I don't think she ever had this situation in mind, and to think about her at all in this moment is too much, and so I just say, "Sorry about the soda stain." And then, a terrible lie: "I didn't get a chance to clean it yesterday."

"No problem," Burly Man says.

Lady Agent doesn't sit down. She is casually making her way around my living room, eyeing its contents. Because I don't yet know that she is there only as a matter of protocol, I take her saunter around my apartment to be a casual collection of information about her suspect.

You have nothing to hide, I assure myself, although I wish I did not have my DVD collection of *The Wire* featured so prominently next to my television set.

Burly Man says that he does not want to ask me any questions that I would prefer to answer with a lawyer. But I can tell that he wants to know if I plan to admit or deny the allegations in the letter.

Burly Man names my co-conspirator. "You did represent him in his criminal case?"

It's common knowledge—a matter of public record, in fact—that I helped represent my co-conspirator in his legal case. Since Burly Man wants some kind of answer from me, to give him this one seems fairly harmless.

"Yes," I say. "I did."

"And you had a romantic relationship with him?"

I swallow. This is considerably less harmless. The answer is also yes, depending on one's definition of a romantic relationship, but something I've shared with virtually no one.

Lady Agent interrupts. She is considering the wall adjacent to my television set. "Did you take these?"

She is pointing to photographs of children in rural Ghana that I took on vacation years earlier. Though I don't understand how these could possibly relate to my crimes, hers is a decidedly easier question to answer.

"Yes, I did."

"They're beautiful pictures," she says, still studying them. I am puzzled, but flattered that Lady Agent thinks much of my photography.

Burly Man's face shows a flicker of annoyance. "I was asking you—"

I interrupt because I don't want to hear him repeat the question. "I guess I can tell you that," I say. "Yes." I add, because it's true, "After the case was over."

Burly Man seems satisfied to have gotten somewhere with me. "Well, I suppose that isn't against the law."

I glance over at Lady Agent. She is now examining my bookcase. She doesn't appear to be listening to my confession.

Burly Man is looking at me as though I should say something more. I know that he'll find out soon enough, so I gesture toward a small carry-on suitcase located near my front door. "Actually, I just got back last night from visiting him." It's not necessary for me to add that I visited him at a federal correctional facility, because this is the only place my co-conspirator can be visited.

"Yes," Burly Man says. "We know."

I feel a chill run up my spine. If Burly Man knows something as benign as this, he has been keeping very close track of me. He has possibly seen my credit card receipts; my flight records; he probably knows the name of the bed-and-breakfast I stayed at in the town where the correctional facility is located; he has almost certainly read my e-mails and has been listening to my phone conversations. He has perhaps looked at my bank accounts, my medical records, my comings and goings.

Over the coming months, I will learn that much of this is true. Now, sitting in my living room alongside two federal agents, only one fact resonates: not only does Burly Man know what I've done, he has also expended considerable resources in uncovering it.

The implications of what is happening swirl in my head. I forget that Burly Man is sitting on my sofa. "You seem very calm," he tells me.

I look at Burly Man but say nothing. On the inside, I am in emotional free fall.

Then, I hear this: "Oh, my goodness, is this your cat? She's adorable!"

Lady Agent has caught sight of my cat, a fluffy white Himalayan. She likes to climb on humans, particularly males, usually resting in and around their crotch region. I think it may have something to do with pheromones and warmth. I usually remember to warn men of her advances before they sit down. Today, however, this has slipped my mind.

While Burly Man and I have been discussing my imminent demise, my cat has made her way into the living room. She has summarily dismissed Lady Agent's overtures and is sauntering over to Burly Man with her eye on the prize.

I pull myself away from my inner turmoil. "I'm sorry. She's very friendly," I say as she rubs against Burly Man's legs. I don't tell Burly Man to watch his crotch, as this seems inappropriate.

"Actually, I like cats," Burly Man says as he reaches down to pet her. "I have two of my own."

Burly Man does not strike me as someone who would have cats. Dobermans, maybe, or a pair of cobras. But cats? All the same, I see that Burly Man has a small smile as he strokes my cat's back. She is elated at the display of affection.

I try to imagine Burly Man at his home with his cats, putting down cat food, cleaning up litter. They curl up with him while he watches TV and drinks a beer. He strokes the tops of their heads, they close their eyes with contentment. I have to leave early, he tells them this morning. I have to go bang on someone's door and wake her up and make her read a letter and ruin her life. I'll be home soon.

My cat has had enough foreplay and is ready to go all the way. I see her poised to jump on Burly Man's lap and quickly grab her. She's not taking this well and is squirming so she can get down and return to pursuing her target.

I can't take much more of this, so I stand up.

Burly Man stands up, too. Because he is at eye level, my cat stops squirming. "Well," he says not unkindly, "I will tell them at the office that you were cooperative with us."

It's an odd segue but I take it. I say what I think to be the magic words, or as much magic that can be conjured in such a hopeless situation. "Please tell them that as soon as I consult with an attorney, I will answer their questions."

This will keep Burly Man away from my door. It is also very likely my only way out.

Burly Man is visibly relieved to hear this. I have just made his life much easier. He throws me a bone. "Hopefully this can all be explained," he says.

I say nothing.

Burly Man and Lady Agent make their way to the door. The relief I thought I would feel at this moment does not come. Instead, I quickly realize that their departure marks what Churchill might have called—if

Churchill ever cared to describe this juncture of my criminal case—the end of the beginning. Now that prosecutors have made me aware of the investigation, I know that the next steps will likely be swift and harsh.

"Wait," I say.

They both turn around.

"Would it be possible to call my parents? I mean, without the call being recorded?"

I don't ask this out of any calculated legal strategy. I ask about being able to talk to my parents because it is all I want to do. Actually, to be more exact, all I want to do is go to my parents' house. Live there, so I no longer have a door for federal agents to pound. Be a child again, so I am able to avoid the series of poor decisions that have led me to this moment.

Lady Agent and Burly Man exchange looks. "Let's say, hypothetically, we are recording your calls," Burly Man says. "If we hear that you are speaking to your family, we know that call is not of interest to us."

"So you won't listen?"

I'm not certain, but I think I see a look of pity in Burly Man's eyes. "No, we won't listen."

And with that, the two federal agents are finished with me for the day. I watch them make their way to the elevator. Out of habit, I wave good-bye as though they are departing dinner guests. I wait for the sound of the elevator. Then I close my front door, sit down on the floor in front of it, and place my head in my hands.

When I finally lift my head, I have to squint to adjust to the daylight. The glare bathes my living room, as though even the sun has placed me under heightened scrutiny.

I know I can't sit here forever. I make my way to the desk where my telephone is located and sit down. Without dialing, I push my ear to the receiver in order to listen for any surveillance. I'm not sure what this would sound like. I decide I should just assume they are there.

I take a deep breath and dial my parents' number. Before it begins to ring, I realize that I have no idea of what I'm going to say. I hang up.

Have you ever had to call your parents to tell them that you are the target of a criminal investigation? If so, you know that this is a task that requires some forethought. The news will likely be disturbing. Also, it would be a mistake to tell them something that the government does not yet know. This would technically make them witnesses to my crime, a thought so terrifying that I consider whether I should call them at all.

I decide that I am too far gone where the government is concerned, that there is no sense in hiding anything from my parents. I make two small caveats. First, there is no reason to worry both of my parents. I will tell either my mom or my dad, but not both. Second, I will not give this parent the full story until after I have consulted with a lawyer.

The only decision that remains is which parent to tell. The issue is a complicated one given that my needs are contradictory. On the one hand, I am in need of a steady hand, one that is guided by common sense, to help me figure this out. On the other hand, I am in need of sympathy, of someone who might understand why I did the things I did.

Logic and common sense are qualities epitomized by my dad. A civil engineer by trade, he has spent a lifetime considering the science of structure, a pursuit made possible only through the avid use of rational thinking. My dad is a man who approaches every issue with an analysis that is as measured as it is detached, the type of person who not only reads the instruction manual that accompanies an electronic device, but enthusiastically highlights it for future reference. The type of person who keeps this manual in a clearly labeled file contained in an elaborate filing system located in the basement. The type of person who maintains a filing system containing four decades' worth of such documents with a level of order akin to that of the National Archives. The type of person who retains a file labeled "Children's Artwork." A file labeled "Greeting Cards." A file labeled "Blank Paper."

That my father leads with logic is probably a product of his upbringing. He was born in an old holy city ninety miles south of Baghdad in an era of Iraqi politics rendered unstable by unsavory influences. Regimes would come and go and then come back again, each time bringing a new set of uncertainties and fears. Nothing was predictable, until the Baathists took over, and then the only thing that was assured was misery. My dad has seen the very worst of what a lack of order can bring, and so it's my hypothesis that this is why he has dedicated himself to a life guided by reason.

I should mention that I have visited the city of my father's beginnings, yet was unable to picture him anywhere near it. The city has a rich religious history, but because reason and religion do not always mix, I can't imagine my father was much taken with this. The air was hazy with smoke wafting from open food stalls, the smell of spiced lamb ubiquitous. My dad invariably smells of Old Spice and refuses to eat anything out of paper or plastic. The dusty streets were teeming with local children running among religious pilgrims, their smiling faces smudged with dirt and their movements carefree. As a parent, my father admonished my siblings and me to sit still and implemented bath time as a non-negotiable demand.

My father's measured approach strikes me as appealing. But when I consider the other side of the coin, I hesitate. For while my father will probably have the most sensible answer as to what I should do next, he will never be able to understand why I did what I did. In my father's universe there is no justifiable reason to disobey the rules. If there is a good enough reason to break a rule, he often says, the rule would not exist in the first place.

How can one argue with this? What I learned over the course of my childhood is that one can't. I thus received no leniency in tenth grade when I was sent to the principal's office because I refused to throw away an apple I was illicitly eating during class. Already condemned by the school to a week of lunchtime detention, in facing my family tribunal I took the adamant position that there were starving people in the world, and to require me to waste a perfectly good apple was unjust, even immoral. My father, unmoved, grounded me for a month. When I protested that this harsh punishment was not unlike those meted out by the oppressive government he had fled, I bought myself an additional two weeks for cultural insensitivity and general smart-assedness.

Remembering my father's unwavering adherence to the rules makes me rethink bringing him into today's conversation. I shift my consideration to my mother. If "logic" is my father's guiding light, then "tradition" is my mother's. To my mom, there isn't any problem that cannot be solved by adhering to the time-tested standards of the ancients. Of these, she is very familiar. Raised in an elegant Baghdad neighborhood in a home that was a stone's throw from the Tigris, my mother was brought up in a sea of adages that can be traced back to the birth of civilization.

The most stringent of my mother's standards regard the conduct of women. A woman is supposed to act in a certain way. When we watched one of the preeminent women on *The Real Housewives of New Jersey* proclaim that "a wife should be a cook in the kitchen, a lady in the parlor, and a whore in the bedroom," my mother's eyes widened. "Listen to her," she ordered me. "This is very true." The conviction in her voice was so cringe-worthy that I was unable to finish my ice cream sandwich.

But even these qualities are not enough. Women must also be academically accomplished. My childhood was replete not only with admonishments to study but also the pervasive sense that I was never doing quite good enough. It was not uncommon for a ninety-six percent on a math test to be met with an inquiry as to the whereabouts of the remaining four percent.

In order to enforce her impossible standards, my mother ran a very tight ship. I am of the opinion that because she lived under Baathist rule longer than my father, she was better versed in its more effective methods of control. There were no individual rights in our household. My mother kept a mental list of all of our significant schoolwork so that she could interrogate us about completion. Personal choices of any kind were subject to her approval. Book bags were routinely inspected. Time in front of the television and on the telephone was regulated and monitored. The closest I have ever come to a fear-induced heart attack—and I include the aforementioned visit by the feds—was when my sister and I snuck out of the house and returned in the middle of the night to find our mother standing out front in her coat, waiting for our arrival. She was always one step ahead, making our efforts to live outside her lines futile.

My mother's traditionalist views make me hesitate again. After all, good girls do not break the law. And there is a romantic relationship mixed in with my case, something of which my mother will certainly not approve.

But I also think about the fact that, like most traditionalists, my mother is a sizable hypocrite. When I visited Baghdad for the first time, I learned that she was a very different daughter than what she expected me to be. She was uniformly described to me as someone with too many friends and social engagements, and with propensities not in academic achievement but in fashion and dance. Although her sisters pursued degrees in medicine and science, little mention was made of my mother's scholastic work ethic. I later discovered that this was because it mostly didn't exist.

When I learned of my mother's double standard, I thought about all of the times in childhood I had to account for missing percentage points. In a brief moment of postmodern thought, I resentfully pondered what kind of punishment my mother would have doled out on her younger self had she been a member of our household. I wondered, too, if her younger self might have served as an effective lookout that night when my sister and I tried to sneak back into the house.

Still, over time I've come to see that my mother's hypocrisy comes from a good place. Her role as parent-slash-dictator is likely an outgrowth of her belief that her children deserve more than what was made available to her. And for all of her insistence on perfection, she is a big believer in throwing caution to the wind. In a vivid memory from childhood, she permitted my brother and sister and me to convert her green metallic Buick Skylark into an imaginary General Lee, the iconic vehicle from *The Dukes of Hazard*, each of us hanging from its windows Bo-and-Luke-Duke-style while she drove us to the day care at her Jazzercise class. In my memory, with my torso extended and my arms outstretched, I felt as though I was flying. I remember looking at my mother in the driver's seat; she was intently observing the road, undisturbed by her children's whoops and hollers. My mother understands that there are times to set aside logic—and child-safety laws—and just be.

So while my mother talks tough, her heart is soft. Even in matters of criminal justice, she cannot bear the suffering of others. She takes the abstract position that crime must always be met with unfettered punishment, yet she will openly weep whenever she watches Sean Penn make the slow march to the death chamber in *Dead Man Walking*. When she served as a juror in a federal drug matter, she could not bring herself to find the young defendant guilty because she did not want to ruin his life. Though she will never say so, my mother believes that everyone deserves second chances, the benefit of the doubt, the presumption of being good.

It is this good place in my mother's heart, and her ability to see virtue where reason can't, where I believe my salvation can be found. She is the parent who wins the unfortunate prize. She will get why I did it, I think. She will understand.

I dial my parents' number. It's still early in the morning, but my father picks up after the first ring. As I expected, he is already preparing himself for the day.

"Hi, sweetheart!" he says. He does not express surprise that I am calling him so early on a weekday. He is possibly hoping that I have finally adopted the sleep schedule he has futilely encouraged since I was young. He does not know that were it not for my rude awakening by federal agents, I would still be asleep.

I ask if I can speak to my mom. "She's still sleeping," he says.

"Can you please wake her up?"

He pauses for a moment. "Is everything all right?"

"Yes," I lie. "I just wanted to tell her something and this is probably my only chance today to call."

I soon hear my mother's groggy voice on the line. "Hi," she says. I can tell that she is still supine, under the covers.

I'm not certain how to begin, so I start with the obvious. "Mom, some agents came to my door this morning."

"Some what?"

"Agents," I say. "From the Department of Justice."

"What are agents?"

"They're like the police," I say. I do not add: but they are much worse.

I hear my mother sit up. "The police? What do they want?"

"They said I broke the law."

My mother lets out a long exhale. "Well, that's ridiculous. There must be some mistake. Just tell them, Jennie, that they made a mistake. They'll sort it out."

Her relief is making this worse. I take a deep breath. "It's actually not a mistake," I say.

There is a long, painful pause.

"How can it not be a mistake?" And then, cautiously: "Did you do something wrong?"

"Yes," I say.

"What do you mean? What did you do?"

"I can't tell you," I say.

"What? Why can't you tell me?"

"Because I don't want anyone from the government to question you." I don't want to say it, but I have to. "Also, my phone might be tapped."

There is silence on the other line. My mother knows from tapped phones, having grown up under a paranoid dictatorship. Hers is a learned response, one that is based in fear.

"I think I really messed up." Saying this out loud causes all residual shock to dissolve. For the first time that morning, I begin to cry. And then, with a tone of self-pity that only a mother can indulge, I sputter through tears, "I think my whole life as I know it is pretty much over."

"Don't say that. Crying is not going to help now." And then, as I cry harder, she says: "No, no. You're a smart girl, a good girl."

This is a phrase my mother repeated to me in my most vulnerable moments in childhood. To hear her say it then made my troubles subside. To hear it now as a grown woman facing criminal charges is decidedly less comforting, possibly because in this moment it is the furthest thing from the truth.

"Mom," I say pathetically, "can you please come here?"

"To New York?"

"Yes," I say. "I want you to come here."

She agrees. She has one condition: "Please, don't tell your father about what happened," she warns. "He will be sick over it."

She's being literal; my father's worry usually manifests as physical ailments. Once, on a cruise vacation when he could not locate my brother and me—we had absconded to the boat's casino in the hopes of finding unclaimed tokens for the slot machines—his fear that we had fallen overboard made him so ill that we had to summon the ship's doctor.

But there is more to it: she is also sparing my father from what she is feeling now.

She seems eager to get off the phone. She tells me to let her know what I can, when I can, and that she will let me know when she is coming.

She is saying good-bye, and I interrupt. "Mom?" I say.

"Yes?"

"I'm so sorry. I promise to spend the rest of my life making this up to you."

She does not immediately respond. I hear a deep sigh. "No," she says.

It's not clear what she is saying no to, and I'm too afraid to ask.

When I get off the phone with my mother, I am not sure what to do with myself. That's the horrible thing about getting tangled with the law: there is everything to think about and nothing to be done. My shock has waned, and I let reality sink in.

I halfheartedly walk into my bedroom. I might as well get dressed, I think. As I rummage through my closet for something to wear, I catch a glimpse of myself in my full-length mirror and freeze.

I'm wearing my standard-issue nighttime clothing: a pair of ging-ham pajama pants and a cotton T-shirt. But what I failed to remember when I ran to the door this morning is that the night before, I had selected a T-shirt that was almost completely sheer. In the commotion of my morning, I've also failed to put on a bra. My breasts are entirely exposed.

I reflexively pull my arms around my body, as though somehow this will erase the fact that I have managed to flash two agents of the Department of Justice. I suppose that being consummate profession-als, neither Burly Man nor Lady Agent let their eyes linger on my chest. Or if they did, I was too distracted to notice it. I clutch my arms harder in the hopes that this will stop the cringing. It doesn't.

What I don't know as I stand essentially topless in front of my mir-ror is that this is a harbinger of things to come. Criminal cases have an inevitable voyeuristic streak. Personal details, even when they don't precisely bear on the relevant facts, always seem to rise to the surface. I've often wondered if this is an intentional prosecutorial tactic, confronting suspects with the sordid details of their personal lives to force them to acquiesce to the government's demands.

I've seen glimpses of this in practice, clients having to admit affairs or fetishes or narcotic proclivities. But now it's me who will be standing in the spotlight. This will seem harmless at first: I will be asked to identify my birthmarks, to provide my weight, to list any tattoos. My pharmaceutical records will be discussed. I will be asked questions about my family, my bank account, the places I have called home.

But over time, the exposure will extend to the most intimate parts of human existence, the spaces that one believes, or at least hopes, will never be public knowledge. E-mails of the romantic kind, both written and received, will be presented as evidence. I will be questioned about the location of kisses, both on earth and on my person. A prosecutor will advise a judge that I maintain that I did not have sex with my co-conspirator and that he is unable to prove otherwise. In an open courtroom, a defense attorney will ask about my vagina. My bra will become the stuff of newspaper headlines. On a message board for lawyers, men will hypothesize about my ability to perform fellatio. I will learn that in the realm of criminal justice, no corners of life are sacred. Everything is for the taking.

As I stand in front of my mirror, however, I know none of what's to come. Instead, I stare at my reflection, at the residues of my beauty regimen from the day before. My hair, perfectly coiffed for yesterday's prison visit, has been reduced to limp waves. My skin is tan from the sweltering summer. I notice smudges of mascara on the sides of my eyelids, faint traces of eyeliner underneath. My face looks as though it was once precisely drawn but then placed in a washing machine.

I gaze at it as though it belongs to someone else. This, I think to myself, is what a criminal looks like.

Without a clear memory of the remainder of the day, I'm later forced to piece together its events through documentary evidence. Taxi receipts and legal bills demonstrate that I meet with my attorney that same afternoon. I note that he is kind and thoughtful and does not appear to openly judge what is undoubtedly my disheveled state. I give him the letter from Burly Man and in painful detail explain exactly what I did and why. As most lawyers do, he speaks reassuringly, but I do not leave his office feeling reassured.

He advises me not to talk to my co-conspirator until this matter is resolved. He also asks me to print out all of my e-mails to him so he can read our exchanges for anything relevant. I know this drill well, but not from this end. I hate the thought of my attorney reading my private exchanges for evidentiary purposes.

Still, a credit card receipt will show that on my way home I stop at a drugstore to pick up a ream of printer paper in order to follow his directive. When I leave the store, I think I hear a man's voice calling me. Trying to avoid human interaction at all costs, I quicken my pace and look straight ahead until the voice fades into the cacophony of the street. When I return to my apartment, I realize that I've left the paper behind.

Home phone records for that day will show that on or around seven o'clock in the evening, my best friend calls me. She asks me about my day, and I report that federal agents came to my door and that I've been informed that I'm the target of a criminal investigation.

At first, she's silent. And then she says: "Damn, Jen, your life is never boring."

It is my first and only laugh of the day. Though I never discussed my crime with anyone—my co-conspirator and I have sworn each other to secrecy—it seems she has a sense of what I've done. She does know about my relationship with my co-conspirator and makes the immediate connection that he is somehow involved.

She is a good friend, and so she comforts me that everything will be fine when it most certainly won't. She says there is nothing to do but try to take my mind off of things. I promise her that I will try. She suggests that these circumstances are extreme enough for me to employ a method of relaxation involving a substance that is currently legal in most states only for medicinal purposes. I tell her that it seems unwise to risk racking up my charges, especially so early into my case.

She says she will call me tomorrow and is true to her word. She will call the next day, and then the next, and then virtually every day thereafter until the middle of winter, when I appear in court to account for my sins. On that day, I will speak to her by phone just before my appearance. In a comforting voice, she will assure me that it will all be over soon, that my life will be boring again. Even though she can't see me, and even though that does not end up being true, I will nod my head in relief.

Finally, U.S. Bureau of Prisons records will reveal that on or around eight o'clock in the evening, a call from one of its facilities is placed to my cellular telephone. The allowed duration of calls from this and any other federal correctional facility is exactly fifteen minutes, after which the line will automatically disconnect. The caller is announced in advance, and I'm required to declare my willingness to speak to him by pressing the number five. At five-minute intervals throughout the call, a female recording will remind me that I am a party to a call from a federal prison. The recording is not without judgment: her accusatory tone makes clear that she is addressing someone who has committed a crime or is cavorting with a criminal, or in my case, both.

The call surprises me. I assumed that he has also been confronted by federal authorities about what I did—what we did—and that he has likewise been instructed not to speak to me. When I hear his upbeat voice over the line, I realize that this isn't true.

"Did you have a good trip home?" he asks. He starts telling me a story about something that I don't quite register because I'm trying to figure out how to tell him that everything has fallen apart.

I finally blurt out, "I actually can't talk to you."

He is dumbfounded. "What? Why?"

"I can't tell you." Because the call is being recorded, I don't want to implicate him any more than he already is.

"What do you mean you can't tell me? What are you talking about?"

"I just can't tell you."

"Why can't you tell me?"

I try to think of a way to tell him without really telling him, but I can't. So I just say, "I thought maybe you already knew that I couldn't talk to you."

"What? How would I know that?"

The silence is eerie. If I listen hard enough, I think I can hear the shift in my life's trajectory, far away from what I had intended it to be.

To block the sound of silence, I fill my mind with questions. I wonder if this matter might go away. I consider worst-case scenarios. I imagine how I would fare as an inmate. I wince at the thought that inmates are required to use the restroom in the most public way possible. I wonder if it is physically possible to refrain from using the bathroom for the entire duration of a sentence. I believe that it is not.

I consider the irony—and hypocrisy—in the fact that in a matter of weeks I am supposed to begin teaching criminal law. I wonder how I will approach my lecture about theories of punishment while possibly awaiting punishment of my own. I think about whether my conduct constitutes a literal teaching moment. I decide that it does not.

I think, too, about what a criminal record will mean for my future. I think about what I will do if I can no longer practice law or teach. I try to remember what I wanted to be before I decided to be what I am. I was so young when I chose a career in law that I think it was something fanciful, like becoming a mermaid or a princess. I think about sitting monarchies across the globe. I think about whether a prince would ever marry a putative princess with a criminal record. I conclude that he would not.

I consider whether I ever expected that my crimes would be discovered. I am certain that I did not.

I think about why I did not think about any of these things before I decided to commit my crimes.

I have no answer.

I lie this way for hours. At some point, I pull my face from the pillow. I squint my eyes and see that the sun is rising over the East River, filling the sky with light. It is already the next day, and my hell persists. There is no escape.

I don't know what to say. I feel my entire body begin t

"I want to know who said you can't talk to me." He is a

I hesitate. I don't know if answering would be saying too

"Jen, tell me who said you can't talk to me."

"My lawyer," I finally say. In acknowledging this—that I h

yer, that I have this lawyer because I've committed a crime,

crime is being pursued by law enforcement—the reality of the s

washes over me. For the second time today, I burst into tears th

devolve into long, self-pitying sobs.

He is stunned silent. After a moment, he says, "It's going to be

Jen. Everything is going to be okay."

He does not ask any more questions.

I suppress my sobs as best I can. We speak as two people mi

when they know they will be separated for an extensive period of tim

But this doesn't last long. I begin to cry again, so hard that I can n

longer form words.

"It's going to be okay," he tells me. "I promise it's going to be okay."

He says it over and over again, as though this might make it true. I

cry even harder, knowing that it won't.

We continue in this manner until the phone abruptly cuts out. Fif-

teen minutes have passed. Our time is up.

There are no further records for the remainder of the day. At some

point, I realize that the sooner I go to sleep, the sooner this day is over.

I decide to reinstate the sleep decree I issued earlier.

The drastic difference in my life from the time of the sleep decree

to this moment is not lost on me. Everything that concerned me then

has been rendered irrelevant. The people I've known, the plans that I've

made for myself are now all things that once were. I try to picture what

happens next. I see nothing.

I dress for bed—in an opaque T-shirt this time, just in case—and

fall into the mattress face-first, my arms splayed, like I used to do as

a child. With my face buried in the pillow, I wait for sleep to come. I

listen for the usual bustle from the street that serves as my lullaby. I

hear nothing.

CHAPTER 2

Meet My Co-Conspirator

Allow me to introduce you to my co-conspirator. His name is Cameron Douglas.

He was arrested in New York City in July 2009 on a non-violent drug offense—distribution of methamphetamine, commonly known as crystal meth—that subjects him to a mandatory minimum sentence of ten years.

In certain ways, Cameron fits the statistical profile for many nonviolent drug offenders. But for his stint as a dealer, he has some, but not much, of a criminal history: a couple of petty misdemeanors. He has spent some time in juvie. Having been removed from private school, the high school he attended—a public high school in a working-class community in southern California—has poor graduation rates. Cameron is among those who failed to graduate with his class. And for most of his life he has been a drug addict, at the time of his arrest a severe heroin addict.

These are where the similarities end.

Cameron Douglas's father is a film actor. You may recall him from popular movies such as *Wall Street* and *Jewel of the Nile* or the critically acclaimed *Traffic*, in which he plays a government drug czar. But if you were a child of the 1980s, you perhaps know him better from a trilogy of sexually imbued movies, each of which is released at pivotal moments in your pubescent development: just prior to undergoing puberty (*Fatal*

Attraction), during the prime of your adolescence (*Basic Instinct*), and just after reaching adulthood (*Disclosure*). Perhaps in seeing these films—particularly *Fatal Attraction*, which predated your knowledge of anything sexual—you become somewhat scarred by the depiction of sexual intercourse as something leading seemingly inevitably to serial stalking and the boiling of bunnies. Maybe you also note that sex looks as though it involves a considerable amount of physical effort. You might even be left wondering if, when you grow up, you, too, will be required to exert such effort slammed against the wall of a loft elevator or straddled over a sink.

Possibly later, as a college student, you study this trilogy of sexy films in a women's studies class. You are taught that they epitomize Hollywood's misogynistic depiction of independent women. A visibly angry professor lectures that these portrayals send a subtle message that when women step out of their essential role, when their actions do not comport with convention, they are no longer worthy of the audience's sympathy.

This assessment doesn't make you think particularly highly of Cameron Douglas's father. Nor do the quotes attributed to him in the required reading for the course, Susan Faludi's *Backlash: The Undeclared War Against American Women*, in which Cameron Douglas's father announces he is "sick" of feminists and that "[g]uys are going through a terrible crisis right now because of women's unreasonable demands."

This quote perhaps leaves you with the impression that Cameron Douglas's father is kind of disgusting. Over time the thought fades, although whenever you encounter his image you note that there is something not quite right about him, but you can't remember what it is.

You only bother to search for the answer when you find yourself representing his son in his criminal case. By then, you are relieved to find that the chauvinist themes evinced in his films do not appear to be easily attributable to Cameron Douglas's father himself. In fact, his avid interest in the well-being of his son is enough to make all of your prior impressions fade, even the impact of his more graphic love scenes on your burgeoning sexuality.

Cameron Douglas doesn't only have a famous father who has starred in sexy films, but also a grandfather who is an old-fashioned film legend. With two generations of famous men preceding him, Cameron is often described with words like "scion," "heir," and "descendant."

You might come to wonder if Cameron's famous lineage helps to explain the DEA's avid interest in his case. This certainly could explain why so many resources were expended on uncovering drug dealing that was short-lived and, by the time of Cameron's arrest, long over. This might also explain why one DEA agent assigned to the case went to such lengths to make Cameron his friend, initiating "bro" talk, conspicuously pointing out attractive women to Cameron as he was dragged through the courthouse in handcuffs.

You possibly find it interesting—ironic, even—that Cameron has been made subject to the same calculated focus by law enforcement that is usually reserved for populations of lower-income communities, that fame has offset the advantages he would otherwise enjoy as someone of his socioeconomic status in the criminal justice system.

I do. I often tell Cameron that I bet that if he had been some run-of-the-mill pill pusher in a well-to-do neighborhood, none of this would have ever happened.

But he isn't. And it did.

I first encounter Cameron Douglas as part of his legal team in October 2009. He had been arrested several months earlier, but his family decided to supplement his defense team, which now includes me.

We meet in one of the attorney rooms of Manhattan's Metropolitan Correctional Center, MCC, the maximum-security prison where Cameron is residing. When he enters, I see that his handsome exterior is rough. When he approaches his seat, his walk is so swaggered that it presents as a limp. He is tall and broad, but his jumpsuit is so oversized that his body seems to drown in it. The few exposed body parts emerging from it are blanketed in tattoos. The most prominent of these appear on his forearms in large print. In actuality, these read "TICK" and "TOCK," an homage to the preciousness of time. But the execution of the Old English lettering is sloppy, particularly the letter "T," and so when I catch sight of his arms I misread them to say "DICK" and "COCK."

His hardened appearance turns out to be somewhat of a red herring. He is exceedingly well mannered, using "sir" and "pardon" at every turn. Throughout our meeting, as his case is laid out for him, his facial expressions often resemble those of a bewildered child. He blushes easily, his cheeks seeped with red when he elaborates on his crimes or doesn't understand what is being said, or, oddly enough, when I offer him my business card.

"Let me know if you need anything," I tell him as I hand it over.

Although there are several attorneys in the room, in my memory of this meeting there is really only Cameron. I observe him as though he is an exotic creature trapped in a cage, different from anyone I've ever encountered. I take note of the way he leans in his chair, folds his arms, grips his pen. I spot the manner in which he considers a thought, tipping his head to one side as though the substance of what is being discussed slides from one ear to the other. Even when he catches sight of my survey, I record his reaction, the smile of his eyes, the sheepishness of his grin. To the naked eye, his mannerisms appear to be masculine but also childlike, alluring but also endearing.

I am rapt as he recounts the facts surrounding his crimes, how he would package drugs inside stereo equipment for safe shipment or would fill a container of bath salts with crystal meth. He describes his use of a burner phone to surreptitiously complete drug transactions in the same manner as one might give directions to the train station. As I listen to him talk, I have a sense that I should probably be appalled; instead, I am closer to mesmerized.

We don't speak much in this first meeting. At one point the remainder of the legal team steps out of the attorney room, leaving us to stare blankly at each other. I am without words, too overwhelmed to think of anything to say. He, too, appears to be at a loss. The moment is so awkward that we simultaneously burst into nervous laughter.

This is the moment, he will later say, that first bonds us together. This is when the proverbial deal is sealed.

But I don't remember it this way. I am too struck by Cameron to form any kind of bond. Later that day, when I review my notes of our meeting, I discover that they are a jumbled mess. In my distraction, I have not bothered to see any of my sentences to their end. After assessing the damage, I decide there is no use in trying to re-create them. I already seem to realize that representing Cameron Douglas is not something I will soon forget.

I'm unable to reconcile what I see in my client with what I presume of his fancy lineage. There isn't much of it that can be explained other than to say that Cameron Douglas is a young man of paradox.

Contradictions surround every aspect of his person. While he comes from unimaginable means, he has not experienced some of the most basic trappings of middle-class existence. Acting is his birthright, but he has never seen a play. He has lived in residences reserved for the highest echelons of society, but also in shabby hotels and on friends' couches. He has traveled the globe, but has spent as much time locked in a room with a needle in his arm.

He suffers from an untreated learning disability, one that is so severe that I find it more efficient to read everything to him. Yet he possesses an instinct for human behavior that allows him to see through any ruse, even the stock lines that sophisticated clients usually accept without question.

He is both prince and scourge, at once loved and hated. I observe the alternating adoration and contempt that is piled upon him by MCC's illustrious staff of corrections officers. On his prison unit, he is so well received that some inmates gratuitously prepare his food, buy him gifts. But others display ire at his presence, rendering him familiar with physical altercation. Prior to his arrest, he was chronically surrounded by a gaggle of adoring women, and yet when he is required to provide an inventory of his physical scars, almost all of these can be attributed to instances of female rage.

It's only the most obvious contradiction about Cameron, that the talented product of a prominent Hollywood family would ever turn to a career in drug dealing, that in the end is probably not a contradiction at all. After all, Cameron's struggles with drugs accorded him extensive experience in the drug trade, and as with any industry research, he had unparalleled knowledge of the players and the products. Thus, when his family gave him an ultimatum to either get clean or go it alone, he defiantly chose a career path in what he knows best.

But I suspect that even this doesn't fully explain why Cameron turned to a life of crime. I privately wonder whether walking away from the family business and into the dicey field of drug trafficking allowed Cameron to demonstrate a perverse but rare fortitude among men. That by traversing the line between celebrity and notoriety, in making real what could only be imagined by his Hollywood family, Cameron managed to step out of an otherwise endless shadow.

Once, when he speaks of reviving his acting career, I joke that it's probably best that Cameron go into his dad's business rather than the other way around.

He doesn't laugh. "My dad could never do what I did," he tells me. I'm not certain, but his tone seems to be one of pride.

And so in the end, it might be Cameron's crimes that make the most sense about him. In this way, Cameron and I present as opposites. My history is void of conundrums, my unfulfilling path up until our meeting the stuff of rigorous rules and copious planning. It is my crime that will present the greatest contradiction of my life, one that try as I might, I cannot seem to reconcile.

In our second meeting, Cameron displays the qualities of what is sometimes called a "difficult client." As soon as he arrives in the attorney room, even before he takes his seat, he is yelling at everyone in the room.

"Where the hell have you been?" he demands.

The legal team has not seen him in a week. He is not angry because he has missed us. He's angry because while he is incarcerated, the only way information can be securely passed to him is in person. Our absence has left him with the feeling that his case is proceeding without him.

Though I am caught off guard by the change in his demeanor, I don't experience the silent resentment I usually do when someone is yelling at me. Instead, as with a crying child, I want only to make it stop. I see in his face exasperation more than anger, and so during a pause in his tirade, I tell him that we understand why he is upset and promise to visit him with more frequency.

At this, he begins to calm. We proceed with our meeting, during which questions are met with answers. As we get ready to leave, I tell him I'll be back in a couple of days to discuss the latest update, and every few days thereafter.

Once he sees his needs are being met, he is contrite. "I'm sorry," he says. "I shouldn't have yelled."

"It's all right." I stand up to leave.

He stands up, too. "It's just . . . I'm having a bad day." He points downward. "Some of the guys wanted to do me a favor by fixing my jumpsuit. But look."

I examine the cuffs of his jumpsuit. Something indeed looks off.

He explains: some well-meaning members of the Gambino crime family noticed that the pant legs of his oversized jumpsuit tended to drag across the floor. In a gesture of kindness, they arranged for their "tailor"—apparently another inmate who is adept at sewing—to adjust the hems to a more appropriate length.

The problem is that the trimmed pant legs make the oversized jumpsuit look misshapen. This is not helped by the fact that, presumably due to a limited thread selection, the brown hems are sewn in white. It's as subtle as the stitching on a baseball.

"I look ridiculous," he says.

He does. I'm not sure what to say, so I try to point out the positive. "The stitching is really even," I say.

I'm not just trying to make him feel better. The Gambino family has landed a plum tailor, one whose stitches are so precise in size and tension that the hem looks sewn by machine. But I do understand Cameron's complaint. I'm able to evaluate the quality of the stitching only because I can see it from where I am standing.

He doesn't care much about the quality of the stitching. "It's just so obvious." He looks down again and frowns.

Because his face is crestfallen, I find it appropriate to offer him a small white lie. "It really doesn't look that bad," I say.

He's not particularly convinced, but becomes aware that he is complaining about something as silly as his outfit. "Yeah, it's no big deal," he says.

He shrugs it off, but I am unsettled by his discomfort. After I leave

him in the attorney room to make my way back to the office, after I
leave the office for home, even after I'm lying in bed in anticipation of
what the next day will bring, I find myself thinking about those hems.

T wo days after this exchange is when I believe that the deal between
Cameron and me is actually sealed. This is not because I have an epiph-
any about his case or even because we see something in each other that
silently suggests our compatibility as co-conspirators. It's because I fix
his jumpsuit.

The idea strikes me as I am leaving my apartment to go to MCC. We
are planning to conduct a client history—an accounting of everything
he's done leading up to the present moment—and as the low lawyer on
the totem pole, it falls to me to take detailed notes. Just before I run out
the door, I rummage through my desk to find a pen. My eye happens
upon a set of Sharpie markers, and an idea pops into my head. I grab
one and throw it in my purse.

When I arrive at the prison, I present my legal pad and Sharpie
marker for inspection and sign into the attorney log. The corrections
officer on duty looks on in annoyance as the Sharpie's ink bleeds
through several sheets of paper when I enter my name and time of visit.
With a heavy sigh, he lets me through.

Cameron is already seated in the attorney room when I arrive. I
announce that I have brought him something.

His face bears a look of misery. "Thank you very much," he says with
disinterest. He doesn't bother asking what it is.

I present the Sharpie to him, but he is unimpressed. "Thanks, but I
can't take that back to my unit," he says.

"Yes, I know," I say. I push the marker toward him. "I thought you
could use it to color in the stitching on your jumpsuit."

He considers this for a moment and looks at the marker apprehen-
sively.

"See?" I say as I remove the lid. "It's almost the same shade of brown.
If you color in the stitching, it will just blend in with the fabric."

He thinks about this and then shrugs his shoulders. He takes the
marker, and then leans over to apply it to the white thread.

I'm leaned over as well, watching him color as though he is perform-ing a complex surgical procedure. Just as I had hoped, when he makes his way around his ankle, the stitching seems to vanish.

We are both still leaned over when he looks up from his handiwork. He rewards my efforts with a small smile.

"Thank you," he says. "It looks better."

I am relieved. "See? We take good care of you." I smile, too.

"You do," he says.

Making my difficult client happy is enough of an accomplishment that I don't mind that I now have to take several hours' worth of notes in thick brown marker.

This seemingly innocuous transaction is one that in hindsight pro-vides a road map of what's to come. I've just demonstrated to my client that his extralegal needs are my concern. That I am comfortable going beyond what is expected. That I am willing to push the rules of confine-ment in order to put things right.

I don't know it yet, but these are the crucial ingredients that will make up my own criminal case. Tending to Cameron's hems is the very first step in my criminal journey. It is only a matter of time for the others to unfold.

I find it difficult to gauge how Cameron is really faring at MCC. The brief glimpses he provides of life in confinement seem to depict two separate worlds. When he describes prison society as one where each inmate supplies and demands the skills required by the circumstances (cooking/washing/fixing) and describes the establishment of a local currency (canned tuna), he makes life on his prison unit sound like a capitalist enterprise out of *Wealth of Nations*.

But then other times he will share stories of inmate behavior that is more consistent with *Lord of the Flies*. "Fighting" in prison appears to often reach the legal definition of attempted murder. In one graphic story, an inmate on his unit used a makeshift shiv hidden under his mattress to slit another inmate's neck from ear to ear. When I ask what happened to the attacker, Cameron thinks I am asking about the victim and explains that he had to get more than a hundred stitches to close up his neck.

"No, what about the guy who cut him?" I ask.

"They sent him to the SHU, I think." The Special Housing Unit is where inmates are kept in solitary confinement.

"Is he coming back to the unit?"

He shrugs. "I don't know. Maybe."

I am conscious not to appear worried for Cameron, but I am. He is very possibly MCC's most conspicuous resident. But that's not all: I'm concerned because in order to avoid a lengthy mandatory minimum sentence, Cameron is serving as a government cooperator.

Cameron's agreement to cooperate with the government was made before I arrived on the case. From the outset, it's apparent to me that this was not a decision that Cameron made for himself, but one that was essentially made for him, albeit out of love, by his family. Cameron himself agonizes about the decision at every turn, not comfortable divulging sensitive information and not wanting to be known as a cooperator for the rest of his life.

Being a cooperator is not exactly a badge of honor. But where mandatory minimums create drug sentences that are longer than those for child pornographers and bank robbers, where cooperation can mean the difference between missing your toddler's first day of kindergarten and missing his graduation from high school, the decision seems almost a necessity. I tell him, too, that because most cases plead out before trial, cooperators rarely have to take the stand in open court. For many cooperators, I point out, no one will ever know.

Of course, the secrecy that surrounds cooperation has a downside as well: it breeds fanaticism among inmates intent on uncovering cooperators. In prison society, it seems any cooperator is anathema, and each inmate must be prepared to prove he isn't cooperating or else suffer very real consequences. When a cooperator in the Bernie Madoff case fails to provide satisfactory answers to such questions, he is physically punished to such an extent that he is transferred to a different facility the following day.

I find it surprising that anyone would care about a fifty-something cooperator in a case against a reviled Ponzi schemer. "Really?" I ask Cameron. "These guys are in solidarity with Madoff, even?"

"It doesn't matter who it is, Jen. In here, a snitch is a snitch." His face displays shame.

I'm concerned for Cameron's safety, but do not say so. Instead, I want to make him feel better. "Well, it sounds like that Madoff guy didn't know the right things to say," I tell him. "If you ever have to leave the unit and need an excuse for why you are gone, just tell me and I will give you an alibi."

This plan seems to provide some comfort, but not much. Cameron is far more interested in avoiding the issue altogether by securing bail. Still, in the coming weeks, I quietly observe in our conversations that he has seemingly implemented his own plan to protect against being discovered. First, he aligns himself with a close circle of friends on his unit, I suspect to subtly create a line of defense on the inside. Second, in having my word that I'll throw off the scent about his cooperation, he accords me a specialized status through which I am entrusted with preventing any leaks from happening on the outside.

I say nothing about either course of action. Both will be integral to my undoing.

As the case proceeds from the fall of 2009 into early winter, I stop by to see Cameron once or twice a week. These meetings are ostensibly to deliver case updates. But in reality they provide Cameron with a welcome change from his obvious presence on the unit. Early into the case, he tells me that the attorney room presents his only real opportunity to enter a space and close the door behind him. And while that door is made of glass, and while everyone who passes gawks at him through it, the attorney room still provides him with a respite that he can't otherwise find.

One evening, our meeting runs long enough that the corrections officer on duty comes to our door to announce that the facility is about to conduct a count of inmates. During the count, no movement is allowed in the facility. If Cameron does not return to his unit now, we have to remain in the attorney room until the count is cleared. The corrections officer wants to know if I intend to stay.

I look at my watch and shake my head. We've gone through everything of interest. But when I look at Cameron, he has a look of concern on his face.

"Did you want me to stay?" I ask.

He hesitates, and then provides an odd response. "It's up to you," he says.

It's perhaps the uncertain inflection in his voice or the faint color of crimson that flushes his cheeks, but the sentiment feels strangely personal. I notice that the corrections officer is standing over my shoulder, watching me as though he is waiting to see if I will say yes to going to the school dance.

I feel my own cheeks warm when I see both men waiting for my response. "You're the client, so it's really up to you," I say. "I can stay if you need me to."

"Okay, then stay."

"What's up?" I ask Cameron once the door is closed.

But nothing, in fact, seems to be up. He spends a few minutes asking questions we've already gone over, the answers to which he appeared to understand the first time around. He just wants to talk. We engage in some chitchat and then, with no real prodding, he begins to tell me stories about his life before he got arrested.

I feel like the one-woman audience to his one-man play, listening with rapt attention because I've never heard Cameron say so much at once. I am captivated by the version of Cameron that emerges from these stories. He is very different from the tough, tattooed client I encountered on my first day. Here is someone more inquisitive and kind, almost vulnerable. Maybe someone who has not yet given himself the chance to be the person he is meant to be.

I am possibly drawn to Cameron's stories for the additional reason that they transpire in a reality that is not plagued by the drudgery of my own. Cameron's way of life presents a radically different framework, that is to say, no framework at all. He exists entirely outside the lines, unhindered by obligation, free of expectation, motivated only by his own desires. As he describes his utterly irresponsible but absolutely alluring world, I can feel myself lean forward in my chair, as though he is literally pulling me in.

When the corrections officer arrives to announce that the count is over, I find that I am reluctant to gather my things. Once I do, I extend my hand to say good-bye.

He takes it and asks me in the voice not unlike that of a small child, "Can't you come here every day?"

I usually bristle at clients who demand a lot of personal attention. "I can't come every day," I tell him. But to my own surprise, I add, "But I promise I'll come as much as I can."

In the cab ride home, I ask myself why I am willing to make such a heavy promise. I tell myself that this client has special needs, that he is forced to harbor a potentially dangerous secret in a fishbowl. His wanting to remain in the relative privacy of the attorney room is understandable. As his attorney, I can provide him with a safe harbor, with refuge from reality.

But looking out the car window at the East River, I know that this is only partially true. There is something about being around Cameron that shakes me from what has become a bland, purposeless existence. Because he needs me, I feel needed. Perhaps my time with him is my own safe harbor. Maybe he is my refuge from reality, too.

I do deliver on my promise to visit Cameron as much as I can. As the case proceeds, the nonlegal portions of our conversations compose more and more of our time together.

These conversations often begin as jumping-off points from the case. Newly sober in every way, Cameron is eager to talk about the clean life he plans to lead once his case is over.

During these discussions, it occurs to me how rarely a conversation like this is uplifting. Due to his privileged circumstances, Cameron will likely avoid the usually impossible task of trying to secure a living in a postconviction reality, where drug offenders are presumed to be bad even when they are trying so hard to be good.

When I watch other inmates file into the attorney room lobby, I take the mostly dismal looks on their faces to mean they already know there is nothing good ahead. I am struck by one inmate in particular in his late teens, who is so slouched in his chair that he is almost supine. He does not make eye contact with his lawyer, but looks down at the ground as though it might hold better answers. The quiet resignation in his body language seems to concede that his young life is mostly over.

Remembering this sight, I can't help but point out to Cameron the preciousness of the second chance he will be allowed because of his family. "Don't blow it," I tell him. "Most of your friends on the unit will never get that chance."

Cameron's face indicates surprise, as though this is something he's never considered. He is quiet for a moment. "Well, I'm going to take care of them so that they have a fresh start, too," he says.

I don't bother pointing out the improbability that Cameron can personally solve the problems of the prison industrial complex. It's not his fault that the system is unfair, and though his offer is somewhat naïve, he obviously means to be kind.

Over time, our conversations become more personal. At first, this does not seem like anything unusual. Many clients show an interest in their attorneys' personal lives, probably because they are required to divulge so much about their own. But Cameron displays an almost anthropological interest in my background. Just as I am fascinated by his unconventional world, he romanticizes the idea of people with ordinary lives. He asks me questions about my family, my job, my travels. When I explain to him my mostly standard existence, he looks on with delighted interest as though he is watching the National Geographic Channel.

But the nature programming I provide Cameron is carefully edited. I don't mention that I've managed to establish a life that is void of any of the things that I wanted for myself, that somewhere along the way, I have managed to squander my blessings, that my sense of purpose has been unwittingly carried away.

Though I don't share this with Cameron, for some reason the loss is more palpable in his presence.

"Are you happy?" he once asks me.

"Of course," I reply. As I say it, I feel a lump at the back of my throat.

After a while, Cameron's questions begin to veer beyond the benign into the very personal. He asks about my relationship status, but when I tell him that I just ended a serious relationship, he does not consider the question fully answered.

"Why did you guys break up?"

I'm not expecting this. "Cameron, I am not going to tell you that."

"Why not?"

"Why would you even want to know that?"

"I don't know. Just curious."

"Well, be curious about something else."

"No, c'mon, Jen, look how much I told you."

"But that's so I can help you with your case!"

"Not all of it. I've told you a lot of personal stuff."

This is true. By this time, Cameron has regaled me with loads of stories, usually about his family, his run-ins with the law, and my personal favorite: endless entanglements with women. One woman breaks into his home, another cracks his skull. In my favorite vignette, a woman rubs Tabasco sauce into his eyes while he is sleeping. When Cameron recounts his way with women, I feel a pathetic sense of superiority in the way I do when I watch *Hoarders* or *The Biggest Loser*. I don't know yet that I will commit acts not much more sane than these.

But I still don't see this as ample reason for me to share something so personal. "Yes, but, Cameron, you offered all that up. I didn't ask you about it."

"Why won't you tell me? Is it bad?"

I'm at a loss for a reason, other than I don't want to. I don't want Cameron to know that I am still reeling from my breakup, that the entire thing was yet another failure to add to a growing pile, that I can't seem to figure out how to move on.

He looks at me intently, waiting for me to provide an answer.

"Cameron, I'm just not going to."

"So it's bad?"

I am exasperated at his relentlessness. "No, it's not bad. He just didn't want to have kids, and I did. Is your earth shattered now?"

As soon as I say it out loud, I wish that I hadn't. I should have made something up, like my ex-boyfriend was in the Russian mob. Or got hit by a bus. This feels far too personal, referencing my reproductive system, and now I'm seated before my client with cheeks warm from embarrassment.

Though my head is down, I can feel him looking at me. I think he might be smiling, but I'm too afraid to check.

I awkwardly change the subject. He allows the conversation to move back to more mundane matters. And then, mercifully, a corrections officer shows up to tell us to call it a day.

I can't gather my things quickly enough. I stand up, head down and hand extended, and tell him that I'll check back in a few days.

He takes my hand. "You know, Jen," he says in a voice laden with bravado, "I think you should know, I definitely want to have kids."

I look up at him, mortified. He has a twinkle in his eye.

What a charmer, I think to myself.

I force an eye roll. "Do lines like that ever actually work for you?"

The bravado remains. "All the time."

I shake my head and say, "I'll see you later, Cameron."

The exchange remains in my thoughts as I make my way out of MCC in pursuit of a cab home. When I flag one down and give the driver my address, he considers my face for a moment. "You have a nice smile, miss," he says. I am surprised. I don't realize that I am smiling.

I'm two months into the case, close to the Thanksgiving holiday, when I encounter Cameron's psychiatrist, an addiction specialist, in the lobby of MCC. He visits Cameron on a regular basis and is assisting the legal team with an assessment of Cameron's rehabilitation needs.

I approach him to introduce myself. "I know who you are," he says with a smile.

I am not quite sure what he means, so I simply smile back.

He asks about Cameron's bail, an issue that will impact his ability to receive drug treatment. I tell him that our plan is to make an application, but we are still trying to determine what kind of opposition there will be.

The psychiatrist is not particularly satisfied with this answer. "This is really a horrible environment for him."

I nod in agreement. "His situation makes him a sheep among some very rabid wolves."

"Isn't there a way for the government to protect him from that?" he asks.

"Not in a savory way. I think they can place him in the SHU, but he will have to be caged up, essentially. No calls with family. No real outdoor time."

"Cameron shouldn't go into solitary confinement," he says.

"I agree, it sounds awful."

"No, I mean, he really shouldn't, as a matter of his mental health."

I have no previous understanding of Cameron's mental health issues, I know only that he struggles with drug addiction. The psychiatrist explains that Cameron suffers from comorbid depression and anxiety disorders. What I grasp from what he is saying is that without treatment Cameron can't be left alone for significant periods of time because he might have a breakdown, or even hurt himself.

I try to compare his description to what I see in Cameron during our visits. It sounds as though he is describing a different person.

My face must display some level of worry. "Look, don't be alarmed. He just needs to get into treatment," he says.

"Is there anything we need to be doing right now for him?"

"Just get him bail as soon as possible."

"We'll do our best, I promise."

He looks at me and smiles. "You know, I can tell he likes you. He trusts you. It's a good thing for him to have someone like you on his case while he is in here."

It is always nice when someone recognizes the admiration and trust your client has for you. It is less nice when this admiration and trust blows up in your face. But as I stand there reviewing Cameron's condition with his psychiatrist, I have no idea that I am ambling toward self-ruin. "Thank you," I say. "I like him, too."

It takes me more than a reasonable amount of time to admit to myself that I have developed romantic feelings for my client. I would like to think that this is because I'm so busy working on his case that I remain unaware. But I'm fairly certain that's not the truth.

I tell myself that I am just devoted to Cameron's case. This is why I am sure to visit him as often as he asks, regardless of what else is happening around me. When he requests a visit the day that New York experiences a snowstorm so severe that the subways shut down and the courthouse is closed, I brave the elements without pause. As I sign into the attorney log, I see that I am the only attorney who visits that day.

I am so dedicated, I tell myself.

When his bail application is pushed until January, I feel sympathy that he will have to spend Christmas at MCC. I can understand that he does not want to spend the long Christmas weekend without contact from the outside. So, en route to Christmas dinner at a friend's house, I stop by MCC for an hour. He is gleeful at the sight of his attorney on a national holiday.

"Merry Christmas, Jen. You smell good," he says.

I am so thoughtful, I tell myself.

I ingest each occurrence on the case as though it is happening to me personally. When I read an initial version of the Presentence Investigation Report that mistakenly states that Cameron's suggested term of imprisonment is up to seventeen years, I promptly get up from my desk, go into the ladies' room, and throw up. When Cameron stands in a packed courtroom to account for his crimes, I am so moved that my eyes well with tears.

I am so passionate, I tell myself.

I also don't give much credence to acts of Cameron's that possibly reflect his own feelings. I take his avid insistence upon our visits to be a practicality given his circumstances. I chalk up the flirtatious things he says to be his general manner of dealing with women. I conclude that his questions about my personal life are born out of curiosity, not any self-interest.

I don't think much of the increasingly frequent calls I receive from various members of his gaggle of lady friends who complain that he has not called or responded to letters and e-mails as of late. "I think he is just nervous about sentencing," I tell them. "Is there any message you'd like me to pass along?"

I also don't think too much about the fact that when I relay these messages, Cameron displays emphatic disinterest, as though solely for my benefit. He's probably just embarrassed because of all the stories he's told me, I decide.

What I do allow myself to see, only because it is too conspicuous to miss, is a silent connection that develops between us. For all of our differences, Cameron and I are unusually compatible. The trust that bonds us is such that he relies on me to gauge his emotions. When he receives news on the case that he fears is worrisome, his eyes fixate on mine to discern the degree to which he should be concerned. When he is given good news, he cautiously looks my way to see if it is acceptable to be pleased.

But there's more than this. Cameron and I share a goofy sense of humor, an affinity for the same movies, the same music, the same reality television programming. And as I get to know him better, I quietly recognize that we share some similar afflictions. We both have an unflagging need to make others feel good about themselves. We both likely have this need because deep down we long to feel better about our own selves. Perhaps relatedly, we both have led lives that have caused us to end up in places where we don't really want to be.

Despite these shared woes—or maybe because of them—there is something about being around Cameron that makes me feel better about being in the world. When I began work on his case, I had recently exited a relationship with a brilliant but tormented man that began as a loving union but, over the years, had devolved into an exercise in emotional abuse worthy of a Lifetime Original Movie. By the end, he seemed to be content only when I was miserable—which was more often than not—and when our problems began to bleed into my work, he almost appeared to be pleased.

After putting myself through this gloom, in Cameron's presence I feel as though someone has finally turned on the lights. Even in his terrible legal circumstances, he is invariably positive and upbeat, a state of being I find not only alluring but also contagious. When I am around him, I remark how long it's been since I've laughed so much. And I am sweetly flattered by his enthusiastic interest in my work; when his friends call me to check up on him, they reveal that he has been discussing my credentials, praising my abilities, expressing gratitude for having me on his case. Cameron reminds me of the good things that I've forgotten. He sees me in the way I want to be seen, the way I want to see myself.

Our compatibility eventually gives way to more concrete signs that we are shifting away from what is normally expected between attorney and client. I find that I would rather spend time with him than with anyone else. I relive our conversations in my head long after I leave him behind. I catch myself thinking about him at the oddest times and in the oddest ways. When I go to see a movie, I wonder if he might like it. When I cook dinner, I wonder if it would be to his taste. When I'm spending time with friends, I wonder what it would be like if he were here, too.

In time, I silently register some changes in Cameron's behavior toward me as well. He will sometimes look at me with such intensity that I feel compelled to avert my eyes. When we say good-bye, he begins to stand so close to me that I can detect the scent of his soap. And even when there are others present, he doesn't shake my hand so much as take it in his own, clasping it in a way that allows him to quickly brush his fingers against my palm.

In a group meeting, as I adjust my sitting position our legs serendipitously touch. When I instinctively begin to move my leg away, he uses his ankle to still it in place, the inside of his calf now pressed purposely against the outside of mine. The move is so swift, so unexpected, that I conspicuously look over to him. His face bears an almost imperceptible smile, but he is otherwise intently listening to what is being discussed, paying me no mind.

I don't move, partially because I fear that wrenching my leg away will cause a disturbance and partially because . . . well, just because. The surreptitious tangle of our legs is like everything that comes to be with Cameron: I know I shouldn't, but I do. Enveloped in the warmth of government-issued canvas, my stockinged leg remains under his domain, happily in exile. When he sees that I don't resist, I feel him press closer, and then closer, as though he is daring me to move away. But I simply look down at my notes, hoping no one can hear my heart beating as loudly as it is.

The entire encounter doesn't last long: a few minutes, not much more. It is a small, silly occurrence, too insignificant to be addressed afterward beyond a smile and a shake of the head. And yet, when it happens, I am acutely aware that this is the closest I have ever been to Cameron, the closest I will probably ever get to be.

While he has a team of lawyers and a fleet of friends and family to support him, Cameron insists on my involvement in almost everything.

I in turn am only too willing to become involved. When I can't make a group meeting, his conduct afterward is described to me as obstinate, unruly, distrusting. Cameron demands to know my whereabouts, refuses to agree to anything without me.

"Jen, please, you can't do that again," he tells me of my absence.

In addition to the hefty legal work required for his case, he begs my help on decidedly nonlegal matters. On his behalf, I enthusiastically pick out a birthday card for his little sister, arrange for his reading material, contact the kennel that houses his dogs. I field phone calls from concerned family and friends. I accompany his mother to select his suit for court.

I eagerly accede to his request to see me as many as five days a week, but in reality I sign over to him every waking moment. I visit him on a Friday and a Sunday, and on the intervening Saturday, my phone rings.

"Aren't you happy to hear from me?" he asks sheepishly.

"Of course I am," I say. "But I just saw you yesterday, and I'm going to see you tomorrow. Is everything okay?"

"I'm bored," he says.

In his demands for my attention, I sense in Cameron a childlike craving to be cared for. He reminds me of a toddler in need of a nap, his arms stretched upward, begging to be held. I sometimes wonder if this is an actual remnant from his unorthodox childhood; the mere speculation is enough for me to feel as though I should try to make up for the difference.

Thus, over time, I take on Cameron's pleas and wants as though my very existence lies in the balance. And, maybe, to some extent, it does: I have so conflated my life with his that I begin to have difficulty discerning where his demands end and my own needs begin. To fulfill somehow becomes fulfilling, to bind myself somehow feels liberating. Even as I do it, something deep inside tells me to stop. But I still push my way in further, irrationally believing that in losing myself in Cameron I can somehow be found.

I embrace the virtual overlap of him over me. I readily accept that Cameron will be my first and last thought of the day. I don't think much of it when my cleaning lady points out to me that I have inadvertently

made her check out to "Cameron Douglas." I don't find it strange that
on the few occasions when I force myself away from him, I'm sure to
place my cell phone closely at my side. Even when I am where I'm
supposed to be—with friends, with family, on reluctant dates with
upstanding gentlemen—Cameron is there, too.

And so, whatever romance there comes to be between us, always
underneath is something darker, more potent. Our dysfunctional
exchange of needs creates a thick rope of codependency; it harnesses
me to Cameron completely, inexorably. In the end, only the most power-
ful government in the world will be able to pull me away.

Like many unconventional romances, ours is over far too soon. Unlike
many unconventional romances, ours is cut short due to our having
collectively committed a federal offense.

Much is made in my case about my relationship with Cameron.
The government refers to ten weeks' worth of e-mails and phone calls
following Cameron's transfer out of MCC as evidence that I committed
my crimes out of love.

I don't think that it was love that motivated me to turn to a life of
crime, at least not exclusively, and certainly not in the moment. The
government doesn't seem to care about the distinction, and I suppose
in the end I don't either.

In our first meeting, my lawyer asks me about my relationship with
Cameron. "Don't be embarrassed," he tells me. "I just need to understand it for when you are asked about it."

"I'm not embarrassed," I tell him. It's something I find myself
repeating over and over again during my case. In truth, I am still not
quite sure which part of having feelings for Cameron is supposed to be
embarrassing. The fact that I started a relationship with a client? The
fact that he is the son of a celebrity? The fact that he has dabbled both
personally and professionally in the narcotic arts? None of this seems
particularly shameful to me, although it's been made clear to me that it
probably should.

In an appeal for leniency, my lawyer will explain to the government
that my personal circumstances contributed to my feelings for Cam-

eron and my decision to commit crimes on his behalf. He will explain that I had recently undergone a painful breakup; that I was miserable both personally and professionally; that I was planning a career change in the hopes of finding a more fulfilling existence. These statements are all true. What they imply, however—that had I not been an unhappy mess when I met Cameron, I would not have developed feelings for him—is probably not.

At the same time, I do not posit that ours is the greatest love story of all time. Or even, really, a love story at all. I labor under no misapprehension that had my crimes not been discovered, we would in any real sense remain together. I am not the one who got away. I am only the one who got arrested.

CHAPTER 3

Welcome to Cowboy Country

One might find it fitting that my conspiracy was born within the confines of the walls of the Metropolitan Correctional Center in downtown Manhattan. Crime is its entire reason for being. Here is the lowdown on MCC: Built in 1975, it is a maximum-security federal pretrial detention center that houses almost eight hundred inmates, most of whom are awaiting trial or sentencing. The prison has housed some of the most dangerous criminals in modern history, including crime boss John Gotti, drug kingpin Frank Lucas, and a number of al-Qaeda operatives.

Although I have spent a lifetime in relatively restrictive institutions, MCC presents something of another order. When I am within its walls, I'm immediately reminded of the experiences I've had at military checkpoints in more conservative pockets of the Arab world. After taking detailed stock of my person, the corrections officer on duty invariably examines my attorney credentials with the same suspicion and incredulity as does the Syrian soldier inspecting my U.S. passport. Both men are outwardly dubious at the presence of a woman unaccompanied by a man. Both begrudgingly grant me permission to pass, yet leave me with the persistent feeling that I've done something horribly wrong in simply being alive.

I must add that for all of the import surrounding its role in the war on crime, MCC is in many ways lacking in the rule of law. While the facility possesses an extensive set of rules, these are never followed the same way twice. The quality of an attorney's visit is entirely contingent on the mental stability of the corrections officer on duty. The odds of an efficient visit are not great. On the majority of occasions that I visit, it feels as though I have entered what I imagine to be the same regulatory framework that exists in the rogue outskirts of Taliban-friendly Pakistan. Complete cowboy country.

Sometimes my lawyerly skirt suit satisfies the dress code. Sometimes the very same suit is deemed indecent, and now I must run to a nearby clothing store to purchase something to pull over it.

Some days the corrections officers are stern but professional. On other days, entering the facility is the criminal justice equivalent of walking past a construction site. In confined and controlled spaces, I'm berated about my marital status, my ethnic origins, my availability later for a drink.

The worst days at MCC are those where I am forced to encounter an elite category of corrections officers seeming to specialize in psychopathy. One officer in particular, whose height I will estimate at six-foot-ten and his weight at 450 pounds, deems it unnecessary to use words. Instead, he chooses to communicate by pounding his enormous fist against the door, causing it to shake so violently that it looks as though it might break.

This gargantuan man comes in a set of two with another officer who is smaller in size but crueler in conduct. He barks orders in such close proximity to my face that I'm able to assess the shoddiness of his dental work.

This dynamic duo does not take much time to make clear their fervent hatred of Cameron and, by extension, me. One evening early into the case, both men are sitting just outside our attorney room, whooping and laughing so loudly that I can barely hear what Cameron is saying. Their conduct seems purposeful, as they eye Cameron in a manner that emphasizes he is powerless to do anything about it. Cameron, too, recognizes that he is being mocked; though he says nothing, his ears are red with anger.

This is bullshit, I think. I get up and walk to the door. "Excuse me," I say.

The laughter stops. Two angry sets of eyes look at me.

I swallow. "It's just, I can't really hear what my client is saying. Would you mind keeping it down a bit?"

Their eyes are still fixed on me, but they remain silent.

"Okay, then," I say with awkwardness. "Thank you." I'm anxious to shut the attorney room door, which serves as the only barrier between these frightening individuals and me.

And thus our beef is born. Apparently, these two men—Cameron and I come to lovingly refer to them as "Fat Fuck" and "Mean Fuck," respectively—don't take well to being asked to do anything and are sure to make us pay. Whenever they're on duty they are sure to place us opposite the venue of their private comedy hour. They permit other inmates to use the restroom, but when Cameron asks he is told no. They continually interrupt meetings to berate Cameron for petty issues, like when he leans in his chair or uses my pen. When in order to show Cameron a chart I sit diagonally from him rather than across, I earn a bellowing scream that echoes in the pit of my stomach along with a fat punch to the glass door. In dreaded elevator trips, I am alternatively harangued by both Fucks about my meetings with Cameron and the status of his case. One time, presumably by accident, Mean Fuck smacks me in the face with the attorney lobby door, causing me to fall over. He does not say a word, he merely steps over me and goes along his way.

I stop reporting the misdoings of Fat Fuck and Mean Fuck, only because it turns out to be a complete waste of time. There is no real recourse in cowboy country. I observe some of the most aggressive defense attorneys in the city completely cower where the imposition of authority of MCC is concerned. It seems to be generally accepted that life at MCC is distinct from that in civilized society, that one must simply grin and bear it.

When I later confess my crimes to the prosecutors in my case, one politely cautions me. "We know that things are done a little differently at MCC," she says. "Don't feel as though you have to edit your experience there."

"I won't," I say. But even then, I don't bother mentioning Fat Fuck and Mean Fuck. By that time, their misconduct constitutes a drop in the bucket of transgressions that surround Cameron's case. This includes, I suppose, my own. When it's time for me to answer for my misdeeds, no solace can be had in pointing to those of others. When my reckoning arrives, it is for me and me alone.

Not long after our beef begins with the Two Fucks, I tell Cameron, "We've got to get you out of here."

He enthusiastically agrees.

It's after the Christmas holiday, January 2010, and we're preparing to make a motion for Cameron's bail. The government opposes the motion based on the not altogether unreasonable premise that Cameron was already awarded bail but violated the terms. We are nonetheless trying again, based on the argument that Cameron's bail violation was not really his fault.

As specious as this may sound, as a medical matter it is true. When DEA agents arrested Cameron, they recognized that his heroin addiction was of some medical concern. They took him to a nearby hospital, where the on-call physician advised that he take a detoxification medicine to avoid severe withdrawal. Cameron had this medicine in his possession when he left the hospital. DEA agents then took him to MCC, where he spent the night.

The day after his arrest, he was granted bail in the form of house arrest, which he served at his mother's house under the supervision of a private security company. But when he arrived, the detoxification medicine was nowhere to be found. When I join the case months later, it's still not clear where the medicine ended up, whether it was lost in the shuffle between MCC and his mother's house, or whether the security company confiscated it. All that's clear is that no one seemed to know what to do next.

Thus, against medical advice, Cameron was left to undergo severe heroin withdrawal without medical supervision. The psychiatrist, out of the country when all of this happened, later explains to us that this situation is physically untenable, that opiate withdrawal causes the brain to turn against itself. The withdrawing addict, believing he is about to die without using, becomes suicidal.

Cameron did not attempt suicide. What he did was call one of the prominent ladies in his gaggle—Mother Goose, if you will—to put him out of his misery. Mother Goose was also a heroin addict and so had some handy to place in a glassine envelope and stuff into the battery cartridge of an electric toothbrush. The toothbrush was delivered along with some other toiletries to the security guards at Cameron's mother's house.

It probably would have worked but for Cameron's desperate need for the drugs. The symptoms of heroin withdrawal do not allow for subtlety, and so when he berated the security detail about the imminent arrival of his toothbrush, suspicions were raised. No one really needs a toothbrush with that much urgency, and so when the toiletries arrived, the security guards examined the battery cartridge and contacted the government.

Cameron was sent to MCC that same day. Upon processing, MCC assigned him to a detoxification protocol. Two weeks later, he was clean.

When I hear Cameron tell the story of how he ended up at MCC, I marvel at how avoidable it all seems. I'm also dumbfounded by his decision to have someone smuggle him heroin while he was under house arrest.

"I mean, if anything, why not just have her smuggle the medication? You were supposed to have it anyway."

"She didn't have my medication."

"I know, but she could probably get her own. It just seems less egregious to bring you what was prescribed to you rather than a street drug."

He thinks about my logic for a moment. "Yeah, I guess that makes better sense."

Though it won't be easy to win bail the second time around, we don't consider it impossible. And so when Cameron pleads guilty before the magistrate judge—the presiding trial judge is tied up in a terrorism trial—we also submit papers asking that he be granted bail.

The circumstances of Cameron's plea make it an ideal time to ask for bail. Because he has pleaded guilty before the magistrate judge but not yet appeared before his trial judge, his plea is not considered "official." This could make all the difference, as there are different legal standards for bail depending on whether or not the defendant has given an official plea. As one might expect, it is easier for a defendant to receive bail before he officially admits to committing a crime—that is, pre-plea—than it is post-plea.

The magistrate judge orders a bail hearing. Sensitive to Cameron's status as a cooperator, he agrees to hold it in a closed courtroom, away from the bustle of the magistrate's court.

But on this day the case takes a turn.

After hearing arguments from both sides, the magistrate judge agrees that Cameron should be awarded bail in order to undergo drug treatment. He also goes so far as to set the conditions of Cameron's release, including a $1 million bail bond to be signed by both of his parents. But there's a significant catch: because a bail decision might be different under the post-plea standard, and because Cameron is really only pre-plea as a technical matter, the magistrate judge freezes the bail order until the trial judge has a chance to weigh in on the matter. In the meantime, because of Cameron's status as a cooperator, the judge orders that all of the proceedings and paperwork in the matter be sealed from public view.

It is a pyrrhic victory. Cameron is no closer to going home, and yet we have to concern ourselves with the minutiae of his bail paperwork. He flashes me a defeated look as a U.S. Marshal escorts him from the courtroom to the inmate holding area.

I begrudgingly assist Co-Counsel, an attorney from Cameron's original legal team, with pulling together information for Cameron's bail bond and ensuring it is placed under seal. Cameron Douglas's mother, who is present at the hearing, signs the bond and goes home. But this is not enough: Cameron Douglas's father must sign it, too.

In the four months that I have been on the case, I haven't had much occasion to communicate with Cameron Douglas's father. He receives regular telephone updates on the case from the legal team, and I participate in these if I am asked to. But this will be the first time I will meet him in person.

Any other day, I would be curious to meet the man whose sink sex scene haunted my preadolescent mind. But I'm drained by the day's events and disappointed in the outcome. I would much rather go home, throw myself under the covers, and put off meeting him to another day.

Co-Counsel and I wait for his arrival at one end of the courthouse. When he enters, he is dressed in black skinny jeans and a black leather jacket, appropriate attire for a man who once starred in sexy films, but odd to me in terms of "dad" clothing. In sizing up the ensemble, I can't help but think of my own father, who tends to favor muted wool sweaters and thick corduroy pants. I try to picture my dad in a similar get-up and bite the inside of my cheek to keep from laughing.

Cameron Douglas's father is not one for remaining under the radar. He walks with purposeful strides and greets every person he encounters, each of whom are outwardly excited by the recognition. As I look on, I wonder what it's like to affect someone by simply saying hello. It appears exhausting. But after I watch for a while, I notice that the relationship might be symbiotic: just as the strangers are touched, Cameron Douglas's father seems touched that they are touched. Perhaps in the end, like everyone else, Cameron Douglas's father just wants to be liked.

After he's done with the receiving line, Cameron Douglas's father walks toward me and extends his hand. In returning the gesture, I give him a quick once-over. I'm struck by how he simultaneously manages to resemble his son but also look so different. Their facial features are exact replicas, as though someone has copied the father's face and pasted it onto the son. But Cameron has fair coloring, and his father's looks are darker, more distinguished. Cameron is built like a natural athlete—tall and broad—but his father's build is that of an actor: smaller in person than what appears on-screen. And while Cameron exudes a rugged masculinity, his father's appearance is more manicured, almost delicate.

My stargazing is cut short by the reality of the circumstances. Cameron Douglas's father signs the bond and then indicates that he would like to talk about what happened in court. I internally cringe. This conversation is not going to be an uplifting one.

Co-Counsel is quietly explaining what happened in court when a man inserts himself into the discussion, joining the circle as though he has something to add. He introduces himself by name to Cameron Douglas's father and asks what he is doing in the courthouse today.

Cameron Douglas's father looks wary but is polite. "I'm sorry, who are you?"

"I'm with the *New York Post*," the man says.

So much for a closed courtroom.

Without looking at one another, we three briskly make our way into the courthouse elevator. Co-Counsel presses a floor at random, so that we can go anywhere else.

In the elevator, Cameron Douglas's father is not pleased. "Great," he says. "Now his bail application is going to be all over the papers."

I'm stupid enough in this moment to open my mouth and speak reassuringly. "Actually, we asked that the entire thing be sealed," I say. "So, it can't become public."

He flashes me a look of derision. "Oh, *really*, Jen?" He yells in a manner that can only be described as dramatic. "You're going to tell me that this isn't going to become public? Please!"

His angry outburst strikes me as so out of place that I actually begin to look behind me in the elevator to see if he is talking to someone else. When I realize that this is directed at me, I am at first insulted and then, quite frankly, a little starstruck. I think: Yes, why don't you please explain to me how a sealed document works, you asshole. I guess playing a lawyer in a string of shitty movies means you know more than an actual attorney.

But then I find myself thinking: How did he know I go by Jen?

I escape my head long enough to speak. "They can't just do that," I finally say. I can hear my voice shaking, and I hate myself for being as intimidated as I am. But my confidence in respect for the judge's order is unwavering. "It would be illegal for someone to make this public."

At this, Cameron Douglas's father says nothing, but crosses his arms and looks angry.

By the time we exit the elevator, we are met with a small group of reporters. A U.S. Marshal offers to escort us into the witness room of one of the nearby courtrooms so we can speak in private. Co-Counsel begins to explain once again what happened in court. I notice that he is trying to put a positive spin on things, just as I had done moments before in the elevator. I bite my lip as he speaks, silently praying that he does not step on the same grenade that I did.

But he does. Cameron Douglas's father, like his son, seems to have an extraordinarily sensitive bullshit meter and is not shy when it has been activated. He wants to know why his son is still incarcerated after

Co-Counsel assured him that he wouldn't be. He also wants to know why Cameron remains a sitting duck in prison when he has dutifully cooperated with the government. He's angry, too, that his own presence in the courthouse may have attracted attention that will place his son in danger.

"We've given these guys everything they asked for," he says, referring to the government. "I don't understand why they are putting him through this." His voice wavers, and I see that he might actually be more afraid than angry. I feel sort of bad for hating him a few minutes ago.

There is an awkward lull in the conversation. I can't take the silence, and so I decide to open my mouth one last time. Without editorializing, and with as little eye contact as possible, I explain to him in dry, technical detail where things stand. Because he does not immediately jump down my throat, and because the sound of my voice fills the silence, I say as much as I can think to say: I explain the two standards for bail and how it is that Cameron stands between them. I describe how the stark difference between the standards probably influenced the magistrate judge's decision to punt the matter to the trial judge. And I tell him that we simply don't know what the outcome is going to be until the trial judge hears the matter. All we can do right now is wait.

In the few moments that I accidentally make eye contact with him, I notice with relief that Cameron Douglas's father is calmly listening. One thing that I learn about him during the case is that he wants only to hear the technical issues, and these in as fine detail as possible.

While Cameron Douglas's father does not seem particularly assuaged by my explanation, he is satisfied enough to end our meeting. When we arrive in the courthouse lobby, I see several photographers posted outside waiting for his exit. Great, I think. This is definitely going to make the paper.

I have no interest in having my picture taken under any circumstances, much less these, so I say good-bye to Cameron Douglas's father and tell him and Co-Counsel to go ahead without me. I watch from inside the courthouse as both are surrounded by a tiny fleet of reporters and press photographers. I look at my watch and try to estimate how much time it will take for me to finally be at home in bed.

I give them an extensive lead and then exit the courthouse on my own. I can see the backs of the reporters' heads as I make my way behind them to the main thoroughfare.

But then, suddenly, the reporters have switched direction and are now rushing toward me. I strain to see what has caused the about-face. That's when I see black skinny jeans and a black leather jacket approaching.

I want to stop the press from taking a single step closer. "Please just go on without me," I call out to him.

But he keeps walking toward me, press corps in tow.

I am holding my breath. Oh, shit, what now? I think. With the photographers headed my way, I'm also wishing I had checked my hair in the ladies' room before leaving the courthouse.

He reaches where I am and extends his hand. "Thank you, Jen, for everything," he says.

"Of course," I stammer. I pause to see if there is something else, but he has already turned around and walked away, leaving me standing among the press.

We collectively observe his departure into a black SUV. I'm still watching him as the reporters surround me, ask me who I am, why he is thanking me. I don't provide any response, but as I slink away from them I find I must suppress the urge to smile. Perhaps in the end, like everyone else, I just want to be liked, too.

At some point I make it home, but my comfort under the covers is short-lived. I'm awakened early on Saturday morning by the telephone—first my cell, then my home phone, then my cell again. I feel my pillow shake, indicating that my BlackBerry is vibrating with new messages.

I don't bother answering the calls or reading the e-mails. Instead, I stumble to the computer and look at Google News. There are a bunch of articles about Cameron Douglas's father's cameo court appearance.

A British tabloid features a photograph of Cameron Douglas's father outside the courthouse, looking none too happy. Far in the distance, I see myself making my way through the revolving door of the courthouse. My head is down, and all that can be seen of me is my red wool coat. I breathe a sigh of relief.

I know this can't be why my phone is ringing. I click on the local papers and see the reason for urgency. The *New York Post* and the New York *Daily News* report that according to a courthouse "source," Cameron had a bail hearing closed to the press, the records of which have been sealed, facts that lead both papers to conclude that "apparently" he is cooperating with the government.

It turns out that Cameron Douglas's father was exactly right. I am not only shocked by the lack of integrity at the court, but also shaken by it. To learn that a transgression of this kind could occur at the oldest and most distinguished federal district court in the country is like finding out that Santa Claus is a pedophile. Nothing is as I thought it to be.

Disgusted, I pull on MCC-appropriate attire. The phone rings again. "I saw the articles," I say as I pick up the phone, already knowing that it will be the legal team on the other end. "I'm headed there now."

In the taxi on the way to MCC, my minds reels back to the confidence with which I told my client's father that the rules in this process are sacred. I see now that Cameron's case is altogether different, that I am in a game with rules I don't know and with stakes that remain uncomfortably high.

"Get me the fuck out of here."

This is how our meeting with Cameron begins.

He has no clue about the articles, he is learning about them as they are being described to him. The legal team asks if he wants us to pursue any additional protection for him at MCC.

His face turns a dark shade of burgundy. "No. Just get me the fuck out of here."

We explain that we have to wait for the trial judge to consider the issue, hopefully in the coming week.

"Then please get out of here."

"Cameron . . ." I say.

"Please leave. Look, if this gets around, I don't want people to see I've been down here meeting with my attorneys."

We leave.

I come back the next day, expecting him to refuse the visit.

He shows up. I notice one of his forearms is scratched raw.

"Are you okay?" I ask, pointing to his arm.

"Yeah, I don't know, it started itching."

"Look, I can go if you want," I say. "I just wanted to check in and see if you're doing okay."

He looks down and shakes his head. "Jen, everyone calls home on Saturdays. Their families have read the articles, and I am getting a lot of questions."

I swallow. "What have you been telling them?"

"Nothing, I just keep denying it."

I think for a minute. "Why don't you just say that your parents asked for the courtroom to be closed?"

"What?"

"Just say that your parents are embarrassed about your case and they pulled strings to have the courtroom closed."

He gives me a look not unlike the one I received from his father the day before.

I state my case. "How would any of them know what kind of influence your parents have? Just say the press assumed you were cooperating because no one at the courthouse wants to say that they gave your parents a favor."

It reflects no more poorly on the court than reality, I think to myself.

He considers this. "Fine, whatever. But, Jen, I have to get out of here."

"I know, Cameron." I give him my stock line. "We are doing everything we can, I promise."

"Jen, you know how important this is to me." His face crumples a bit. This ordeal is trying him.

"Cameron, look at me."

He does. His face is flushed, as though it might burst.

"Just hang on as best you can. You are not in this alone. I promise you I am going to do everything I possibly can for you."

It turns out I am a woman of my word.

Cameron appears for a bail hearing before the trial judge the Thursday before President's Day Weekend, 2010. I have plans to go skiing upstate for the long weekend, and I'm hopeful that Cameron will be bailed later in the day, leaving me plenty of time to pack.

It feels like it could be a good day, but it isn't.

There is a smattering of press in the courtroom. We ask that the courtroom be closed, but the trial judge denies the request. Instead, he kicks the press out of the courtroom while matters pertaining to cooperation are discussed, and then opens the court back up for the remainder of the hearing.

After hearing arguments, the judge asks to hear from the psychiatrist, whom we've prepared to deliver testimony about Cameron's medical needs. He gives a reasoned explanation of Cameron's condition and his serious need for treatment. He also, probably without even thinking about it, gratuitously adds in open court that Cameron was placed under house arrest "because he was going to be an informant."

When I hear him say it, I think I've heard him wrong. But I see that the backs of the two prosecutors at the table in front of ours have straightened up ever so slightly. The two other attorneys at the defense table exchange quick looks. Cameron, who is seated next to me, hangs his head down and simply says, "Wow."

When the hearing is over, Cameron is whisked out of the courtroom. A reporter for the *New York Post* then approaches the legal team to say that he plans to run a story that Cameron is an active cooperator. Do we have any comment?

So, this is happening. There isn't much that can be done. We've asked the judge that the comment be stricken from the record. We also tell the government that if they plan to take any steps to protect Cameron that these not include placing him in solitary confinement. I also call the manager of Cameron's unit and leave a message begging her not to deliver tomorrow's edition of the *New York Post* to his unit. After I get off the phone, I feel a brick in my stomach. What on earth will happen to Cameron now?

With few other options, I head home. I make a lame attempt at packing my suitcase, but end up sitting on my couch, my arms crossed, my thoughts jumbled. I think about how Cameron is about to be branded as something he never wanted to be. I also try very hard not to think about the vicious attacks that are regularly meted out against cooperators in prison.

I am there for hours when I hear the familiar "thud" outside my door of the morning paper being delivered. I look at the clock. It is almost five a.m.

I wait until the newspaper deliveryman enters the elevator, and then in my pajamas and socks step out into the hallway. I don't subscribe to the *New York Post* and so I wander the hall to see if any of my neighbors has a copy lying in front of their door. They, too, prefer to get their news elsewhere, and so I take the elevator to the top floor of the building and work my way from floor to floor in search of the day's edition.

After four floors, I finally find a subscriber. I grab the paper, take a mental note of the apartment number, and then ride the elevator back to my apartment.

The cover story is somewhat haunting: the designer Alexander McQueen has committed suicide after suffering from anxiety and depressive disorders. After a few pages more, I see the headline:

SINGING ROLE FOR CAMERON

Then I start to read the story:

> The cat's out of the bag—actor Michael Douglas's son is a rat.
>
> Cameron Douglas's shrink let slip the closely guarded, potentially dangerous secret during testimony yesterday at a Manhattan federal bail hearing. [He] confirmed speculation that Cameron was released to house arrest last summer "because he was going to be an informant."
>
> Defense lawyers asked—

And then I stop reading.

• • •

Cameron has been placed in the SHU.

I find this out when I drag my sleep-deprived self to MCC later that morning. On the Attorney Visit form, the number of his prison unit has been replaced with the letters S-H-U. I assume he has already gotten into a fight over what happened and has been sent there for disciplinary reasons.

It takes a full hour for Cameron to be brought to the attorney room. Accompanied by three corrections officers, he is wearing a bright orange jumpsuit and is handcuffed. The officers explain that because Cameron is now a ward of the SHU, the attorney room must be locked from the outside.

Cameron's face is pale and sweaty, he is breathing deeply. "What happened?" I ask gently.

"You tell me," he says curtly.

"What do you mean? Didn't something happen?"

"No. They just pulled me out of my cell in the middle of the night and brought me here. I asked them why and they said to ask your lawyer."

"We told the government not to put you in the SHU and they agreed."

"Well, I'm here."

"You're not supposed to be."

"Please just go find out why."

I motion for the corrections officer to unlock the door. He lets me out, and then locks the door after me. Before I head out to the elevator, I look back at Cameron. His head is in his hands.

The decision to place Cameron in the SHU was made unilaterally by the Bureau of Prisons. He was placed in "Protective Custody" so that no harm befell him on the unit.

Getting to this answer provides its own adventure. As I exit the attorney room lobby, I ask every corrections officer I encounter why my client is in the SHU. No one can tell me anything. Finally, one corrections officer suggests, "Ask his lawyer."

"I am his lawyer," I say.

The officer looks me up and down. "I mean his actual lawyer," he says.

"That's still me."

"Well, okay. You can call our legal office, they should be able to tell you."

"Can I call them from here?"

"No."

I trudge back to my office. On a phone call with MCC's Legal Department, I explain to the attorney on the other end that Cameron's treating psychiatrist has explicitly warned against his being in the SHU.

The woman I speak to in MCC's Legal Department possesses the same congeniality as most of its corrections officers. "Don't you care about your client?" she asks me condescendingly. "Do you want him to get hurt?"

While on a day with decent sleep I might have answered with some diplomacy, today is not that day. "I didn't ask you how to represent my client," I snap. "I asked you why he is in the SHU and how I can get him out."

"We are investigating his safety," she says. "We can't let him out until we are certain that conditions are safe for him."

"Yes, but doesn't his presence in the SHU essentially confirm to the other inmates that he is definitely a cooperator? Aren't you making him less safe?"

"It's a risk we have to take. We can't let him be a sitting duck. We know that if he's in the SHU he'll remain unharmed."

I hate that this sort of makes sense. But the psychiatrist was clear about this. "I'm sure that's true of other inmates, but not this one. His doctor has specifically said that he can't be left in solitary."

Silence.

"Well, can this determination be made today?" I ask.

"No."

Of course it can't. "When do you think it can be made?"

"Well, it's a long weekend." She pauses, as though she is looking at a calendar.

I suddenly remember my ski trip. What a naïve fool I was to think that I could have enjoyed a weekend away.

"The earliest will be Tuesday after the holiday weekend. Maybe later in the week. It depends."

I sigh. "Thank you," I say, and hang up.

Cameron Douglas's parents have seen the *New York Post*, and they are beside themselves.

Soon after I finish my phone call with MCC, Cameron Douglas's mother calls me sobbing. She is terrified that something will happen to her son. I try to comfort her as best I can without mentioning that deep down I am worried about the same thing.

She insists on meeting immediately with the legal team. What seems like moments later, she appears perfectly coiffed in our office lobby. I extend my hand to greet her, but she refuses to take it. Too tired to care, I stuff my snubbed hand into my dress pocket.

When we sit down for the meeting, she asks that we conference in Cameron Douglas's father by telephone. He is out of town and has been pulled off a ski slope in order to participate.

The meeting begins as one might expect. There is ample yelling, both from the Douglas in the room and the Douglas on the phone. The Douglas in the room manages to cry and yell at the same time.

We explain that what has happened—that Cameron is now in the very place we said he should not be—is because of a unilateral move by MCC. The Douglases don't understand how it is that their son has been put at risk twice over, first by the article, then by MCC.

I don't find the yelling to be particularly pleasant. It isn't until I have my own criminal case that I develop a full understanding of why clients react this way. In my own case I yell plenty, albeit outside the presence of my attorney, mostly at outcomes for which he bears no responsibility. Sometimes yelling is all one can do, and so one does it, usually at full volume.

Over all of the shouting, we manage to get in that MCC's move is likely temporary, that they've determined that for now he is safer in the SHU, and that as soon as they can confirm that it is safe for him to return they will let him out.

At learning that this is a protective measure, the Douglases change their tone from anger to worry. They don't doubt Cameron should be punished for his crimes, but they don't think he should be physically harmed for them, either.

"I just don't want him to get hurt," Cameron Douglas's father says.

"How do we even know he can make it through the weekend?" Cameron Douglas's mother exclaims through tears. "He can't even call us to tell us how he is."

The drama is a bit unbearable to me, I want only for this meeting to end. After a moment, I say: "I will go and see him this weekend."

Cameron Douglas's mother looks at me with big, wet eyes. Perhaps due to the pervasiveness of her crying, her voice is that of a little girl. "You will?"

I had already said a mental good-bye to my ski weekend when I was on the phone with MCC. I nod. "I'll make sure he spends as much time outside of the SHU as possible."

This seems to calm her down. The phone is silent, and I take this to mean that Cameron Douglas's father has calmed down, too.

I'm anxious to get out of the room. I quickly try to tie any loose ends. I ask Cameron Douglas's mother if there is anything she'd like me to relay to Cameron. She asks for a piece of paper and begins writing him a letter.

The phone is still silent, and so I ask the same of Cameron Douglas's father. He doesn't respond right away. It takes me a moment to realize that this is because he is crying.

"Please send him my love," he manages.

Between the chain of events of the last twenty-four hours and my lack of sleep, I quite frankly want to join him. Instead, I promise that I will update everyone on how Cameron is doing.

As she gets up to leave, Cameron Douglas's mother grabs my hand with both of hers, possibly compensating for the lack of her hand at the start of the meeting. She is thanking me profusely, but my mind is on what's to come. You know your case has taken a turn for the worse when your most immediate task is to make sure your client doesn't have a breakdown and you've just made both of his parents cry.

• • •

I begin my marathon session at MCC the next day around noon and end up staying until ten p.m. I am ready: I have brought twenty-five crisp single-dollar bills for the vending machine. Since we will be locked into the attorney room for the duration, I purchase most of its contents and place them on the table in the attorney room in a sort of prison picnic.

When Cameron arrives, he is still upset about what has happened. He also has a severe cold, owing to the fact that it is the middle of winter and the SHU is not properly heated. But he is certainly communicative, and after some time passes even relaxes a bit. He manages a laugh when I note that the orange shade of his jumpsuit so resembles the color of the nacho cheese Doritos we are sharing that he can just wipe the crumbs on his sleeve.

There are no legal issues on the table, at least not imminent ones, and so I am really there to kill time. We play a series of games, classics such as hangman and tic-tac-toe, and a new one I invent that I call Who Would You Rather Punch? It is both cathartic and educational and invariably involves employees of the federal government.

When I leave Cameron at the end of the day, he seems to be in decent spirits. We agree that I will return the next day for more of the same.

In the cab home, I note that my head is heavy with congestion. In the dry air of the attorney room, I think I've caught Cameron's cold. Still, the day went smoothly. Cameron seems to be doing well enough that I wonder if the psychiatrist has possibly exaggerated his condition.

But the next day, things have changed.

When Cameron is brought into the attorney room, his skin is covered in deep red welts. He scratches these as he slumps into the chair across from mine. He looks at the floor and says nothing.

"I'm back," I say cheerfully.

He barely looks up.

I try for some chitchat, and while he does engage with me, I can tell that it's a struggle. I relay to him a series of messages from friends and family and ladies of the gaggle in the hopes that these might lift his spirits.

They don't. Instead, he begins to cry.

I have had clients break down on me before, and so I know to remain silent and supportive. After a moment, I say, "Cameron, you're going to get through this."

He tries to bring himself back to the conversation, but seemingly can't. The more that he tries to control his emotions, the less he is able to. He begins to breathe deeply. And then it seems as though he can't catch his breath.

"Cameron, just try to calm down and breathe."

That's when I notice that he isn't having trouble breathing because he is overcome with emotion. He is having trouble breathing because he is hyperventilating.

He has pushed his chair away from the table so that he is turned away from me. He claws the hives on his arms, the skin scratched raw. I can also hear him struggling to breathe, his breaths becoming quicker, almost urgent.

My own heartbeat rushes as I watch this unfold. This situation calls for something far different from legal assistance.

"Cameron, I am going to ask the CO to get a medic."

"No," he says. "Please, I just need you to go."

"Cameron, I am not going to go when you are like this."

"Please, Jen."

"I'm not going." I know I am not helpful to the situation, but I am also not about to leave him while he appears to be coming apart.

He looks at me and sees that I have no intention of leaving. He turns back to the wall. We sit in silence, the only sound is his breath. I watch his shoulders rise and fall in short, rapid movements. After a few minutes, they start to slow.

I think it is all over and feel a wave of relief pass over me. "Do you want me to get you some water?" I offer.

"No, I'm all right." He is still facing the wall.

"Okay, well, let me know. We can just sit here if you want."

The calm is short-lived. In a moment, the hyperventilating returns. The attack is apparently not over.

"Please," he says in between gasps, "I'm begging you to just leave."

"I can't leave you like this."

"Just *go*. Please. *PLEASE.*"

His shouting is disturbing enough that I feel my only choice is to go.

I jump up from the table and pull at the door, only to remember that I'm locked in. The fact that my departure is stalled only causes him more distress. I begin pounding on the door to get the corrections officer's attention on the other side of the lobby. When the door is finally opened, I burst out of it.

I leave Cameron in this state of unhinge. I try to catch his eye as the corrections officer locks him in, but he is still facing the wall. As I wait for the elevator, I crane my head to see if he might look up. He doesn't. All I can see is a glimpse of the back of his nacho cheese jumpsuit. It rises and falls, up and down, with no end in sight.

When business resumes after the holiday weekend, MCC determines that it is safe for Cameron to return to his unit.

He's pleased by this development. He doesn't make mention of his anxiety attack. And although I describe the incident to the psychiatrist, I don't bring it up with Cameron.

The following week we appear back in front of the trial judge. He takes the bench and issues his ruling:

```
First of all, I think the submissions here have
been  exemplary,  strong  submissions,  both  in
the papers and in the testimony, and certainly
heartfelt.
```

It's not a great sign when a judge begins a ruling with what sounds like the lead-in to a breakup. The judge confirms this moments later, stating that he will not award bail. But he is sympathetic to Cameron's medical condition:

```
I would be happy to sign an order and to make a
recommendation based on medical advice, so that's
something for you to consider. [ . . . ] In par-
ticular, I think medication, but if there is any-
thing more specific that you all want me to include
in that, I would certainly be happy to do that.
```

The judge also suggests that Cameron's sentencing be expedited—scheduled in forty-five days rather than ninety—so he can be moved to a facility with improved medical and rehab facilities as soon as possible.

It's not what was hoped for, but there is solace to be had. While Cameron will not be released, he will finally be treated for his condition. And his stay at MCC is soon coming to an end. Relief is on the way, for Cameron and also for me.

Not long after the hearing, the psychiatrist calls me. In light of the judge's decision, he would like to prescribe medication for Cameron and wants to know what the procedure is.

After some digging, I tell him that in order to prescribe medications to an inmate, the pills and dosages must appear on the Bureau of Prisons formulary. I ask him what medications he had in mind, so I can check them against the formulary. He names a medication he would like to prescribe Cameron.

"What category of medication is that?" I ask.

"It's an antidepressant."

I thumb through the formulary, but the name of the medicine does not appear. "He can't have that," I say. I read to him the name of the antidepressant that does appear on the formulary.

"That's fine, I'll prescribe that."

In addition, he would like to prescribe Klonopin.

"What category of medication?"

"It's an antianxiety medication. It's basically Xanax."

I look at the formulary, and the medicine appears. "Yes," I say. "He can have that."

The psychiatrist says that he will write the prescriptions and give these to us to forward along. The prescriptions are faxed to MCC later that day.

"Hey, did you get your meds?" I ask this of Cameron several days later, when I am visiting him to discuss the details of his sentencing papers.

"I got one," he says. "An antidepressant."

"They didn't give you your antianxiety meds?"

"No," he says.

I don't think much of it. "Well, I'm sure they will."

A week later, I arrive at MCC to find Cameron in the attorney room with the psychiatrist. They invite me into their meeting.

"Look at this," the psychiatrist says, pointing to Cameron.

I look over. His neck and arms are covered in welts. He continually leans over to scratch his legs, which are splotched with hives.

"Do you know why he hasn't gotten his medicine?" he asks.

"You still haven't gotten it?" I ask Cameron.

"Clearly he hasn't," the psychiatrist answers for him.

"I'll follow up," I say.

I brace myself for a journey into cowboy country.

It takes several days, numerous calls per day, to finally get a human being on the phone who can actually find out why Cameron has not received his antianxiety medication.

It takes another two days to receive an answer. "We didn't fill the prescription," the gentleman tells me. "We frankly thought it looked fake."

I don't understand. "How did the prescription look fake?"

"Because it was photocopied."

I close my eyes but continue to speak. "Do you mean because it was faxed to you?"

"Let me look. Yes, it was faxed."

"So is it that you need a prescription with an original signature?"

"Yes. You'd better use the mail."

I want to ask: Is there a reason that you didn't just call us to request an original? But I know there's no place for such questions in cowboy country.

I get the mailing information and call the psychiatrist, who sends over new prescriptions to be mailed out later that day. I begin to turn my attention to something else but then am struck with a thought.

If they thought the prescriptions were fake, why did they fill one of them?

Here is MCC in a nutshell. "Fucking cowboy country," I grumble to no one.

It's Saturday afternoon, about a week later. I'm spending the day in my apartment, reveling in an MCC-free day relaxing on my couch.

My cell phone rings. I recognize it to be a call from MCC. I'm assuming it's Cameron calling.

But the call is not from Cameron. The recording announces another man's name, one that I recognize as being a friend of Cameron's.

I accept the call, and a man's voice appears on the line. "Hello, is this Jen? Cameron's lawyer?"

"Yes," I say. "Is Cameron okay?"

"Yeah, I'm gonna need you to bring Cameron's transcripts the next time you come here."

"His what?"

"His court transcripts. Cameron says he isn't a rat. And if that's true, let's see the transcripts."

I hold my hand over the receiver and take in a breath.

"He's not a cooperator," I finally say.

"Yeah, so you say. Let's see the transcripts."

"Look, I'm his lawyer, I would know."

"So then it should be no problem to bring the transcripts. Right?"

He sort of has me there.

I find it odd that he is calling for this in the middle of a Saturday. What is the urgency?

"Where is Cameron right now?" I ask.

"What?"

"Where is Cameron?"

He pauses. "Why?"

I feel myself start to panic. "Just, where is he right now? I'd like to speak with him."

"Are you going to bring the transcripts?"

"Are you going to tell me where Cameron is?"

"Are you going to bring the transcripts?"

"Are you going to let me speak to Cameron?"

"Are you going to bring the transcripts?"

"Yes, I will bring the transcripts!" I yell. "Now please, where is Cameron?"

The voice yells out into the distance. "Hey, Cameron. Say something so she knows it's you."

Silence.

I press my ear to the phone.

"Hey, Cameron!"

I hear what I think is his voice, far in the distance. I can't make out what he is saying.

"Is he all right?" I ask. It is a stupid question to ask of this person, who clearly does not have Cameron's best interests at heart. But I ask him at any rate.

"Yeah, he's fine. Friends fight, you know. He'll be better when you bring me those transcripts."

He hangs up.

My mind races as to what to do next. I consider the possibility of alerting the legal team so that the government can step in. But then what? All roads lead back to the SHU. I decide that the best way of dealing with this hostage-taker is to meet his demands.

I comb through the transcripts of Cameron's various court appearances. Most contain references that a seasoned inmate would know refer to cooperation. But the most recent transcript is clean. I print it out and make several copies.

On Monday evenings I teach a class at my old law school that runs until eight p.m. Due to the exigency of getting the transcripts to Cameron, I cut class short so as not to miss MCC visiting hours. The class—a delightful group of first-year students—is outwardly elated at the reprieve. Their reaction makes me smile. I want to be a student again, and not have to confront whatever is waiting for me at MCC.

When Cameron arrives in the attorney room he looks awful. He also doesn't mince words. "Please tell me you have the transcripts."

"I do," I say, passing them over. "What happened?"

Cameron recounts what happened: he was confronted in his cell by a group of his friends about being a cooperator. After backing Cameron into a corner, the men decided that all of this could be verified through his transcripts. That's when someone decided to call me. The rest of the group was keeping their collective eye on Cameron while the phone call was made, which is why his voice sounded so distant—he was calling out from his cell, unable to get close to the phone.

When I confirmed that transcripts would be provided, the group of men disbanded. Afterward, they individually apologized to Cameron for joining the fray, each blaming someone else in the group for getting everyone worked up. Apparently snitches can be found in groups that are in hot pursuit of snitches.

I shake my head at all of it. "You scared the shit out of me. I wasn't even sure what to do."

"Well, whatever you said, it worked."

"For now, anyway."

He nods, but says nothing. I look at his arms, red with hives.

"Still no meds?" I ask.

"No."

"I'll try again tomorrow."

But try as I might, without much explanation, MCC will not dispense Cameron his medication. And I am hearing about it every week.

"Did Cameron get his meds?" his mother asks me in one of her regular phone calls.

"No, not yet," I say.

Then I call MCC. Then nothing happens.

The psychiatrist calls about an unrelated matter. "By the way," he says. "It looks like they haven't given Cameron his meds yet."

"Still? Okay, I am going to follow up."

Then I call MCC. Then nothing happens.

"Why hasn't Cameron gotten his meds yet?" Cameron's mother calls again, this time agitated. "I just went to see him, and he's a mess. He hasn't slept in days."

"I'm really not sure. I keep calling and everyone promises that they will follow up on it, and then they don't."

"Is it that they don't have any in stock? Can we just supply it to MCC so they can dispense it to him?"

"I don't think that's the issue. I am pretty sure they stock it, because it's on the formulary."

"Well, then, why don't they give it to him?"

"I really don't know. I'll follow up tomorrow."

Then I call MCC. Then nothing happens.

One day, I run into the psychiatrist in the halls of MCC on my way up to see Cameron.

"Still no meds, I see," he says.

"I honestly don't know what the problem is," I say.

We agree that Cameron is in the very position we hoped he wouldn't be. With his upcoming sentencing, there have been regular press articles about his case, many of which discuss his possible cooperation. Rather than become increasingly immune to the allegations, Cameron seems to take each installment with more difficulty.

He says he's noticed that Cameron is particularly reliant on me. I agree. I tell the psychiatrist that I now visit him every other day, that if I wait any longer than that he becomes unsettled.

The psychiatrist puts his hand on my shoulder. "It is good that he has you," he says. "You are saving his life. You really are."

"I wish there was more that I could do," I say.

"Just keep doing what you're doing," he encourages.

The exchange gives me a headache. As I wait for Cameron to arrive, I realize that I can no longer see the line between his interests and my own. When tragedy befalls Cameron, it also befalls me. His suffering is my suffering. I feel as though I am unraveling alongside of him.

You are saving his life.

There is a gentle tap on the attorney room door. There stands a corrections officer, looking at me with sympathy. "Are you all right?" he asks through the door.

I have apparently been staring out into space with tears in my eyes. I quickly wipe my eyes with the sleeve of my jacket.

"Yes, thank you," I say. "I'm fine."

I am finally put through to someone of stature in the mental health department at MCC in April, a few weeks before Cameron's sentencing. I explain to her that we have been trying for over two months to have his prescription filled. I also describe what I observe in my meetings with him: emotional outbursts, hives, and his anxiety attack.

The MCC doctor—I assume she is a doctor of some kind—seems to be writing all this down. "That sounds awful," she says with perfect bedside manner.

"It is," I say.

She says that she would like to meet with Cameron herself to make her own assessment of his needs. She says that if she observes what I describe, she will see to it that he receives his medication.

"Either way," she says, "we will get him the help he needs."

I breathe a huge sigh of relief. "I can't thank you enough," I say. "This has been ongoing for months, and he is truly in a bad way."

"It's not a problem," she reassures me. "I'll let you know how it goes."

I relay the good news to Cameron about his appointment. He says that the MCC doctor has already scheduled an appointment to see him later in the week. His relief is my relief.

A few days later, I receive a call from Cameron's unit manager. She is following up with me about a separate matter. I am surprised when she asks me whether Cameron has met with the MCC doctor.

"I think he did," I say. "Did his meds finally get administered?"

"Oh, I don't know about that. I just wondered because I overheard some people talking about him."

"You mean the fact that he saw the doctor?"

"No," she says. "About things that Cameron told her."

I am silent.

"You have to be careful who you talk to here, you know. Everyone talks. Cameron is too trusting."

I can feel the blood rushing to my face in anger. But there is no reason to discuss this further. "Thank you for letting me know," I tell her.

After I get off the phone, I shake my head at my own gullibility. How naïve I am to think that sincere steps would be taken to alleviate this problem. How stupid I was to think that there could be anything other than this in cowboy country.

Most people would find these events a reason to walk away. That while it is not right, there is nothing that can be done. The only recourse is to rise above.

Unfortunately, I am not most people. I immerse myself in the fray, sink into its depths.

I will outdo them all.

CHAPTER 4

Meet My Conspiracy

It doesn't surprise me when MCC decides that Cameron doesn't need the medication the psychiatrist has prescribed.

It doesn't surprise me when they decide the better course is placing Cameron on a medication that had previously been administered to him but that he was advised to stop taking because it did not ameliorate his anxiety and caused severe side effects.

It doesn't surprise me when a simple web search of this medication, Remeron, reveals that one of its chief side effects is "acute anxiety."

It doesn't surprise me that the medicine causes Cameron to sleep sixteen hours a day. I suspect it has been prescribed to him because it will keep his waking hours to a minimum. He's over an hour late to our next meeting because he's unable to wake up, and when he arrives, the sight of him is enough for me to involuntarily look away: his face is drenched in sweat, his skin is covered in hives, and his pupils are vertical, like a cat's.

It does surprise me, however, when Cameron asks me if I can personally bring him his meds.

At first, I don't understand. "What do you mean, 'bring' them to you?"

"Just bring them to me," he says. "Bring them with you next time."

"Um, no, Cameron. I cannot bring you your meds."

He looks at me as though I should explain.

There is no explanation necessary. "No. No. No." I shake my head for emphasis.

But he persists. "Why not?"

"Cameron, you know why not," I snap. "The whole reason you are sitting here is why."

But I have engaged him enough to make his case. "Yeah, but everyone has said I am supposed to have it. There's no reason for them not to give it to me."

"I know, it's not right," I tell him. "But this is not the answer. Don't you remember what happened last time?" I am referring, of course, to Mother Goose.

"Yeah, but that was heroin. Even you said it would have been better if she had brought me my medicine."

How did he even remember that? "Well, I meant it wouldn't have been as bad."

"Please, Jen. Please."

"No," I say. "Please don't ask me that again."

I believe the issue to be dead and buried. In fact, it is only lying dormant while I attend to other issues in the case.

We are finalizing Cameron's sentencing papers for submission, a process several weeks in the making. Because his cooperation with the government is a key factor in his sentencing, it's something that is emphasized throughout the submission. However, it still must remain a secret. This makes the filing of his papers a bit of an ordeal.

Trial judges have different rules about making sentencing paperwork public in advance of sentencing. Cameron's judge decides to make the papers public but allows us to redact any references to Cameron's cooperation. Being the most familiar with their contents, I am placed in charge of this task.

I approach this mission with pinpoint accuracy. I black out anything that could possibly be construed as a reference to cooperation. If a paragraph makes a single mention of cooperation, I black out the whole thing. I black out cites to legal decisions where the defendant is a cooperator. I also black out a sentence or two in sections that are not about cooperation, just to throw the reader off the scent.

I review each page over and over again, redacting as I go. By the time the papers are filed, they resemble a highly classified CIA dossier.

The day after we file, the trial judge makes the redacted version of the papers available for public view. We are told that a reporter from the *New York Post* has already situated himself outside the clerk's office in anticipation.

I am in my office admiring the papers in their final form. It is on this casual pass that I encounter, in the public version, an unadulterated reference to Cameron's cooperation that I've left exposed for everyone to see.

Given everything that's happened up until this point, my first instinct when I see what I've done is to open up my office window and jump out of it. Of course, this will do little to correct the error, and so, with my stomach in my throat, I contact the judge's chambers to see if it's too late to switch out the page.

The judge's clerk graciously offers to run down to the court's administrative office with a corrected page to see if the offending page can be switched out. She reminds me that the press has already been waiting for the papers and so she will see if they've made off with them yet and call me back.

While I wait, I place my head on my desk and sob.

After a small eternity, the judge's clerk calls back to say that she was able to switch out the offending page, making the papers clean of any references to cooperation. She says, however, that a reporter from the *New York Post* has already walked away with a "dirty" copy.

I breathe a heavy sigh. I throw on my jacket and head down to MCC to warn Cameron of what might be coming.

When I tell Cameron what's happened, he is furious. I remain stoic, owing only to the fact that this is my fault. I halfheartedly comfort him by saying there remains a possibility the *Post* will miss the reference just as I did. "Maybe they won't read the papers the whole way through," I offer.

"Yeah, right," he mumbles. He wipes his angry face. "Who did this?" he demands.

For a moment I consider hedging, but I know the truth will come out eventually. "It was me," I say. "Cameron, I am so sorry."

He does not say anything. He does not look at me.

"Do you want me to ask if I can go?" I ask. The afternoon prison count is in progress, so we are otherwise stuck in the attorney room together.

He shakes his head. We sit in silence.

While we do, I think about the fact that I've managed to negate all of my previous efforts to hide Cameron's cooperation. After the transcript debacle, things seemed to have smoothed over. Now I've made things worse, maybe even gravely so.

I see in Cameron's face that he's possibly thinking the same thing.

When time is up, there isn't much to say. I tell him again how sorry I am. He nods but says nothing.

When I make my way out of MCC, I'm in need of fresh air. I walk to the nearby federal courthouse and sit on its steps. I wrap my arms around my knees and see that my hands are shaking. I am afraid. For Cameron, yes. But I am more afraid for me. I selfishly do not want to bear the burden of causing him harm. I know that my error was inadvertent, that excuses could be made and reassurances could be offered. But I also know that the human conscience does not split hairs this way, it sees only the outcome and its cause. In making the error I've made, I am ultimately hurting myself.

You are saving his life.

There is really only one thing left to try, one last argument to pursue. I remember that while God and State are legally separated, they are never really divorced. And so, seated on the courthouse steps, I pray that I have not placed my client in danger and ruined my own life.

God is in the vicinity of State that day, because my prayer is answered: the *New York Post* does not mention my slip in its coverage about Cameron's sentencing papers. And while the *Post*'s website links to an electronic version of the brief, it's miraculously not a scanned version of the "dirty" brief they obtained earlier that day, but the courthouse "clean" version.

In the end, I suspect the reporter did not carefully consider the portion of the papers where the offending reference was made. Instead, the article focuses on the celebrity aspect of Cameron's sentencing, citing letters by the famous people who have written on Cameron's behalf.

When I put the article down, I savor my dumb luck that my carelessness has been outdone. I relish that the *Post* has so distracted itself with petty matters that it has let something precious go to waste.

I don't know that I'm about to do the same thing.

Soon after the bullet is dodged, Cameron resurrects his request that I bring him his meds.

His sentencing is fast approaching, and he is understandably on edge. But I tell him that what he asks me to do is simply not a good idea.

On several occasions, the conversation ends there. But Cameron starts coming up with bolstered arguments about why he needs his medication.

I wonder to myself why I let this conversation happen as often as it does.

In fairness, his condition is real and has been eating away at him for months. He has stopped taking the medicine prescribed by the MCC doctor so that he can prepare for his sentencing, and his insomnia has returned.

I plead with him to hold on for just a few more weeks, when he is sentenced and transferred out of MCC to another facility that will honor his doctor's request.

"It's just a few weeks more, Cameron," I say. "Just hang on a little longer."

"Please, Jen. Please. I can't take this." He begs me over and over again.

In his final plea, he argues that the risks involved are remarkably low, particularly to me. "It could never be traced back to you," he presses. "I wouldn't tell a soul."

He looks at me. I don't say anything, but shake my head.

"Jen, even if I did get caught, I would never let anyone come after you," he says. He presses his hands to his chest for emphasis. "It'll be all on me."

I find myself listening to this, and then stop myself. "No," I say. "I'll see you tomorrow."

That night as I lie in bed I find myself thinking about what Cameron has asked me.

Breaking the law is not something I regularly contemplate. I consider myself to be mostly, but not entirely, law-abiding. I have made more than one illegal U-turn, jaywalked across more than one street, concocted more than one mix tape. My sophomore year of college, I used a fake ID with relative frequency. I once got a speeding ticket. But on the whole I have stayed within the lines of the law, not out of any great respect for authority but because usually I see no reason not to.

So why am I still thinking about this?

I can't help but think about the pointless hoops that I have jumped through over the past few months at MCC. About the repeated phone calls that remained unanswered or without follow-up. About the amount of time it took to discern why the prescription had not been filled. About all the cowboy-like conduct that surrounded Cameron's session with the MCC doctor.

As I toss and turn with resentment, I feel justified in at least considering it. Two distinct voices emerge: the rational part of my brain, which tells me to stop thinking about it and go to sleep; and the less rational part of my brain, which says there is no harm in following the thought.

This isn't your problem, my rational brain tells me. *It's not up to you to fix this.*

This situation is bullshit, less rational brain says. *You see how much he needs it. He's been stripped of the ability to take care of himself, and the people charged with providing him care simply won't.*

Rational brain counters: *That doesn't matter. It's a crime.*

Less rational brain says: *It just doesn't seem that wrong.*

Rational brain says: *That doesn't matter. It's a crime.*

Less rational brain says: *It wouldn't hurt anybody.*

Rational brain whispers: *That doesn't matter. It's a crime.*

Less rational brain says: *It would be easy. And it would put an end to all of this.*

Rational brain is so muffled I can barely hear it: *That doesn't matter. It's a crime.*

Less rational brain says: *But what if no one would ever know?*

There is no reply.

I begin to drift to sleep, feel myself letting go. My thoughts begin to dissolve, but one last one seeps in, escorts me to unconsciousness.

How would anyone ever know?

The next day, as I am getting ready to see Cameron, I slip two small Xanax pills in my jeans pocket. Remembering the comparison drawn by the psychiatrist, and after doing some quick googling, I determine that these are equivalent to one dose of Klonopin.

I have a bottle of generic Xanax that has lasted several years. I take it when I have to fly long distances and for occasional panic attacks. I mentioned this to Cameron months ago, when I assumed that MCC would be following the judge's ruling. "I take something similar to that sometimes," I told him. "I bet it will help you a lot." He remembers this when he asks me to bring it to him.

I decide that I will carry the pills in my pocket to MCC that day. If they're discovered, I will answer honestly that these are mine and offer to dispose of them. If they aren't discovered, I will, knowingly and intentionally, give these to Cameron.

I take a deep breath as I prepare to go through MCC security. This requires going through a sensitive metal detector. Should the detector be activated—and it always is, due to the underwire of my bra—the MCC guard is required to use a wand. I have noted that this wanding is particularly focused on the offending area and usually for a considerable amount of time. Actually, the wand lingers for so long that I sometimes wait for it to make conversation.

It's never particularly pleasant. But today it provides me with a plan.

By placing the pills in my pocket, I know that they will go unnoticed. The guard will be so preoccupied with his comprehensive tour of my chest region that he will not pay any attention to my jeans. Even if he does, he has never asked me to empty my pockets.

I am proved correct: after what seems like minutes, without any scrutiny to my jeans, he instructs me to pass through.

It turns out I am quite the criminal mastermind.

When I make my way to the attorney room lobby, I'm directed by the officer on duty to an attorney room precisely behind him. As I often do, I put down my papers and pen and walk out of the attorney room to survey the vending machine. I purchase the regular fare: water for Cameron, diet Coke for me, and a bag of pretzels that we share.

Once I'm back in the attorney room, I open the bag of pretzels. I put my hand in my pocket, put the pills into my cupped hand, and then put these into the bag.

As I wait for Cameron to arrive, I'm perfectly calm. Perhaps too calm. I'm stunned by my own conduct, incredulous at the ease with which I have completed this set of acts.

It isn't too late, I tell myself. Just throw out the pretzels and this will have never happened.

But I don't. A minute later, Cameron enters the attorney room lobby.

Last chance, I tell myself.

I don't move.

When Cameron sits down, I say, "I bought you some pretzels."

"Thanks, Jen," he says flatly.

"No," I say. I nod my head toward the pretzel bag and change my wording. "I *brought* you some pretzels."

He looks at me for a moment, confused. I nod my head toward the pretzel bag again.

He opens the bag and sees the two pills. He looks up at me, his face full of shock.

I say nothing. We stare at each other for a moment, silently acknowledging what has happened. What is happening. What is about to happen.

He pulls out a pretzel along with the pills and places both in his mouth.

After a minute or two, he does seem less anxious. And it is perhaps my guilty imagination, but I think I see the hives on his arms reduced from red to pale pink.

We say nothing for a while. And then he says quietly, "Thank you, Jen. Thank you so much."

I'm glad at the relief I see in his face. But his emphatic thank-you only emphasizes the magnitude of what I've just done. "You're welcome, I guess," I say. "I'm sort of disgusted with myself."

"Please don't say that."

"Look, it was my choice. I decided to be disgusting. I just couldn't stand any of this anymore."

I'm not proud of what I've done, but I've done it. And when I walk out of MCC, I'm surprised to find I don't feel any shame or regret. I feel relief.

When I get home, I sit on my sofa and watch TV. In many ways, it feels like any other evening. But of course it isn't. Even though I feel relief that Cameron could take his medication. Even though I can try to justify what I've done. The undeniable truth is that I have committed a crime. And after this, my life will never be the same.

I have a bad habit of doubling down on bad behavior. It manifests whenever I am trying so hard to be good, but then slip and fall down. Rather than pull myself back up, I figure that since I am already on the ground I might as well stay there.

I have already had one slice of cake; I might as well have another.

I'm already late; I might as well call and cancel.

It's based on a warped and self-serving logic: you can break a glass only once. After that, there is nothing to do but look at the pieces.

I've already broken the law; I might as well do it again.

When I next see Cameron, I follow the same protocol. Once again, it proceeds flawlessly.

After I place the pills in the pretzel bag, it dawns on me that I should have some kind of endgame. How long is this going to go on? Am I just going to keep this up until the case is over?

I have no exit strategy.

After Cameron takes the pills, I tell him that while I think it's fine for him to have the medication, it's risky for me to bring it so often. I suggest that I bring it to him one last time before his sentencing, after which he can tough it out until he is finally transferred.

"I was going to talk to you about that," he says. "I was thinking, why can't you just bring me enough medicine until sentencing all at once, just one more time?"

He seemed ready with that, I think to myself.

"All at once?"

"Yeah, just bring me enough for a few days and then you only have to do it once."

I have been very sympathetic to Cameron's condition, but for the first time I feel uncomfortable. By asking me to bring him a dozen pills—three days' worth—he is changing the game, turning my role of makeshift nurse into a smuggler. A mule. He is trying to make an ass out of me.

"Cameron, I can't bring you a whole bunch of pills all at once."

"Why not?"

"You know why."

"Because you think I am going to take them all at the same time?" His face looks hurt.

I don't care. "Maybe, yes."

"Why would I do that when I need this medicine every day?"

Because you're an addict, I think to myself. But I say, "Cameron, you could get sick."

"You don't trust me?"

"I guess I don't," I say.

I continue the train of thought, how bad this idea is. "And anyway, what are you going to do with a bunch of pills on the unit? Isn't someone going to ask you where you got them?"

"I'll put them in the bottle with my other meds."

"That's really risky."

But he is insistent that it's better for me to do it this way; I just have to bring it one last time, and it is all over. He will space them out, and he will not ask me to bring any more to him again.

"Cameron, even if all of that's true, it feels like you would get caught."

"How? I won't tell a soul. And even if I get caught I won't bring your name into it."

"Even if you don't tell anyone, how would you even take the pills from here to your unit?"

"You just put them in a balloon." He says this like the answer should be obvious.

At this, I am floored. "And what, Cameron? You're going to swallow it and poop it? If it doesn't explode in your stomach first?"

"No," he says matter-of-factly. "I will just put it up my ass."

I stare at him and shake my head. How did I get here?

"Why are you looking at me like that?" he asks.

"Cameron, this isn't an episode of *The Wire*. This is real life. I'm sorry, I just can't do this for you. It's dangerous."

"Please, Jen—"

"Look, I think you should have your medicine. But not like this. You could get caught, I could get caught. You could get sick."

"But this is better for you," he pleads. "You just bring it once, and then I won't ask for it again. Even if I ask, you can say no."

Does he mean I can't say no right now?

Have I ever said no to him?

"Just one more time, Jen."

I sit in silence.

"Just one more time, to get me through to sentencing, and then it's over."

I say nothing.

"Jen, please, this is it.

"Just one more time.

"Please.

"I won't ask again. Just one more time.

"Please.

"I won't tell anyone.

"Please.

"It'll be all on me.

"It would never come back to you.

"I promise."

More than any other, this is the portion of the story I wish I could write differently. I wish I could write that I leave MCC that day, pack my bags, and move to an ashram in one of India's lower provinces.

But I don't. Instead, I convince myself that this is not much different from what I've done before, and that while I am taking a sizable risk for Cameron, by agreeing to take the fall he is taking an even bigger risk for me. I don't really buy my own argument. I know that what I'm being asked to do goes well beyond what is reasonable. Still, I don't say no. Instead, I tell myself I just have to do this once and then it will all be over.

And in a way, I am right.

The next day, I purchase a bag of balloons from the dollar store. I measure out twelve pills, enough for three days. I select a long green balloon, the kind that is blown up and twisted into balloon animals at children's birthday parties.

I am not even sure how to do this. The most logical course of action—aside from not doing it, of course—is to stretch open the mouth of the balloon and slip the pills in one at a time, so that they fall one on top of another, like an illicit roll of candy.

I clear off my desk and pour out the pills onto a piece of paper. The tablets are perfectly round, tiny in diameter, the palest shade of pink. Piled together, they do present as something as innocuous as candy. For some reason, this makes what I'm doing a little easier.

When the last tablet has been dropped, I tie the end with a secure knot and observe my handiwork. I have packed the balloon so tightly that its green skin is taut against the curve of the pills. The resulting apparatus is about a quarter inch in diameter, two inches in length. Though I have no point of reference, I decide it will suffice in size and shape for Cameron's butt.

I put on my jeans and slip the balloon deep into my pocket, examining myself in the mirror to ensure it does not protrude or otherwise show. When I arrive at MCC, I follow the same procedure as I did two times before. Predictably, the officer on duty pays my pockets no mind. When I get to the attorney room, I slip the balloon out of my pocket and place it in the bag of pretzels. Then I wait.

When Cameron arrives, he tells me to go to the restroom so that I'm not a witness to what is about to transpire.

I've been avoiding the restrooms in the attorney room lobby for months, but now I walk in and lock the door behind me. The bathroom is large, obviously meant to accommodate both an inmate and a corrections officer to observe the proceedings. There is a faint stench of urine in the air. The facilities are as filthy as I imagined them to be, which I suppose makes this an appropriate place for me to be.

I remain standing, not sure how long I should wait. I consider my reflection in the mirror over the sink. I examine myself as though I will be able to figure out why I have done what I have done, why I keep doing it, why I have let things go this far. My reflection has no answers.

When I look back on this moment, I am reminded of one of my favorite books from high school, John Knowles's *A Separate Peace.* Jealous Gene and the inimitable Finny, two boyhood friends in World War II–era New England, climb a tree together with the intention of jumping off its limb into a river. Gene watches as Finny makes his way out onto the limb, but does not join him. Instead, he remains by the base of the limb and suddenly jostles it, causing Finny to fall and to eventually die. Gene does not act with premeditation or overt maliciousness—he is not an "evil" character—and yet in that moment he chooses the evil thing, he acts in a way that he knows will bring harm to the friend that he both envies and loves.

In English class, we learn that the book is a commentary on war— the war on the battlefield and the war in man's heart. That because of man's propensity to choose the evil thing, even toward the people he loves, his worst enemy will always be himself.

As I stand in the grimy prison bathroom, my shoes sticking to the tile floor, I know that I, too, have done the evil thing and have chosen the wrong path, a path almost certain to cause harm to someone whom I ostensibly love. I am Gene. And I am Finny.

• • •

Once the unpleasantness of the balloon is behind me, I file it away in the nether regions of my mind. I decide that I have good cause to do so, given that Cameron's sentencing is in a matter of days.

I go over with Cameron the comments that he will deliver at his sentencing. He has put a lot of thought into these and is understandably nervous about delivering them in front of a global audience. He practices his remarks over and over again while I don the stern look of a judge.

I examine his appearance to see if he has abused the pills I've given him. I google the symptoms of Xanax abuse and scour his eyes for pinhead-sized pupils and monitor his conduct for anything erratic. It seems he has kept to his promise.

The spectacle surrounding his sentencing is unlike anything I've ever seen. The barrage of press is what one would imagine for a visit by the president, not the halfhearted drug-dealing son of a movie star. Reporters are lined into the jury box of the courtroom and spill out into the gallery. The courtroom is so overflowing with spectators that a second one is opened up for closed-circuit viewing.

Before the proceedings begin, I visit Cameron in the inmate cell adjacent to the courtroom. He's wearing the suit selected for him by his endlessly stylish mother. He looks like an entirely different person outside of his jumpsuit. "I told you I clean up nice," he says with half a smile. But it's a vain attempt at lightheartedness; when I look at the hand holding his dog-eared remarks, it is trembling.

"It's going to be okay," I say. "It's almost all over."

He nods and gives a nervous smile. He says that he is ready.

Co-Counsel arrives to greet Cameron and let him know he's ready, too. He examines Cameron's appearance with an approving look. Through the bars, he helps Cameron adjust his tie. It's a touching gesture, one that Cameron seems to appreciate.

Soon after we return to the courtroom, a U.S. Marshal opens the door with Cameron at his side. The entire courtroom is straining to see. I give him a supportive smile as he takes a deep breath and sits down.

In sentencing proceedings involving cooperators, the government is required to make a motion asking the court to consider the defendant's cooperation in calculating his sentence. Where the cooperation is still a secret, some judges perform this motion outside of the courtroom in chambers. Cameron's judge instead calls a sidebar, so that the motion can be made outside of earshot of the participants, unavailable for public consumption.

As all of the attorneys get up to approach the bench, I consider staying behind. There is nothing for me to say or do. But when I look over at Cameron, he nods his head toward the bench as though to indicate I should go, too.

The sidebar motion is brief—in quiet voices, the government makes the motion and the judge accepts it. All of it is recorded by the court reporter. It's over almost as soon as it starts and then the group disbands.

The proceedings are otherwise rote. The judge is tough in his words but ultimately recognizes Cameron's need for rehabilitation. The government makes no statement. Co-Counsel gives an impassioned presentation about how Cameron now has a support system that will help him get his life on track. And then Cameron stands up and tearfully apologizes for what he has done and pleads for an opportunity to make things right.

The judge delivers the sentence: sixty months. He indicates that Cameron should be given rehab at the earliest opportunity. He also recommends that Cameron serve the remainder of his sentence at a low-security prison camp. All said and done, given the time he's already served, plus the credit he will receive for good time and for completing rehab, this means Cameron will be released in about two more years.

And then, it seems, it's all over. We file out of the courtroom and meet briefly with his family to discuss the outcome.

During the meeting, his mother leans over to me and says, "He looked great in his suit, didn't he?"

"He did," I say. "You did a great job."

"Did you see how healthy he looked? Better than he has in months!"

I nod and smile, but say nothing.

When I see Cameron later that evening, he is the happiest I've ever seen him. In a couple of months, he will be transferred out of MCC.

He will finally escape the scrutiny that this ordeal has brought him and can begin thinking about starting over in earnest.

I'm also about to start over. In a few short months, I will be leaving law practice behind to start a new teaching job at a law school in the outer boroughs. Even before this case I felt I had my fill of practicing law. But Cameron's case and the lengths I have allowed it to take me make obvious to me that I need to get out.

I arrive home that evening to an inbox full of congratulatory e-mails: news of Cameron's sentencing has made him the fifth most googled person of the day. I hold off on responding. Instead, I put on sweatpants and melt in front of my television, emptying my DVR of months of unwatched television programming.

At around eleven p.m., my BlackBerry announces a new e-mail has arrived containing the sentencing transcript that I had ordered earlier that day. I decide to peruse it on the device as I watch TV, scrolling through several pages at once.

My eye catches something and I scroll back. I look twice more. Then I stand up, go to my computer, and pull up the full document.

I'm sure I'm reading it wrong. But this transcript contains the entire contents of the sidebar motion, including an official statement by the government that Cameron is cooperating.

The day has been going so well that instead of panicking, I decide this isn't what I think it is. The sidebar is included in *my* version, I tell myself, because I am on the legal team. There is no way it is included in the public transcript.

I try to go back to watching television. After a few minutes, I shut it off and sit at my computer. As soon as I see that everything's fine, I say to myself, I'll go to bed.

I scour press stories online about the sentencing—there seems to be no mention of the sidebar motion. I check every twenty minutes for new stories. Nothing.

I continue in this manner for over an hour. Then I see the *New York Post* has published a front-page article about Cameron. And there it is: Cameron's cooperation and the full text of the sidebar motion in quotes. Of the hundreds of news outlets that cover Cameron's sentencing, it is the only publication that chooses to print what was obviously meant to remain off the record.

This is what I get. I am being punished.

I try to sleep, but I can't. The night seeps into the next day and with it comes a flurry of activity aimed at damage control. In addition to the usual fare, we've asked the government to take the extra step of seeing to it that Cameron is transferred out of MCC as soon as possible, rather than in a matter of months.

I brace myself for what will happen next. Cameron Douglas's father has his regularly scheduled visit with Cameron that morning, and so the legal team asks him to alert Cameron as to what's happened so that he isn't caught off guard.

I am charged with checking up on him that evening. I am dreading his arrival in the attorney room. But when he enters, he is surprisingly chipper.

"You look awful," he says to me. "Did you go out last night or something?"

He doesn't know. It turns out that Cameron Douglas's father misunderstood what we were asking him to do. So Cameron is taking this news in for the first time as I explain what has happened and show him a copy of the paper.

His reaction is predictably angry. I explain to him that the passage was not supposed to be in the transcript—the whole point of a sidebar is that it is conducted outside of the public.

This provides cold comfort. He is silent as he composes himself. Then he says, "Jen, how could you let this happen? I told you to go up there just to make sure you were looking out for me."

I would normally lodge a defense on my behalf, but he is only saying what I have been thinking all day. "I know," I say.

This does not make him feel better.

I tell him that we are making arrangements to have him transferred out of MCC in advance of the usual months-long waiting period. "Do you think you'll be okay until then?" I ask.

He thinks for a moment and nods. I suppose he knows he has to be.

I look at the clock—the prison count is already under way, and so we must remain in the attorney room for another half hour. I start to make small talk and he interrupts.

"Would it be all right if we just didn't talk right now?"

"Of course," I say. "I know all of this is difficult."

We sit in silence. I do not look up and suspect he is doing the same.

When the prison count is over, I tell him that the rest of the legal team will be there in the morning to check in on him again. He asks me to tell them not to come. "I am going to take the Remeron," he says, "and sleep as long as I can."

I nod in agreement and offer a carrot. "I can come tomorrow evening to check in on you, if you want," I say.

"Okay," he says without looking up.

Another carrot: "I can actually come as many days as you'd like before you get transferred. I don't have much more to do before I'm done with work."

"Okay," he says again.

The next time that I visit him, racked with guilt, I provide a third and final carrot. It is contained in a long green balloon, the type that is often blown up and twisted into balloon animals at children's birthday parties, tied with a secure knot.

I continue to visit Cameron daily until he is transferred a month later. Although I am at first wary about how the disclosure of his cooperation will play out, I notice that in a matter of days he is back to his chipper self. I ask him how things are going on the unit, and he is surprisingly upbeat.

When he is designated to a facility in Pennsylvania to serve out the remainder of his sentence, his case officially approaches its close. I am outwardly relieved for Cameron, happy for him that this difficult chapter of his life is over. But when by myself, I discover that I am utterly broken up over his departure. That for all of the stress his case has provided, I still don't want to return to my stale existence—to any existence, really—without him. My feelings are too raw to hide, and so when I am at home pulling materials together about his new facility, the thought crosses my mind that he will no longer be a part of my life, and I spontaneously burst into tears.

When I arrive at MCC on what I believe to be his last day, I am stoic. I'm sure to display enthusiasm when I show him the materials that I had collected the night before. We revel in how much nicer his new facility will be. When we talk about his new life, I swallow the thought that it will be separate from my own.

I try to avoid looking at my watch to see our few remaining minutes pass, but I can't help myself. When I look up, the expression on Cameron's face indicates he is about to ask for something. "Jen, will you come visit me?" he asks.

I am steeling myself not to cry. "Of course," I say. "Just give me a call whenever you want me to come down."

"I mean a personal visit. Not an attorney's visit."

"Yes, Cameron, I will."

The corrections officer comes to the door to tell us that it is time. I begin to collect my things.

"Well, Jen. I guess this is good-bye. I'm going to miss you."

I look away in the hopes that this will make things easier. It doesn't. I can feel that tears are on their way.

I clear my throat to speak. Through the glass door, I see the corrections officer gesturing that he has summoned the elevator to take me back to my old life. It's time to go.

I turn to him and blurt out, "I love you, Cameron." I am shocked at my own outburst, and, in a quick glimpse through my tears, see that he is shocked, too.

The milk has been spilled, there is no point in saying more. The corrections officer is now yelling, and so I wipe my face as I run to the elevator. I don't look back, and I wait until I am several blocks away from MCC before I start crying again.

It turns out this is not Cameron's last day.

I find that out the following afternoon when his mother calls to ask if I might go down and relay a message. I debate making up an excuse, but the truth is my desire to see him one last time outweighs my embarrassment.

By now, our routine is familiar. He is smiling as he walks into the attorney room. I am feeling sheepish, but as soon as I see him, I am happy that I came.

He has lots of swagger as he sits down. "Well, hello, Jen."

"Hello, Cameron."

"So, you love me, huh?"

"Yes," I say. "I guess I do."

"Well, I love you, too," he says.

"Well, that's good," I say. And it is.

He gets out of his seat and walks over to me. The act is so unexpected that I feel as though I am watching him move in slow motion. When he leans over my chair, I am acutely aware that I have never been this close to him. His breath smells of toothpaste, minty fresh. He has tiny freckles on the bridge of his nose. He seems taller, greater, than when he is sitting across from me.

"What are you doing?" I ask.

He grabs me. And kisses me. And I kiss him back.

I like this good-bye much better.

When Cameron is finally transferred from MCC to his facility in Pennsylvania, the issue of his cooperation has become an ancient relic. Once he is gone, I marvel at how the advent of the newspaper article did not in the end seem to impact Cameron's safety. That even when the very worst came to pass, he managed to escape unscathed.

I do not consider the thought for very long, at least not then. The thought will come back to me much later, when I learn that Cameron shared the contents of one or both balloons with his circle of friends. Whether this was in putative exchange for protection or forgiveness, or for neither of these things, I will never know for sure. What I do know is that in sharing both his medication and my identity, Cameron manages to expose our crimes to his fellow inmates, men whose names I do not know, one of whom is a government informant.

CHAPTER 5

Reckoning

I am often asked if my experience as a defense attorney provides some useful familiarity to my own criminal case. It doesn't. Inherent in this question is the presumption that ushering someone through the criminal process is the same as personally living the experience. It isn't. When my turn to walk the line arrives, everything is starkly, painfully new.

I am asked, too, if my interest in the study of criminal law makes this experience valuable from an anthropological perspective. It doesn't. Inherent in this question is the misguided supposition that I somehow stand apart from other criminal defendants, that the process is something I can look at in the abstract. It isn't. I'm not Barbara Ehrenreich researching the reality of the minimum wage in *Nickel and Dimed*, nor am I a supermodel in a fat suit waddling around town marveling at the plight of the overweight. I don't go home at the end of the day to a "real" life. This *is* my real life.

There are no upsides. The only thing I allow myself to think about when my criminal case arrives is getting out of it. There is an adage that says: "You're not sorry for what you've done, you're only sorry you've been caught." This couldn't be more right. When my future flashes before me as nothing more than a blank page, I'm exceedingly sorry that I have been caught. I leave other regrets for another time.

I discuss with my lawyer the best way to make all of this go away.

While I was blithely playing Clara Barton, I didn't consider what I was putting at risk. Now all that I can think about is nailing down whatever I can before it is ripped away.

I consider the full gamut of possibilities, starting with the fact that my target letter does not technically require a response. I don't have to admit my guilt simply because the government asks me to. One possibility is to let things play out, force the government to make its case against me.

But this is not a realistic option. I am, of course, guilty in the most patent sense. More importantly, I have no idea what evidence they have of my guilt. I don't yet know that Cameron shared his medication or told anyone where he got it, and so for all I know they have play-by-play video footage of everything I've done. If this is the case, all the government needs to do is assemble a grand jury and press play.

A grand jury indictment would be calamitous. It makes the matter not just public, but because of Cameron's involvement, very public. This publicity would ignite a chain of events—loss of job, loss of license, loss of reputation, loss of sanity—that could not be undone. I would like to avoid the press altogether, or at least put it off as long as I can.

To play by the government's rules means the matter will remain private. Because this is what is most important to me, it seems the best course. I hold out hope, too, that by being forthright they might let the matter go. So for reasons that are entirely self-serving, I agree to sit down with the government and give them an honest recounting of what I've done.

A little over a week after the feds arrived, I am to meet with the government under the terms of a proffer agreement. The agreement does not offer me immunity or even leniency, but it allows me to tell my tale without immediately being placed in handcuffs afterward. Based on the disclosures I make, the government will make a decision as to how to proceed.

I wake up the morning of my proffer session as though it is just another day in the life of the law. As I have many times before, I get dressed and head down to the U.S. Attorney's Office. Though this presents the first time the proffer session I'm attending is my own, for some reason preparing for it is no less tedious. As I walk toward St. Andrew's Plaza in downtown Manhattan, I recoil at how much I have wanted to leave this world, only to end up in the worst possible place in it.

I am in the midst of this thought when I hear a young woman's voice.

"Professor Ridha!"

I turn and see one of my students from my class last semester. She is running toward me in her crisp suit, her face full of sunshine.

I paste a smile on my face. "How is your summer?" I ask.

She is spending her summer interning for a federal judge, a job that I had suggested she might enjoy. She is bubbling with enthusiasm about learning the inner workings of the court and is telling me the things from class that she has seen in real life.

I tell her that I am happy she is getting so much out of the experience. I can remember a time when observing the law in motion made me that excited. Now, as she chirps with admiration about her judge, I consider the possibility that he will be assigned to my case, that I will be required to appear before him, beg for his mercy. I wonder if my former student will be there, too.

This thought prompts me to look at my watch to make sure I am not late for what is waiting for me. I tell her that I unfortunately have to get to a meeting—this is technically true—and sincerely wish her a happy rest-of-summer.

At this, without any warning, she throws her arms around me in a hug. I am not in a particularly hugging mood, but the gesture seems so heartfelt that I surrender to it. We stand there, clutching one another as scores of attorneys file around us, to and from the nearby courthouse, ensuring that the wheels of law continue to turn.

That is who I used to be, I think to myself as I watch them pass. I can tell that my student is saying something, but it is muffled by her hug. I am not really listening anyway. I grab her just as tight and savor giving my old life one final embrace.

When I make my way into the dank and familiar conference room at the U.S. Attorney's Office, I meet the team of individuals assigned to bring me to justice. First is Burly Man, who is the investigator on the case. When he says hello, I search his face for signs he's seen me half naked. I learn nothing.

Next is a female prosecutor. She more or less resembles every female Assistant United States Attorney I've ever encountered: attractive, athletic, conservatively dressed. If there ever was an Assistant United States Attorney Barbie, her hair would be dyed an inoffensive shade of brown, she would wear a pantsuit in black or navy, and her face would bear makeup so subtle that she could easily be mistaken for fresh-faced. She would carry a tiny copy of the Federal Criminal Code. AUSA Barbie would make herself pretty, but not so much that it distracts juries. She would fight crime, but not in a manner that is considered hostile or distasteful.

Finally, there is Some Prosecutor, the illustrious author of my target letter. He, too, resembles one of two generalized categories of male Assistant United States Attorneys that I have observed. Category One male AUSAs bear the plain and thoughtful attributes of a quiet bookworm. Category Two male AUSAs are objectively handsome and outwardly aggressive. Category One male AUSAs use their legal acumen to prosecute complex securities and tax crimes; their reserved demeanor and high nerd factor lulls the defendant into the false belief that he will get away with it. He won't. Category Two male AUSAs usually prosecute more conventional crimes—drugs, guns, gangs—and use their unpredictable temperament and exaggerated arrogance to scare the defendant into believing that his freedom is contingent on the prosecutor's personal whims. It isn't. Some Prosecutor is a Category Two male AUSA.

I always smile when famous defendants attribute the bad outcomes in their criminal cases to the specific prosecutor trying the case, as though there were a sympathetic, less zealous prosecutor waiting in the wings. They don't seem to realize all prosecutors are unsympathetic and zealous, not because they share some unfortunate birth defect—at least none that has been uncovered—but because apparently this is how it is supposed to be.

I remind myself of this fact before the proffer session begins. Having sat in on dozens of these in practice, I know some of what to expect.

I know that the prosecutors will be stern about being honest. I know that there are only four possible answers to a question posed by the government—(1) yes, (2) no, (3) I don't know, and (4) I don't remember—each of which will put the burden on the prosecutor to develop all of the facts.

I know, too, not to bother trying to get on anyone's good side. It's natural for someone in such a vulnerable position to try to ingratiate himself with the prosecutors. But sucking up never gets clients far, first because a client's likability has no bearing on how prosecutors will choose to proceed and second because prosecutors usually exploit these opportunities to get more answers. Some might also do the dreaded "fake handshake"—extend their limp hand and then refuse to make eye contact when the client actually takes it. I think the gesture is meant to say, *I am extending my hand to be professional but you are a piece of shit.* At least that's how clients seem to interpret it.

To avoid the fake handshake, I walk into the room and quickly take my seat, hands at my sides. While my lawyer makes small talk with the prosecutors—he is a former prosecutor who has left behind an impressive legacy—I am deliberate in not joining the conversation. I am not another lawyer in the room, I know what I am there for, and so I simply look down at the table until the proceedings start.

When we begin, Some Prosecutor says something along the lines of, "Ms. Ridha, I'm sure you know that you are required today to tell us the truth. This is not the time to cover up for someone else's actions. If we discover you are not being forthright, we will take that into consideration in how we proceed in your case. If you are not prepared to be honest, we should not sign the agreement and go forward with this meeting. Do you understand?"

I have heard this spiel perhaps fifty times before. And yet now, when the statement is directed at me, the gravity of my situation strikes me so hard that my legs begin to shake. I have to place a hand on my lap to control the movement. I can't even formulate an answer to his question. Instead, I helplessly look to my attorney. He tells Some Prosecutor that I understand and we both sign the agreement.

I repeat in my head, over and over again: Yes, no, I don't know, I don't remember. Yes, no, I don't know, I don't remember.

Female Prosecutor starts the questioning. "So, why don't you tell us what happened?"

I look at her for a moment with surprise. I consider reminding her that she is supposed to be asking me yes/no questions. But she seems to recognize that I know how to make this easier on myself. At least this is what her face appears to say when I look at her in the hopes she will rephrase.

And so, I have little choice except to start the story at the beginning. My explanation is far from lawyerly. With the onus on me to provide all relevant facts, I simply try to get everything out there. With the more difficult facts, this is done through tears. I keep looking at Female Prosecutor for signs that I've left anything out.

As I tell my version of events, Female Prosecutor and Some Prosecutor occasionally interrupt to ask questions. Burly Man sits and listens. Female Prosecutor has in front of her a large file folder filled with documents. She shows me my pharmaceutical history, which she has obviously obtained by request or subpoena from my local pharmacy. When I subsequently visit the pharmacy I will examine the familiar face of the pharmacist to see if she knows the feds have been asking about me. I see nothing, other than her obvious discomfort at the fact that I am studying her so closely.

The document from my pharmacy contains a listing of all of my other medications that have been administered as of late. For each medication, it also lists the prescribing physician. In the case of a recent antibiotic prescription for a throat infection, the prescribing doctor is my brother. When I see his name on the exhibit, I tear up in shame.

Some Prosecutor has in front of him a legal pad. He seems to be in charge of jotting down any relevant facts from the meeting. In my experience, there appears to be a direct correlation between the amount of notes taken during a proffer session and the seriousness with which the government takes the matter. In those meetings where few notes are taken, the matter tends to go away. But when a prosecutor goes to the trouble of writing extensive notes, this often means he is making his case against you even as you speak.

Partway through the questioning, I steal a glance at Some Prosecutor. He is slightly hunched over his papers, writing in a small, deliberate scrawl. Easy to read later, I think with a flash of worry. I crane my head to see his notebook. It is bursting with notes, page after page, as though these can barely contain a description of what I've done. I try to count the pages, but there are too many. I have to refrain from asking him to please stop writing down what I say.

I am so distracted that I can't look away. I notice the silence in the room and turn my attention back to Female Prosecutor. She is looking at me expectantly.

"I'm sorry," I say. "Can you please repeat the question?"

"What now?" I ask my attorney as we exit the U.S. Attorney's Office.

"We wait," he says.

And so, with an albatross about my neck, I wait. My attorney tells me that there are three possible outcomes. First, in a best-case scenario, the government can simply let the matter go. Second, in a not-best-case scenario, they can offer to enter into a deferred prosecution agreement, where they would bring charges but agree to drop these in six months if I satisfy certain conditions. Third, in a worst-case-I-wish-I-had-fled-to-a-country-without-an-extradition-treaty scenario, the government prosecutes me, full stop.

I sit in my living room, the three scenarios rolling in my head. I have multiple conversations with myself. Can this really go away? Should I quit my job? Will I have to serve jail time? How on earth will I use the bathroom in front of other people?

I also fixate on Some Prosecutor's notes. I develop a detailed fantasy where his office is flooded, and though there is no serious structural damage—I am not a monster—his notebook is submerged in water, its contents now illegible.

Somewhere in the midst of considering all of this, I notice a dull pain at my side. I ignore it so that I can focus on obsessive thinking. After a while the pain grows sharp. I take two Aleve so that I can go back to obsessive thinking. After around an hour, I am keeled over in pain and realize something may not be right.

I call my brother and give him my symptoms. He is at a loss and says that if the pain is increasing I should go to the emergency room.

It is a Friday evening in New York City, and the emergency room is teeming with disease and disorder. My pain has reached a level where all I can do is cry. I have a brunch appointment the following day with my ex, and so I call him to see if he'd rather go to the emergency room instead. He kindly sits with me for fourteen hours while we await a proclamation of the cause.

I have not seen him since before Cameron's case began. "How have you been?" he asks earnestly.

This question makes the pain even worse.

A nurse gives me an IV of fluids and an injection of Dilaudid. I am instantly covered in a blanket of bliss, adrift in a space where there is no such thing as criminal charges. I lie on the hospital cot with a huge Cheshire grin, oblivious to all sources of pain, professing my love to the nurse who checks in on me every hour.

The following morning, the verdict is reached: there is a calcified stone in my left kidney trying to escape through my ureter. The resident on call asks me if I've ever had a kidney stone before. I have not. Has anyone in my family had a kidney stone? They have not. Do I consume extraneous amounts of sodium and/or creatine? I do not. She is stumped.

I wonder if my fear of impending public urination has caused my entire renal system to cease proper production. I do not mention this to the doctor.

She discharges me and refers me to a specialist. I say a wistful good-bye to my IV and we leave. Within an hour or so, the pain—all of it—is back.

A few days later, I stumble to New York Presbyterian's Kidney Stone Center to find out why I have developed a kidney stone without apparent cause. An endourologist considers my medical history in depth and asks me a series of questions that he says touch on burgeoning areas of kidney stone research. He calls in two of his young medical fellows to discuss my case. The three men discuss my renal health at length. One fellow is based at the computer, looking at my electronic medical records. The other holds a manila folder containing my X-ray and checkup details from earlier that day. They seem to forget that I am sitting there. After a while, I forget that I am sitting there, too.

The specialist sighs loudly. He discovers that I am still in the room. His face changes expression as though an idea has just occurred to him. "Have you been under any significant stress as of late?" he asks.

I consider the events of the past ten days. "Yes."

"Severe stress?"

"Yes."

He looks at me as though I should explain.

"Well, I recently found out that I am the target of a criminal investigation."

At this, the two other doctors stop what they are doing and look at me. The medical fellow who is holding the manila folder closes it.

The specialist has a look on his face that can only be described as relief. "Yes, well, I think this mystery has been solved."

Indeed it has. I have not had a kidney stone since.

On my way out of the hospital, the elevator stops on a lower floor. A large sign proclaims it to be the hospital's pediatric cancer unit. I am still putting these words together in my head when two pretty tween-aged girls enter the elevator, each donning a knit beanie on her bald head. They are decked out in skinny jeans—extra skinny, as both are disconcertingly thin—and glitter nail polish. I observe them as they giggle to one another and discuss what kind of snack they intend to purchase from the concession stand downstairs. When they exit the elevator, they link arms in a manner that suggests they are BFFs—best friends forever—whatever the duration of that forever might be.

I watch these girls for a moment before heading to the subway. I will sometimes find myself thinking about them during my case. This is not because they somehow make me grateful for my circumstances or because their cheery disposition in the wake of something so awful provides me with perspective. I am far too self-involved for any of that. I think about them because they remind me of the logic of my circumstances. It is common sense that bad acts would beget bad consequences, that a perpetrator of crimes would find herself at the center of a criminal case. But there is no amount of logic that can explain what I see in the elevator that day. There is something reassuring in knowing that my misery is a product of my own making.

Not long after my trip to the hospital my mother arrives. To be on the safe side, I ask her to come after my proffer session. This way, I don't need to tell the government that I've told her anything, thereby possibly subjecting her to questioning.

At first it feels like any other visit. This is probably because neither of us wants to acknowledge the existence of my case. Instead, as we normally do, we cook and work on various home projects while watching my mother's favorite television channel, HGTV. My mother has already seen most of the programming but likes to personally narrate it to me in case I miss something.

She is particularly taken with the reveal at the end of each home makeover program, how the ugly before becomes the beautiful after. As we watch, I find myself wishing that I, too, could be completely made over into something new in forty-five minutes, not including commercial breaks.

The programming reaches its end, and we turn off the TV. Now, I think, is when my mother will ask me about my case. But she has put on her pajamas, pulled out one of my magazines, and does not seem to be gearing up for any big conversations.

I sit next to her on the couch. "Mom," I say, "aren't you going to ask me what I did?"

She looks up. "I thought you would tell me when you want to."

I explain to her what I've done in broad detail, although I deliberately leave out the specifics about the balloon and Cameron's anal cavity.

"That's it?" she says incredulously.

"Well, it's kind of a big deal." I explain to her the three possibilities for the resolution of my case. By this time, I am numbed to the stakes involved, so I am blunt about the possibilities.

"What if you lose your job?" she asks me.

"I guess I'll just have to get another one," I say.

"But what if you lose your license?" she presses.

"I suppose I'll have to do something else," I say. I don't have better answers than these.

My mother will later tell me that the most chilling part of this conversation is the calmness with which I speak. How inured I am to the possibility of losing so much.

"I am going to pray for you," she reassures me. "I don't think God will let any of this happen."

I give her a hug. I'm relieved to have told her but also feel bad that she has to hear any of it. Had I thought of her in the moments when I was deciding to break the law, I don't think we would be having this conversation.

We go to bed. She insists on the couch, and I go to my bedroom so I can lie on my bed with my eyes wide open. After a while, I decide to get a glass of water. Although the living room is squarely between my bedroom and kitchen, my mother is a deep sleeper, so I know I will not wake her.

But when I poke my head into the living room, I see that she's not asleep. She is sitting up on the couch, looking out the window, crying.

I freeze at the sight of her, abruptly turn, and then tiptoe back into my bedroom. I don't know what to do with what I've witnessed. I shove my head under the pillow, hoping this will somehow erase what I've just seen.

Under the pillow, I think about how for all of her impossible expectations and Baathist directives, for all of her relentless pushing into a life I didn't particularly want to live, the only thing my mother has ever wanted for me is a life of choices. Now I've managed to choose so wrongly that I may have made all of my good choices fall away.

Of all the repercussions of what I've done, it is the image of my mother, her back to me, her shoulders gently shaking, that is forever frozen in my mind. Every time I think of it, even now, I ask myself: What kind of piece of shit makes her mother cry?

For the remainder of her visit, my mother and I do not talk much about my case. We certainly don't discuss the fact that I saw her crying.

Instead, we resume our daily diet of television and cooking and crafting and pretend that everything is as it always was.

But I notice that as we are reorganizing the contents of one of my closets, she is eyeing me for quite a while. This usually means that an interrogation is looming.

She brings it up casually, as though making conversation. "So," she says. "It sounds like there was something going on with this Cameron."

The first rule of my mother's interrogations is to always play dumb. "What do you mean?" I say. I'm careful not to look up from what I am doing, as that might arouse suspicion.

"It seems like actually you love him."

I knew this would never get past my mother. If the federal government could come to this conclusion, my mother probably got there sooner, even without subpoena power.

I decide to go with what is the most true. I take a deep breath and conjure up the strength to look her in the eye.

"I guess so."

The look on her face is one that I haven't seen since I was a teenager, when I attempted to leave our home wearing immodestly cut jean shorts and a pair of surreptitiously purchased thigh-high stockings. My mother, having sniffed out my escape, was waiting for me at the foot of the stairs in staunch stance, a barrier between me and the front door.

On that day, my mother said nothing. Her look was enough for me to scurry back up the stairs and change. That was the last time I ever saw the stockings; when I returned they were gone, perhaps sent away to a sanctuary for slutty attire.

Today, when I don't cede ground, my mother's look changes to one of incredulousness. And then she says what I know she will say:

"But he didn't go to college!"

This response is as irritating as it is expected. My mother subscribes to the Iraqi philosophy, coined some thousands of years ago, that an individual's worth is based on his profession. She adheres to a strict doctrine that I call the List: doctor or lawyer or PhD. End. Anyone who is unable to check an item off the List—Nobel Laureates, for example, Pulitzer Prize winners, technology moguls, world leaders—belongs to a nebulous category of "other."

This is a backward principle for reasons that are self-evident. But for me, it has always been particularly senseless for the additional reason that my mother, a college-educated homemaker, does not pass her own muster. Sadder still is that this is an outcome she readily accepts, that she agrees she offers less to society than someone who practices podiatry or chases ambulances.

And so while there is in fact a valid reason why Cameron did not finish his college degree—he decided to move to New York to pursue acting and music—for me to justify anything against the List would presume its validity. And because my mother is not on the List, and because I am facing the real possibility of being kicked off of it, I have no interest in doing this.

Instead, I say: "He's a drug dealer, Mom. You don't have to go to college for that."

Her face displays a level of shock that if not directed at me would make me burst out laughing. I bite my lip to contain the urge and wait for her response.

She stares at me a moment longer and then starts laughing.

"You are really an idiot, Jennifer."

I laugh, too. Unlike the List, there is nothing to argue there.

When it's all over, my mother and I will have many more arguments over the things that I've done, the majority of which will not culminate in laughter. One of us will say: "You have fucked up your life." Another of us will say: "Maybe you should get your own life so I can fuck mine up in peace." There will be arguing and intermittent yelling. Periods of détente. Tearful apologies. Then more yelling.

This particular argument is among one of the more pleasant ones that occur. And while these are certainly easier to endure, in the final analysis each and every one of our battles leads me to the same inexorable conclusion: if you truly want to test the bounds of your parent's unconditional love, I highly recommend getting arrested.

The days of summer pass and there is still no response from the government. My attorney calls me regularly to clarify various factual issues and discuss contingency strategies.

Though I know he is only doing his job, I hate hearing from him. I gain a fuller understanding of Kafka's Josef K., his continual incapacitation by thick, stale air whenever he is confronted with his criminal case. I gather this is a physical manifestation of the weight of the law bearing on his chest, slowly suffocating him. In my case, the law has migrated south to my stomach, causing it to curl so much that I keep a wastebasket by the phone should I feel the need to vomit when my attorney calls. I use it on more than one occasion.

Each day I do not hear from the government is agony. And each day I must speak to my lawyer is also agony.

By the end of August, I am supposed to begin teaching at a new law school, and classes are about to start. I have to make a decision as to what to do. My lawyer calls Some Prosecutor—Female Prosecutor has left the U.S. Attorney's Office, and with it my case—to see if I should go forward with my new job or if the direction the government plans to take would make this ill-advised.

"That's up to her" is Some Prosecutor's very helpful response.

I ask my lawyer what he thinks I should do. I do not want to abandon my new job but also don't know if I should teach while all of this is hanging over my head.

My lawyer believes there remains a possibility that this entire thing can go away. He posits that the matter is still private and will continue to be until a decision is made. There is no reason not to assume this might all work out.

I memorialize his advice on the back of an envelope that I later throw into the file of documents I keep related to my case. In green-inked scrawl, somewhat sloppy due to the precarious hand of its writer, it reads: "go in and go to office. go about business."

*W*hat is a crime?

This is the question posed at the start of every course in criminal law. It is the same that I use to begin my class.

The students raise their hands, eager to make a good impression. A crime is something that is immoral. A crime is something that harms another person. A crime is something that harms society.

None of these answers are entirely right, and yet none of them are incorrect. It is a trick question. A crime might address immoral conduct, but it might not. There are plenty of crimes on the books that address conduct—like, until recently, sodomy laws—that is not generally thought of as immoral. A crime might address conduct that causes harm to another person, but it might not. There are many crimes involving consensual conduct—drugs, prostitution—that are without victims. A crime might constitute a harm to society, but it might not. Antimiscegenation laws made it a crime for blacks and whites to marry, and yet we know with certainty that this does not cause harm to society.

In the end, a crime is whatever the law says it is. A crime is only what we are told it to be.

What is punishment?

This is not a trick question. Punishment is a penalty for committing a crime.

How should we punish crimes?

For this question, the students have read for class the section of the textbook describing two schools of thought on punishment. One theory says that crimes should be punished only insofar as it keeps the defendant from committing future crimes. The other theory says that crimes should be punished only insofar as the specific crime requires.

The first theory takes as its starting point the criminal and looks forward. What sort of punishment is needed to prevent her from committing further crimes? Can she be rehabilitated into something other than a criminal? She should be punished only as long as she poses a threat to society, and no longer.

The second theory takes as its starting point the crime and looks backward. What is the harm she caused? She should be punished in a manner proportional to what she did. She should pay back to society what she has taken, and nothing more.

Both of these theories operate in our current system of criminal justice. The students soon understand that under the second theory the punishment is usually harsher. This is because it is based on the notion that the criminal has no value beyond what she has done. Under this theory, a criminal essentially *is* her crime.

Fringe proponents of this second theory consider criminals to be something separate and distinct from the human race. I assign a passage from a nineteenth-century British jurist named Sir James Fitzjames Stephen. "I think it highly desirable," he writes, "that criminals should be hated, that the punishments inflicted on them should be so contrived as to give expression to that hatred, and to justify it so far as the public provision of means for expressing and gratifying a healthy natural sentiment can justify and encourage it."

When I review the assigned reading in advance of class, I notice that this is the only section in forty pages that I've underlined.

In class, the students consider various crimes in the textbook under the two theories. In groups, they must place themselves in the judge's robe and explain the punishment they will deliver and why. As expected, the students tend to veer toward the second theory. This is said to be because students overidentify with the victim. I personally think it's because the exercise presents the first time in their short lives that they have been given authority over others, and there is a human impulse to exploit this to the fullest extent.

Because the duty of the teacher is to shed light on all sides of the discussion, and because no one seems interested in advancing the perspective of the criminal, I end up serving as a makeshift defense attorney to all of the defendants in the textbook. This is a shoe that fits. Predictably, the majority of the students are unmoved by arguments that criminals should be given second chances, regardless of the circumstances. They are not aware that a putative criminal defendant is responsible for their final grade.

Though their sentencing schemes are severe, the students are in general a pleasure to teach. They show real interest in the subject matter and bear passionate opinions. There are days when I return home, satisfied with class, convinced that the greatest travesty on earth would be if I were denied the opportunity to do this for a living.

On other days, I see another side of teaching at this law school. The students insist that legal concepts be spoon-fed to them like infants in high chairs, the more complex doctrines scraped from their chins and offered as something more easily digested. They show little interest in exerting effort that will not be rewarded on the final exam. They groan when they are required to do anything other than sit and listen. I suspect the ennui has something to do with the fact that they have found themselves in a mountain of student debt in one of the worst job markets for young lawyers in modern history.

When I tire of feeling like a law waitress, when I grumble like an old lady about kids these days, when I wonder why I am dedicating myself to a system of education that leaves a significant percentage of bright and capable students poor and unemployed, I question the virtues of teaching law. On these days, when all I can see in teaching is a lifetime of drudgery in a lawyer mill, I think to myself with perverse hope: maybe I will just get indicted.

I arrive home from school late one evening. As I am about to make my way to bed, the phone rings. I look at the clock and frown. It is past one a.m. I warily pick it up.

"Is this Jennifer Ridha?" a male voice asks. I am later asked to identify this voice as either "black" or "white."

"Yes?" Unsure of how better to describe it, I will say that the voice is "not black and not white."

"Is this Jennifer Ridha who represented Cameron Douglas?"

"I don't represent him anymore," I say.

"Look, I'm responsible for the criminal investigation against you, about you giving drugs to Cameron Douglas. I'm the one who started the investigation. And I can end the whole thing if you want me to."

It's a shocking statement, one that knocks me out of my body and into the same default settings that I used when Burly Man arrived at my door. I am silent for a moment, and then ask, "Who is this?"

"Never mind, that's not important. Do you want this investigation to go away or what?" His voice is laced with menace, as though he is threatening me with hardship if I don't want the investigation to go away.

Nothing about this seems right, but my mind is unable to process the reasons why. All I know is that I don't want to talk about this. "I'm sorry," I say calmly. "I don't know what you're talking about."

"You don't have to play dumb. Everyone already knows what you did.

TMZ already knows. So there's no point in pretending that you don't know what I'm talking about."

I do not react to his claim that a tabloid news outlet knows who I am. At least not outwardly.

"Well, I don't know what to tell you," I say.

"Do you want this investigation to go away?"

I want all of this to go away.

"Is there a reason you won't tell me who you are?" I ask.

He ignores this. "Would you rather do this by e-mail?"

Do what, exactly? But I don't bother asking. Instead, I say, "I'm really sorry, I don't know who you are or what you are talking about. I wish I could be more helpful, but I can't."

He doesn't seem to have any cards left to play. He says in a disappointed voice, "Okay."

I hang up. Panic sets in.

I'm not even sure where to focus my fear. I start with the most immediate shock: Who was that? How does he know my name, know that I represented Cameron? How does he know anything about the tabloid press? How does he know my phone number? Does this mean he knows where I live?

As if on cue, the phone begins to ring again. I do not pick it up.

After two minutes, it rings yet again. I turn off the ringer. Over the course of the next twenty-four hours the phone will ring almost two dozen times.

As I accept the reality of what's happening, I decide that this man is either trying to (1) extort something from me; and/or (2) sell a story to the tabloids. I can't decide which possibility is worse.

I'm also not sure what to do next. Should I call the police? The caller claimed to be involved in my investigation, which I take to mean he is in law enforcement of some kind. It doesn't seem like a good idea to call the authorities. I decide I should contact my lawyer.

It's late August, and everyone who is not facing criminal charges is away on vacation. Shortly before two a.m., I e-mail my attorney. Then I go to the bathroom and throw up.

I don't even bother attempting sleep. I sit on my couch, hugging my knees and noting how my decision to commit a crime seems only to surround me with more crime, or whatever unsavory thing this caller is trying to do. I think about Cameron's vow to take the blame, about how all of this is seemingly falling on me. I also consider the possibility that what I've done could become public even before the government decides what to do with me.

I'm still awake when daylight arrives. My attorney calls and tells me to hang tight, that he will call the government to let them know what has happened and then call me back.

I call Best Friend to tell her what has happened. I'm on the phone with her when the call waiting announces a second call. Thinking my attorney is calling, I click over. It is the nonwhite/nonblack gentleman from the night before.

He is angry. "Look, I am sick of fucking around with you. Stop asking stupid questions and running around on the phone and listen to what I am telling you."

Can he see me? Does he know that my attorney has called the government? Just to be safe, I slink into the windowless hallway between my living room and bathroom.

"Now do you want to end this investigation or not?"

I am without sleep and will to live. I am scared and angry. "I don't know who you are," I say, "and for some reason you refuse to tell me. I've already told you that I don't know what you are talking about. Stop calling me."

I hang up.

I call my lawyer again and ask if I can change my phone number. Even as I dial, the call waiting beeps in. I don't pick it up.

My attorney advises against changing my number, since it's within the realm of possibility that the government may seek to monitor the line.

Wonderful.

I do call the phone company and delist my number from the public directory. It's like purchasing flood insurance the day after a hurricane. In the meantime, my phone continues to ring.

Finally, an associate from my attorney's office calls. He relays that Some Prosecutor could confirm that a call was placed by TMZ to the press office of the U.S. Attorney's Office, to which the government gave no comment. He offers no further answers, does not appear to need any additional information.

Soon after this information is relayed, the calls abruptly stop.

To this day, I don't know who was calling me and why. It's unclear if the calls stop because Some Prosecutor heroically plugs an MCC leak—I persist in the theory that the caller's menace and emotional instability reek of cowboy country—or if the random caller simply gives up.

TMZ does not publish a story about my case. I am inexplicably spared, but hardly reassured. I am left with the stark realization that my crimes have taken me to unfamiliar territory, and that there is no going back. All I can do is continue to wait for news of my fate.

A month later, the government reaches its decision. The summer has given way to autumn, and the leaves are beginning to turn. I am hoping that this is a good sign, that perhaps I, too, will be able to turn over a new leaf.

It turns out there will be no turning. When my attorney calls me with the news, he phones me from home and takes a deep breath. I already know this is not good.

"They've decided that they just can't let this matter go," he says. "Given the public stature of the people involved, the government feels compelled to take some action."

Great. My life is about to alter course because Cameron Douglas's father fucked Glenn Close over a sink in a movie. That scene has now haunted me in more ways than one.

"I guess I understand," I say. I presume this means they have agreed to the middle option, a deferred prosecution agreement.

He follows my thinking and takes another deep breath. "They actually have also decided not to do a deferred," he says.

This means, of course, that they will bring charges, that since I have already confessed to my crimes I will have to plead guilty, that since I have to plead guilty I will be convicted of a crime, that since I will be convicted I will be sentenced before a judge, possibly to time in prison. And all of this under the watchful eye of the press, recorded for eternity. It is the worst-case-I-wish-I-had-fled-to-a-country-without-an-extradition-treaty scenario realized.

I can't muster up much to say, so I whisper, "Oh, my God."

He reassures me that he is not going to let this decision stand. He is going to make a presentation to the U.S. Attorney's Office urging them to reconsider. This isn't over yet, and don't lose hope, and some other encouraging words that I am not really listening to.

When we hang up, I call Best Friend and burst into tears. She is as reassuring as she always is, but I can hear in her voice tones of disbelief.

"I just don't know how I will be able to handle prison," I tell her. "And it's not just peeing in front of people. Have you heard about how women's prisons can be? Those girls are mean."

For some reason, perhaps the image of me attempting to defend myself from the evil overtures of mean girls, this makes us both laugh. She tells me it's not going to happen. I tell her that I have seen the government do much more for much less. I know she agrees, but in allegiance to me she says it can't end this way.

I spend another sleepless night thinking about what will happen. Tossing and turning, my tears turn into anger. I am angry at myself. Angry for what I've done, where I've managed to end up. I am even angry that I bothered telling the truth, angry that the outcome here is possibly worse than had I just denied everything.

Tired of despising myself, I shift my ire to Cameron, drifting in and out of consciousness, hating him in ten-minute increments. I think back to the game I invented for his benefit, Who Would You Rather Punch? In this moment, there is no question that I would rather punch Cameron, closed-fist, square in the face.

Several days later, the anger—at myself, at Cameron, at every-thing—begins to fade. I allow myself to hope that this story will have a different ending. That the government will see that my ill-advised conduct was not born out of anything other than a misguided desire to help someone in a bad situation.

I repeat this to myself as though saying it will make it true. But I do not altogether dismiss the possibility of the alternative. I decide to add kickboxing to my workout regimen. Just in case.

About a week later, the day before my attorney is to make his presentation, I am lying on my couch. My face is slathered in a beauty mask, my feet are wrapped in moisturizing socks. This is actually an exercise recommended by my therapist called "self-care." The practice has something to do with preventing the onset of clinical depression, but I think it is really meant to keep you from letting yourself go when everything around you is crumbling. Either way, it seems to work.

My afternoon of self-care is replete with the latest installment of Oprah's Farewell Season. I am elated when she announces that her guest for the day is Martha Stewart.

I have always loved Martha. I relish her intricate lessons on how to create all things handmade, something that Martha manages to do so effortlessly. Her cookbooks line my kitchen shelves and her craft books are stacked next to my sewing machine. During my case, in an attempt to distract myself, I put them to good use. By the time my case is over I will have sewn an entire new wardrobe, knitted half a dozen sweaters, and tried enough new recipes to feed a small village.

Today, Martha is talking about how to make the perfect grilled cheese sandwich and properly fold a fitted sheet. But before she does, she sits down with Oprah to discuss her time in prison.

Martha's criminal case is one that I followed with great interest, both because I am a dedicated devotee and also because the case was so very strange. Martha's crime took place at a proffer session like mine—perhaps, even, in the same stuffy conference room—but in a case where she had no real criminal exposure. In other words, her crime transpired in a place where she did not need to be. According to an article in *The New Yorker*, the reason why Martha's attorney ended up escorting his client to the scene of her crime is because he believed that declining to participate—in other words, pleading the Fifth—is not something you could suggest to someone like Martha Stewart. I find this reasoning odd, especially because corporate moguls like Martha exercise the right to remain silent all of the time. The Fifth

Amendment is as integral to the criminal process as flour is to pie, preferably one with a flaky crust.

During the proffer session, Martha apparently misrepresented the nature of a stock sale. And in a refrain similar to my own case, because of her public stature the government said it could not let the falsehood go.

So Martha catches a case. And when that case goes to trial, her best friend testifies against her. Back when it happened, I was disgusted on Martha's behalf. But thinking about it now, while my attorney is preparing to make a last-ditch effort to save me, I can't imagine being able to conjure the strength to endure such a betrayal. Unlike her pot roasts, Martha is as tough as they come.

Sitting on Oprah's stage, Martha has clearly moved past everything that's happened. She regales the audience with lighthearted tales of prison, how she managed to whip her entire facility into shape. I imagine myself serving time with Martha, learning at her side in the prison kitchen and during craft time. We swap stories from our cases and commiserate about the dismal décor in the U.S. Attorney's Office. I possibly get thrown in the SHU for following her around so much.

Her interview is winding down and it's almost time for grilled cheese. Then Oprah asks Martha whether she carries any residual shame for her crimes, and whether it weighs on her, what has happened, what she did.

I sit up at the question. I have grappled with this myself, wondering if I will ever be able to move on from all of this. I want to know if Martha has any advice as to how to remove this particular type of stain.

Oprah asks something like: Did you feel that you had let yourself down, or let other people down?

Martha pauses for a brief moment, and I hold my breath.

"No," she says, and then talks about something else.

I rewind the exchange and watch it again.

I breathe a sigh of relief. Martha gives me hope that one day I will be able to let go of what I've done. When, just like her, I will be able to discuss what I've done with the same ease as making a grilled cheese sandwich.

I carry this moment with me for the remainder of my case, and for

long after. I consider it yet another invaluable lesson from Martha, and
yes, a very good thing.

My attorney calls me after his presentation.
  "What now?" I ask.
  "We wait," he says.

And so, once again, I wait. I continue to be consumed with worry
about my case, my fate. My thoughts also inevitably wander to Cameron, whether he is undergoing the same sequence of events, whether
he is also waiting, whether he is wondering if I am waiting, too.

  Our communication completely cut off, he still manages to show
up in a strange dream. I am running through a hospital, knowing he
is there, trying to find him. The hospital has an enormous screen
announcing patient rooms and visiting hours in the same way that airports announce arriving flights. I scan the names but can't decipher
any of them. I then rush from floor to floor, frantically throwing open
patient room doors, asking hospital personnel where he might be found.

  I'm about to give up when I turn a corner and see a door slightly
ajar. I look inside. Cameron is lying on a hospital bed, barely conscious,
visibly in pain. I'm terrified that he might be dying.

  "Don't worry," I tell him as I rush to his side. "I'm here, and I'm getting you a doctor right now."

  I run back into the hallway in search of a doctor. I'm shouting for
assistance, but none of the doctors around me stop what they are doing.
I finally see a doctor, a beautiful woman in a sterile white coat, looking
at me expectantly. I go to her, grab her arm. I tell her that Cameron is
sick, that he is in need of immediate medical attention, that I need her
help.

  Though I feel nearly unhinged, the doctor is calm, almost serene.
She follows me into Cameron's room, looks at the manila file containing his chart. "Well, he's very sick," she says.

  "Do you think you can treat him?" I plead.

  "I can," she says. "But are you sure that you want me to?"

I look at her with confusion. "Why wouldn't I want you to?"

She gestures at herself, as though to indicate that in allowing her to treat Cameron, he may find her more alluring than me. That by bringing her to Cameron, I might ultimately be harming myself.

I don't bother considering such a stupid, selfish thought. "Are you kidding me?" I scream at her. "Don't just stand there! *Help him!*"

She quietly nods, says she will help him get better, that she will be back in a moment. With her words, relief washes over me. I run to Cameron, put my arms around him. I tell him that I've found him a doctor, that she will make him feel better, that his pain will be gone soon.

Cameron leans in close, turns his head toward my ear. As he begins to speak, I am startled. His voice is louder and clearer than anything else in the dream, as though someone has suddenly adjusted the audio levels in my brain. He sounds exactly as I remember, so much so that even in the dream I realize that his voice is something I have otherwise forgotten.

He says this: "Jen, I don't deserve you."

And then the dream ends.

In November, the government finally decides what's to be done with me. They have agreed to enter into a deferred prosecution agreement that will result in the dismissal of my charges in six months.

In keeping with protocol, the government does not provide reasons for the change of heart. If someone told me it was because they determined my conduct was not in the end worthy of prosecution, I would think this might be true. If someone told me it was because disproportionate benefits were conferred upon me because of the stature and prowess of my attorney, I would think this might be true, too. Either way, I am grateful and relieved.

The general terms of a deferred prosecution agreement are these: for the next six months, I am required to remain crime-free. I must report in person to Pretrial Services on a weekly basis, my whereabouts recorded, my employment verified, my urine tested. A home visit will be conducted at my apartment to ensure that I live where I say I live. Also, specific to my agreement, I am required to continue seeing my therapist, a provision based on the not altogether unreasonable proposition that my conduct could have been prevented by regular therapy. After the six-month period passes, if all hoops are jumped, the charges will be dropped.

The next steps are these: I will have to formally admit my conduct to the government. I will have to surrender to the U.S. Marshals and then appear in court for my arraignment. During processing, I will be entered into the criminal justice system, my fingerprints and mug shot taken, my vitals registered. I will be held in lockup as the Marshals work through my paperwork. I will possibly be drug tested. I will then go to court, my rights read, my charges announced, my deferred prosecution agreement filed.

The proceedings, obviously, are open to the public.

I am ready to go into court and get this over with. Unfortunately, Pretrial Services has to approve me as someone they would be willing to monitor, and so there is yet more waiting.

In order to be approved by Pretrial Services, I have to provide answers to a questionnaire and collect a series of documents. It is almost Christmas by the time the questionnaire arrives. Eager to get the process moving, I scan through the form. But when I read what it asks, I begin to cry.

By this juncture in my case, I am prepared for the government to know everything there is to know about me. But I am not at all prepared for extensive personal questions about my family. I am required to provide their ages, occupations, and current whereabouts. It asks how long my parents have been married. It asks whether my father has ever hit my mother, whether anyone in my family has ever grappled with drugs. It asks if I have told my family about my criminal activity. It asks about their reaction upon learning of my criminal activity. It asks what my reaction was to their reaction. It goes on and on for pages.

Even though the answers are benign, I feel horrible that I have dragged my family into my wrongdoing, that my crimes are essentially their crimes, too. I feel an added layer of guilt because of my parents' beginnings under a totalitarian regime. I learned over the course of my childhood that the fears instilled by dictatorship don't easily subside. My father did not discuss the nature of his vote with anyone, not even his children, lest our big mouths broadcast it around town. When my mother mistakenly believed my brother was a missing person—he was in fact behind the football field with the rest of his class observing a fistfight—she still refused to call the police, adamant that if she did we would be placed on some kind of list. And now, I am providing indelible details about their private lives to the government.

Given that the answers are required of my deferred prosecution agreement, my choices are few but to complete the questionnaire and to collect the dozen or so documents required. After the law school's Christmas party, I use the Xerox machine in the faculty lounge to copy all of the required documents. The next day, I pull everything together and send it off.

A few days later, I receive a message on my cell phone from my putative Pretrial Services Officer. Her voice is kind. She's calling to tell me she's received my materials and thanks me for providing them in such an organized manner. Apparently, these tend to come to her in a disheveled state, and I have just made her job much easier. She also wishes me a Merry Christmas.

Her message gives me an odd sense of pride. Perhaps it is the shame I feel in dragging my family through the court system with me. Or maybe it still means something to me to do a good job. Either way, I decide that this is proof that I still have something to offer to the world. I may have faltered in my duties toward society and family. But I am good at being a criminal defendant.

CR 12 (Rev. 5/03)　　　　　　　　　WARRANT FOR ARREST

United States District Court

	DISTRICT
UNITED STATES OF AMERICA v. JENNIFER R. RIDHA	SOUTHERN DISTRICT OF NEW YORK

DOCKET NO. **11 MAG 0047**　　MAGISTRATE'S CASE NO.

WARRANT ISSUED ON THE BASIS OF: ☐ Order of Court
☐ Indictment　☐ Information　X Complaint

NAME AND ADDRESS OF INDIVIDUAL TO BE ARRESTED

JENNIFER R. RIDHA

DISTRICT OF ARREST
Southern District of New York

TO: UNITED STATES MARSHAL OR ANY OTHER AUTHORIZED OFFICER　CITY New York, New York

YOU ARE HEREBY COMMANDED to arrest the above-named person and bring that person before the United States District Court to answer to the charge(s) listed below.

DESCRIPTION OF CHARGES

Providing Contraband in Prison

IN VIOLATION OF	UNITED STATES CODE TITLE 18	SECTION 1791(a)(1) & (b)(4)

BAIL　　OTHER CONDITIONS OF RELEASE

ORDERED BY
JAMES C. FRANCIS IV
UNITED STATES MAGISTRATE JUDGE
SOUTHERN DISTRICT OF NEW YORK

SIGNATURE (FEDERAL JUDGE/U.S. MAGISTRATE)　　DATE ORDERED JAN 06 2011

CLERK OF COURT　(BY) DEPUTY CLERK　　DATE ISSUED

RETURN

This warrant was received and executed with the arrest of the above-named person.

DATE RECEIVED	NAME AND TITLE OF ARRESTING OFFICER	SIGNATURE OF ARRESTING OFFICER
DATE EXECUTED		

Note: The arresting officer is directed to serve the attached copy of the charge on the defendant at the time this warrant is executed.

CHAPTER 6

I'll See You in Court

My court date is set for January 7, 2011.

The day before, I'm trying to select an appropriate outfit for court. This is a less straightforward task than one might think, particularly given the possibility of press. I do not want to wear something that might attract attention. But if I do end up attracting attention, I must prepare for the probability that what I wear will be recorded in history. It's going to be hard enough to look back on this day. I don't need to also lament my appearance.

Earlier in the week, I go to a women's clothing store and browse through the racks. A salesgirl politely offers her help, but as I consider her young face and innocent smile, I conclude that she would know nothing about whether her store carries anything for an arraignment-like occasion. I decide that my court ensemble is one that I already own.

I examine the contents of my closet in order to start pulling things together. Given that photography is not allowed inside the courthouse, outerwear is of salient interest. I select a black wool coat with fat buttons. I pull out a pair of black pumps with formidable heels: if I am going to be publicly humiliated, I would at least like to do so while looking tall.

I begin to pack my usual going-to-court bag with my belongings and then realize that both the bag and its extensive contents are not necessary. I instead select a small purse of forest green leather and place inside only my wallet and a lipstick.

For my courtroom attire, I decide I should dress less like a lawyer and more like a defendant. I forgo my suits and select a plain black turtleneck and a pleated skirt of green Marimekko fabric. The skirt is born from my ordeal, stitched by my hand as I awaited news of my fate.

I choose a pair of silver earrings, purchased on vacation in southern Turkey in a different lifetime. I grab a pair of black tights. Now my outfit is complete.

Except. I am unsure if processing will require a drug test. I rack my brain through old cases to recall if this is required. I know that these are conducted before sentencing—I have an uncomfortable memory of a mortified client emerging from the Pretrial Services bathroom alongside an officer holding a jar of her urine—but I can't remember if it is required for arraignment. I am too embarrassed to call my attorney to ask, and so I decide to assume that a test is forthcoming, and with it the dreaded advent of having to pee on demand. After considering the contents of my underwear drawer, I pick out the plainest pair.

I lay all of these items out on my dresser, except the skirt and the coat, which I hang in a nearby closet. The entire collection looks like the adult version of what my mother used to prepare every night in my era of elementary school. In a matter of minutes, jumpers and undershirts and white tights would be gathered and precisely arranged so she could move on to other tasks that would ensure our academic success. At this thought, I refold and straighten everything in a manner more worthy of her, as though this might compensate for something.

Later in the day, my attorney calls to give me a rundown of what to expect over the next twenty-four hours. He tells me that by the close of business, Some Prosecutor will file the charging instrument—a criminal complaint—along with a warrant for my arrest. It's official: I have to appear in court tomorrow or else I will be considered a fugitive from the law.

"Where do I meet you tomorrow?" I ask my attorney.

He has arranged with Some Prosecutor a time to meet. "We'll all meet in the courtroom at ten a.m."

"But wait," I say. I have already prepared myself for the order of events for the day. "I need to surrender and be processed before I go to court."

"Oh, right," my attorney says. "I'll call him and call you back."

He calls me back later in the afternoon. Processing had apparently been forgotten. Some Prosecutor has arranged for me to meet Burly Man at the U.S. Attorney's Office at nine-thirty a.m., who will in turn deliver me to the U.S. Marshals for surrender.

When I get off the phone, I roll my eyes in nervous annoyance at the fact that I essentially requested that I be processed. I already spelled out the case against me; now do I have to prosecute myself, too?

There is something in the air the day of my arraignment. When I wake, I'm in higher spirits than I ought to be. Here is the day I've been dreading, and yet I find myself poking my head out of my bedroom window, breathing in the crisp air. Although the clouds overhead promise snow, the sun is shining. I look up and tell it, "I am being arraigned today."

I leave my apartment early so as not to be in violation of my arrest warrant. When I do, an available cab pulls up to my doorstep as though waiting for me to emerge. The driver, an elderly Chinese man, makes pleasant if incoherent chitchat as I direct him to the U.S. Attorney's Office. When he deposits me near the entrance, he says without sequitur, "I think you might be an angel."

If he only knew where I am headed.

I arrive at the security station of the U.S. Attorney's Office at nine-thirty a.m. on the dot. I give one of the three U.S. Marshals standing guard Burly Man's name, and, per usual, I am instructed to place my purse and coat on the conveyor belt and provide photo identification.

Apparently, there is no immediate answer at Burly Man's line. "Are you here for a meeting?" the U.S. Marshal asks.

"No, I'm here to surrender," I say.

The three men stop what they are doing and consider me with what appears to be shock. There is silence for a moment.

"Are you sure you mean surrender, dear?" one of them says.

"Yes, I'm sure," I say. And then, to clarify, I say, "I did something bad."

They allow me to pass. As I walk toward the main lobby, I glance back and see that the men are watching me make my way. They smile in unison, and I can't help but smile back.

Burly Man meets me in the lobby. When he greets me, he hardly seems like the menacing man who once stood at my door. Instead, he is pleasant and conversational. In fact, he seems very much like someone who would own and care for two sweet-natured cats.

He first takes me to his office. The walls are papered with newspaper clippings of prominent criminal cases, I presume those that he has worked. He seems to have spent his entire career in law enforcement. He confirms as much when we make small talk on the walk between the U.S. Attorney's Office and the courthouse. On our walk I note that we do not exit through the main doors of the U.S. Attorney's Office, but through a basement exit that makes our entry to the courthouse less conspicuous.

"We don't need to attract any attention to you," he explains when I am looking around to see where we are.

I look at him for further explanation, but there is none to be had. He is staring straight ahead.

I expect that when I am delivered to the Marshals Service I will be placed in lockup until they are ready to process me. But Burly Man waits with me outside the office until they are ready for me. He regales me with stories of law enforcement—chasing after fugitives, running stakeouts, tracking down defendants. It is in this conversation that I learn Lady Agent was not assigned to my case, but was only present at my apartment as a matter of DOJ policy.

I feel comfortable enough to tell Burly Man, "I sort of wondered why she was so interested in my photographs." He shakes his head and smiles.

The Marshals indicate they are ready for me. Burly Man escorts me inside. The time for my surrender has arrived. I picture myself being asked to fall to my knees with my hands in the air. Instead, I am led into a large room that bears the stale but familiar smell of MCC. I am so turned around geographically that I cannot tell if this office is somehow connected to MCC or if this is how all lockup facilities in Manhattan smell.

Normally, any reminder of MCC would turn even the sweetest moment sour. But I am distracted by what I see. My only interactions with the U.S. Marshals Service have been in connection with the security they provide at federal buildings. These Marshals tend to be older, distinguished-looking gentlemen who examine the contents of your briefcase and stow your phone while you are inside the courthouse. I have never been able to reconcile these stern but seemingly harmless men with what I understand to be the bulk of the Marshals' work: apprehending dangerous fugitives and persons of interest, enforcing federal arrest warrants, and running various tactical missions.

Now that I've arrived for processing, the mystery is solved. Here presides an entirely different caliber of U.S. Marshal—each one younger, taller, more rugged than the next. It does not at all stretch the imagination to imagine these stalwart individuals physically fighting crime, wrestling crime to the ground, making crime wish it had been born into something more virtuous. The sight is so unexpected that I can only stare at my surroundings like a teenager.

I am knocked out of my daze when one of these Marshals directs me to a small office. As he sits at a computer, I answer a series of questions he reads from a questionnaire. I give responses about my social security number, my address, my marital status. Some of these the Marshal simply answers for himself. "Do you do drugs? No. Any tattoos? No. Wait, do you have any birthmarks?"

When he asks me for my occupation, because my crime occurred while I was practicing law, I tell him that I'm an attorney. When he asks for my place of business, I explain that I'm now a professor and work at a law school.

"So you're a lawyer and a law professor?"

"Yes," I say. I do not add: for now.

He looks back to an earlier portion of the document.

"How are you single?" he asks.

At first, I think this is part of the questionnaire. I'm not sure how to answer. How much space is available on the form?

He sees my confusion and explains with a smile, "I'm saying that you are a perfect package."

I feel my cheeks burn. "Well, I'm getting arraigned today," I say. "So, probably not perfect."

After this, I am brought to a tiny room where fingerprint- and mug shot–taking occur. I catch sight of Burly Man: he is sitting on a chair, my purse and coat in his lap, looking bored. I'm second in line to provide fingerprints; ahead of me is a young Russian man charged with a

drug-related crime, and after me is a pedophile who is there on a violation of supervised release.

When it's my turn to supply fingerprints, I'm told to place my hands
on what looks like an enormous Xerox machine. The Marshal presses
my hands down as the machine seems to scan their image. But it doesn't
take on the first attempt. Or the second. Or what I count as the eighth.
I try to press my hands harder onto the glass to possibly make things
easier, but this only makes the machine stall.

"Stop trying to help," the Marshal admonishes me.

"I'm sorry," I say.

He sighs. "It's this fucking machine," he tells me. He calls in another
Marshal, this one with a heavy Boston accent, and tells him that he's
unable to fingerprint me. The second Marshal sizes me up.

"Whaddaya here fah, a fackin misdemeenah?" he says.

I nod.

The two men fuss with the machine. They look at each other as
though they are at a loss. They look at me again. They don't seem to
know what to do next.

"Maybe I could just promise never to commit a crime again," I offer.

This suggestion is ignored. The second Marshal catches sight of my
shoes. "By the way," he asks, pointing down at them, "did anyone tell ya
there's a fackin blizzaad outside?"

He is likely referring to the fact that my black high-heeled pumps
are not suited for the gathering snowstorm.

I shrug my shoulders.

He shakes his head at me and looks over at the other Marshal. "Just
give ha the ink."

This means exactly what I think it does. The first Marshal produces
an old-fashioned fingerprint card, a box for every finger. "Watch that
you don't get ink on yourself," he says as he presses my hand into an
inkpad. When I look at the black on my fingers, he assures me that the
ink can be wiped off with a tissue.

He returns me to Burly Man, who hands me back my coat and
purse. He explains that we now have to go to Pretrial Services before
heading to court.

"That's it?" I say. This was less painful than a trip to the DMV.

One of the Marshals leads us to an internal elevator that will take us upstairs to Pretrial Services. The elevator is meant for law enforcement and contains a large cage to carry criminal defendants.

As we make our way into the elevator, I step toward the cage.

"What are you doing?" Burly Man asks.

"I'm going in here," I say, pointing inside the cage.

"No, absolutely not. You stand right next to me," he says protectively.

"Okay," I say. I look up at him, but he is once again staring straight ahead.

When we arrive at Pretrial Services, we walk into a room full of people waiting to check in with their Pretrial Service Officers. This will be me in a week, I think to myself.

Burly Man walks me through the waiting room to a hallway on the other side. "We don't want to sit in there," he says. "It's filled with defendants."

But *I'm* a defendant, I feel tempted to say. But I don't. I'm unclear as to the reasoning behind his care, but feel that he is being kind.

While we wait on Pretrial Services, I ask Burly Man questions about law enforcement, how he can tell a perp is lying, how he knows if someone is up to no good. "It's just something you know," he tells me with pride.

In the midst of my questions, Burly Man looks at his watch. "I'd better get you over there," he says, referring to the magistrate's court. "You can come back here after you're done."

"Okay," I say.

He leads me into the courtroom, where I catch sight of my attorney. Once we've said our hellos, I turn around and Burly Man is gone. I find myself feeling wistful at his disappearance, almost sad that I did not have an opportunity to say good-bye.

My attorney and I sit down in the gallery. I survey the room for possible press but don't see any. My eyes circle the room every few minutes to detect whether this changes.

On my visual tour of the courtroom, I watch a group of gentlemen get arraigned on tax crimes. One of them looks over at me as the extensive charges against him are being read and rolls his eyes. If I weren't awaiting the announcement of my own charges, I would probably laugh.

I also catch a glimpse of Some Prosecutor on the other side of the aisle. I had forgotten what he looked like, I recognize him only from the scowl he gives me when our eyes meet. I greet his disapproving look with a small smile that I have perfected in consultation with Best Friend the night before. The smile is not so large as to be arrogant but not so weak as to concede complete defeat. It assumes a middle ground, possessing a calibrated level of contentment that says merely: this did not break me.

By the time I execute it, Some Prosecutor has turned his attention to the papers in front of him. I decide that this still counts.

I continue to scope the door for entering reporters, but there appear to be none. Lawyers and defendants mill in and out of the courtroom, but as it becomes closer to lunchtime most of these have filed out. By the time my case is called, the courtroom is otherwise empty.

The court clerk announces: "The United States of America versus Jennifer Ridha." It is the worst thing I've ever heard in my entire life. Everyone? I want to ask. Is there no one who isn't against me?

The proceedings begin as the magistrate judge takes the bench. I keep turning around to see if any reporters walk in. My attorney shoots me a look that says I should stop.

The magistrate judge reads me my rights. I am to confirm my understanding of these rights. He explains the charge against me. I am to confirm my understanding of this charge. He explains to me the terms of my deferred prosecution agreement. I am to confirm my understanding of these terms. He asks me a series of questions, the answer to all of which is "Yes, Your Honor" or some variation thereof.

It is quick and painless, over in less than ten minutes. The courtroom remains empty for the duration.

There is nothing out of order, nothing out of place. But something odd happens to me at the end. As the proceedings are about to close, the magistrate judge addresses me thusly:

THE COURT: The Government has provided you with an important benefit and opportunity here. I trust that you will comply with the terms of the agreement and the case will be dismissed.

A sensible statement such as this one is expected for any defendant who is fortunate enough to avoid pleading guilty. And yet, as terrible as it is to admit, when I hear these words, I am internally consumed by a burst of anger. My own reaction is so unexpected that I feel as though I am possessed by someone else, someone who is so defensive about what she's done and so resentful of authority that this small admonition causes her only to curse in my head: "Why don't all of you take an opportunity to go fuck yourselves?"

This internal reaction lasts only a moment, but given the easy events of the day is so misplaced that I'm somewhat unsettled. The intensity of my anger, the velocity with which it has arrived, the ease with which this feeling could take me over, all of this leads me to the brief but troubling conclusion that what I've done is possibly not an isolated error in judgment as much as it is a flaw in my construction, a part of who I really am.

As I see everyone awaiting my response, I push away the thought. I look at the judge, seated on his bench, and with this harnessed focus my demons are seemingly exorcised. I am thus able to respond to his suggestion of gratitude with pitch-perfect acquiescence, like the obedient young woman I was raised to be.

The court transcript captures it this way:

THE DEFENDANT: I will, Your Honor. Thank you.

With the proceedings over, I walk out of the courtroom and begin to breathe a sigh of relief. I suck it back in quickly when I see standing in front of me the same reporter from the *New York Post* who interrupted the impromptu meeting with Cameron Douglas's father in the very same spot a year before.

For a brief moment my body seizes with fear that the reporter is here to ask about my case. But he does not look up from the conversation he is having with another gentleman. I tiptoe around the two men and then move to a strategic spot close to the clerk's office. I motion to my attorney to join me and then position myself so I can keep my eye on the reporter's movements without having to crane my head or otherwise make myself conspicuous. If he comes my way, it's my plan to dart into the nearby ladies' room.

Some Prosecutor follows us to discuss some housekeeping issues. He and my attorney chat for a bit, and then he enthusiastically takes my attorney's hand and shakes it. I am only half paying attention because I am keeping my eye on the reporter.

I at first don't notice that Some Prosecutor has extended his hand toward me. When I do, I realize that the time has come for the fake handshake. I don't want it. I stare at his hand for a moment, until I see my attorney giving me a look. I begrudgingly take Some Prosecutor's hand, and, as if on cue, he dramatically turns his eyes away.

Dammit, I think to myself. I was so close to getting through my case without it.

Some Prosecutor walks away, and shortly afterward my attorney leaves me to deal with the odds and ends. At Pretrial Services, I am told that my Pretrial Services Officer (PSO) is away conducting home visits, that I should call her later in the day to arrange for my reporting schedule.

I step back into the main hallway of the magistrate's court and take a quick look around. The *Post* reporter is gone. I exit the courthouse undisturbed, not a camera in sight. I begin to run from the courthouse, my heels pressing the snow, running as though if I don't move fast enough I will be apprehended and the whole thing will start all over again.

I don't stop running until I am several blocks away. When I return to my building, I see that the blizzard is approaching—the sun has departed and the sky is gray. I have narrowly escaped the storm.

I enter my apartment and immediately go to the computer to check the news: there is not a single piece of press about my case. Relieved, I call my PSO to check in. She is confused as to why I am calling.

"Didn't you get your reporting instructions?" she asks.

The man at Pretrial Services did hand me a form, which I had stuffed into my purse without reading. "Yes, I'm sorry, I don't think I realized what that was."

"Well, you're supposed to call in once a month, the first Friday of the month. Don't call me until then."

"Okay, but when do I have to come in?"

"You don't."

"I don't have to come in?"

"No. Talk to you next month." She says good-bye, and then hangs up.

I'm puzzled. I had prepared myself for weekly meetings, random drug testing, home visits. I feel so certain that these are required that I consider calling her back to make sure I understood her correctly.

I decide to leave the matter for now. My court date is officially over, and I feel unprecedented relief. Not because I survived something today—a kid sent to the principal's office would have it worse—but because this is no longer the point in my case that Churchill would call, if Churchill ever cared to describe this juncture of my criminal case, the end of the beginning. Instead, I believe this is the beginning of the end.

I kick off my weather-inappropriate high heels and stand at the foot of my bed. I fall into the mattress face-first, like I used to do as a child, like I did the day the federal authorities came to my door. This time, I am smiling. For the first time in months, sleep arrives in mere moments. As though making up for lost time, it pours over me like dense syrup, absorbing me to such an extent that when I finally wake, the brightness of the day will lead me to wonder if all of this hasn't simply been a dream.

My PSO was not exaggerating. The sum total of my obligations to the Pretrial Services Office consists of six phone calls, one for each month of the term of my deferred prosecution agreement. Each of these calls consumes something on the order of forty-five to ninety seconds.

On five occasions, I call her on the first Friday of every month. On the sixth occasion, she tells me that she will provide a recommendation to the U.S. Attorney's Office to drop the misdemeanor charge that had been lodged against me.

There is no in-person reporting, no home visits, no drug testing.

It is an odd incongruence, the start of my case as compared to its ending. The brute arrival of the feds, the possibility of prosecution, the fear of the press, and the threats of extortion all seemed to portend my status as a criminal worthy of heavy punishment. And yet, this is hardly what transpires.

My family and friends insist that I should be happy about the apparent exceptions that have been extended to me. It could have been so much worse, they say. But as it is happening, I find myself distrustful of the disparity. That I have been spared what even the most privileged defendants are forced to endure makes me question why I have been put through it at all. I feel as though this has been more of an exercise in humiliation than an attempt to address wrongdoing.

Over time, I gain better perspective. I come to the conclusion that of the two theories of punishment, I am subjected to the approach in which the criminal is punished only insofar as needed to prevent her from committing further crimes. And in determining how the interests of justice could be served in my case, the system did not consider my conduct to be that of a repeat offender as much as that of a complete idiot.

What really matters, I tell myself, is that it's all over.

Or so I think.

CHAPTER 7

Thank You for Your Cooperation

Wen my case is over, I hold out hope that I can move forward with my life.

It doesn't work out the way that I intended.

Once the charges are dropped, my lawyer calls to check in with me to see how I'm doing. I tell him that I am making the most of my second chance. I am elated, I tell him, that my case has come to an end.

"There's just one thing," he says.

And that thing is cooperation.

When boiled down to its essence, cooperation is an exchange of evils. It operates on the straightforward premise that the cost of leniency for one act of evil is worth the ability to harness two such acts.

Cooperation is usually heralded as a situation in which everyone wins. The cooperator gets off easier than he normally would. The government saves precious resources. Crime rates go down. Cooperation is quick, it's easy, everyone is happy.

But.

Because cooperation deals in evils, it has many of its own. Cooperation has a bad reputation for promoting dishonesty. One often finds that individuals who are comfortable (a) committing crimes, and (b) turning in their accomplices for personal gain, are just as comfortable

(c) lying about it. Cooperation can, and sometimes does, harm the innocent.

Cooperation's evils can obviously befall the cooperator as well. For some cooperators the leniency offered by cooperating can come at the price of one's own life. Cooperation can, and sometimes does, harm the guilty.

When you really think about it, cooperation's evils can be traced throughout history. Jesus Christ himself was famously ratted out, his identity and subsequent arrest provided by a paid informant who sold him out at a dinner party. And although that particular instance doesn't end too badly—it did bring about one of the world's great religions—similar betrayals have brought about nothing less than mass atrocity. Cooperation is the fuel in genocide's engine. Cooperation is how death marches and pogroms come to be.

Because of these evils, our legal system recognizes that cooperation has limits. This is why husbands and wives, doctors and patients, attorneys and clients, clergy and congregants have all been deemed sacred relationships in which loyalty is protected. Left unfettered, cooperation tears at the social fabric, rips through community trust, causes more harm than it seeks to prevent.

I have seen in practice the filthy residue that cooperation can leave behind. So when my attorney tells me that cooperation bears on my ability to move forward with my life, I am right to be concerned.

In order to explain how cooperation comes to touch my criminal case, I need to go back in time to the summer of 2009, months before I even join Cameron's case. Shortly after his arrest, Cameron identifies his drug suppliers as two brothers named David and Eduardo Escalera. The Escaleras befriended Cameron when he moved to California in 2003 and are alleged to have served as Cameron's personal dealers before joining him in the drug conspiracy that is being pursued by the government.

The expected next steps after Cameron provided this information were these: The Escalera brothers would be arrested; they would decide to either plead or go to trial; if they chose to go to trial, Cameron would take the stand. If they pleaded or were found guilty, they would be sentenced. Then, after all of this, Cameron would be sentenced, the full fruits of his cooperation taken into consideration by the judge.

But this is not what happened. The Escalera brothers somehow managed to elude arrest. Perhaps owing to the publicity surrounding Cameron's arrest, they made themselves scarce, possibly absconding to their native Mexico. For the duration of Cameron's case, they apparently were nowhere to be found.

This was good news for Cameron. He had been dreading any arrest of the Escaleras, not wanting to cause them harm and also not wanting to reveal his begrudging decision to cooperate. Because his sentencing was expedited, true to his wishes, he was sentenced without any arrests having been made.

After his sentencing, I tell a hopeful Cameron that maybe they will never be arrested at all. Maybe, I tell him, this is all over.

But I'm wrong. The very day that Cameron was transferred from MCC to his facility in Pennsylvania, the Escaleras were arrested near their homes in California. They were then brought to New York City to be tried along with the other members of the conspiracy.

When I learn of the Escaleras' arrest—one month after Cameron is sentenced and two months before Burly Man arrives at my door—I am inexplicably disturbed on Cameron's behalf. There seems little reason to be: with guilty pleas from everyone else in the drug conspiracy and with the existence of multiple government cooperators it seems reasonable to expect the brothers to plead guilty as well. As Cameron's lawyer, there is little cause for concern.

And yet, I am left with a persistent queasiness that something is not quite right. It is as though I already know that the filthy residue from Cameron's cooperation is about to become my own.

The first order of business after the Escaleras' arrest in May 2010 is to let Cameron know that it has happened. This is a delicate task, not only because any phone communication we have at his new facility is monitored, but also because he will undoubtedly find the information distressing. I decide it best to discuss the matter with Cameron in person. To do that, I will make a prison visit.

Soon after he arrives in Pennsylvania, Cameron mails me a visitor's form, the subject of which we have discussed in advance. The form asks how long you have known the BOP inmate. Cameron, fearing we haven't known each other long enough for my visitation to be approved, insists on putting a date prior to the start of the case.

"We had to have crossed paths before that," he says.

I shrug my shoulders. I believe this to be technically true. We compare notes as to our whereabouts in New York City over the past few years and the various nightclub events we have both attended over that time. Most of these date back to when I was in law school, when Cameron was a DJ in the city. But I feel uncomfortable putting on the form that we've known each other for ten years. I agree with him, though, that our first meeting was technically before his case began and so, perhaps somewhat inexplicably, I split the difference and put "2008."

(It's not a great move. The government later shows me the form during my proffer session, doubts that this entry has any truth to it. Some Prosecutor goes so far as to threaten to bring a charge for making a material misrepresentation on a federal form, but at some point the issue is dropped.)

I'm looking forward to our first visit. It is early July 2010, nearly two months since we have last seen each other. This experience provides a brand-new context for Cameron and me: the visiting room. According to the visitor's manual, because this is a personal visit, Cameron is permitted to sit at my side, hold my hand, and even provide a kiss "that is conducted in good taste" at the start and close of the visit.

Though by this time our feelings for one another are out in the open and have been readily discussed in detail, I find myself somewhat nervous at the prospect of being in such close proximity to him. In this way, our meeting is the stuff of Victorian novels, if ever there was a Victorian novel about prison visits between a reformed drug dealer and his attorney.

In truth, I have found something comforting in the forced distance that is always between Cameron and me. In his restrictive environment, our interactions are necessarily restricted, too. Cameron can only call me at certain times and for certain durations. He can only see me when I am willing to see him. Our manner of intimacy is set forth by strict federal regulation. As someone who has come to possess a clinical fear of emotional intimacy, I find my relationship with an incarcerated felon to be one of the safest choices I can make.

When I arrive on the prison's grounds, I discover that Cameron's facility is appended to a larger, maximum-security institution. I encounter this facility first. Its facade is actually stunning; one would presume it to house inmates only because of the large tower at its center and the eerie silence that surrounds it. A voice from an intercom commands me to state my business and allows me to pass through.

The minimum-security prison camp presents much differently. As I walk down the hill to its entrance, I see three flat buildings with some sort of sporting event transpiring in between. With its institutional smell, the drab buildings present less as a correctional facility than an underfunded middle school. I line up with the other visitors and feel as though we are waiting to go to a decrepit study hall.

I survey the line, consisting mostly of women and children. The women look comparable to those who would stand on the sidelines of my second-grade soccer games. They don't appear as what I imagined women cavorting with incarcerated men to be, but I suppose I'm not what I pictured either.

When it is my turn to encounter security, the corrections officer is exceedingly polite. I find this almost disconcerting. He asks to see my driver's license and checks my name against Cameron's visiting list. He then motions me toward the visiting room.

"That's it?" I ask.

"That's it, ma'am."

The visitor's room resembles a large cafeteria. Filled with tables and chairs, along one wall are a series of vending machines and an old microwave. In the center of the room is an elevated podium from which our lunch monitor—a corrections officer—can observe the proceedings. Off to the side, there is a small room with a television set and toys, lest children become bored with the visit. There is also an enclosed outdoor area with picnic tables.

I observe the scene but am not sure how to place myself in it. This does not seem like an ideal place to sit in someone else's seat. I watch the women scramble as they await the arrival of the inmates. They methodically storm the vending machines, retreating with armfuls of junk food that they then arrange on the visiting tables as though setting the table for dinner.

I remain standing, hedging as to what to do next. A woman stands a few feet away, examining the contents of a vending machine. She resembles a friend of mine, but for her cherry red–dyed hair, which accents her pretty face.

I approach her with some timidity. "Excuse me," I say. "This is my first time visiting here."

"Okay," she says.

I am not sure how to phrase my question. "What exactly should I do?"

She smiles. As she points out to me the preferred seating, two other women join our conversation. One woman indicates the most sought-after vending machines and warns that these are the quickest to sell out.

"You might want to get your stuff now," she advises.

"Oh. I'm not really sure what he would like."

The women look at me. It seems as though I should know this.

The women also explain to me the visiting calendar—some weekends the inmates have two visits, some weekends three, and some weekends none at all—and advise me about places to stay nearby. It turns out that by staying at a bed-and-breakfast one town over I'm located farther from the facility than I need to be. I stop short of explaining that I preferred to stay in the quaint college town so that I could enjoy my free time away from the visiting room. This doesn't seem like the right thing to say.

The women ask me about my inmate. "How long has he been here?" one asks.

"Less than two months."

"So you're new to this. You poor thing. How long is he in for?"

"With good time it works out to a little over two years, I think," I say.

"It's hard at first," Cherry Red tells me. "But it does get easier. In the beginning I used to have trouble sleeping, but now I'm much better."

I have had no trouble sleeping, at least not yet. But I nod anyway.

"Do you guys have kids?" she asks me.

"Oh, no," I say. I do not add that we've only just kissed, that it's quite possible that I am just a goose in a gaggle. "Do you?"

"No," she says. "Not yet."

The other women look at her sympathetically. This seems to be a topic that has been discussed before. "He'll be out soon," one of them says.

"I know, I know." Cherry Red is smiling, but her eyes look sad.

I have no real standing to say anything, but want to fill the awkward silence. "If you guys can make it through this, you can definitely handle children," I offer.

"I know, I know," she says again with a smile. "You're going to make it through, too."

She is heartfelt in saying so, and I thank her. But I am obviously a fraud standing among these women. I know nothing of their hardship. They have had to sacrifice plans and pick up slack and put on brave faces. They regularly drive hundreds of miles so that their family can be together for a few hours.

I've heard people say that the families of the incarcerated serve time alongside their inmate. As I listen to these women and observe the children of the visiting room ready to burst with excitement at the imminent arrival of their fathers, I see that this might be painfully true.

I have made no sacrifices. I am serving no time. I am here to simply see Cameron, sit next to him rather than across, and find out what happens next.

Speaking of which, I notice that inmates are starting to slowly stream into the visiting room. I turn to tell Cherry Red and the others that I should probably find a table, but they are already dispersing. It is something unsaid, like the flickering of lights at intermission, that indicates that the time has come to take a seat.

Cameron emerges from the crowd with a smile on his face. His new prison attire consists of khaki pants—oversized, of course—and a matching khaki shirt. He looks as though he has just returned from safari, a supposition bolstered by his sunburned face. It seems that after spending most of the previous year indoors, his skin has forgotten all about natural light.

I can't help but smile back at the sight of him, and we are both grinning when we embrace. When he leans in to kiss me, I keep my eyes open to get a good look. He senses this and opens his eyes, too. With our faces pressed together we look at each other and both start laughing.

"Let's try that again," he says. And then we do. We then take a seat outside on one of the picnic tables.

There is much to catch up on, but I first want to tell him about the Escalera brothers. I am technically departing his legal team, but I know he might have questions and is flustered when he does not have enough of an opportunity to ask them.

His face displays shock and dismay as I relay what has happened. He had filed all of the unpleasantness of his case away, and I have just forced him to reopen the file. He looks down at the picnic table for some time, rubbing his thumb against the metal. Though we are outside in the summer sunshine, holding hands, it feels as though we have suddenly relocated to the attorney room. I remain quiet as he processes the news.

"So, what does this mean?" he finally says.

"For right now, it means nothing. You've been sentenced, your case is over. The government will only want you if they go to trial. And that's unlikely."

He looks up. "Is it really unlikely, or are you just saying that?"

"That's what everyone says. That the brothers would be crazy to risk going to trial, that they will be much better off if they plead."

I don't mention the inexplicable bad feeling I got when I learned of their arrest, but Cameron appears to have caught wind of it.

"Okay, everyone tells you that. What do you think?"

"I have no reason to think they're wrong."

"You didn't really answer my question."

I sigh. "Cameron, I don't know," I say. His face looks worried. "But yes, I think they will plead."

I don't think I've convinced either one of us, but we let the topic go.

I notice Cameron eyeing the vending machines through the window. "Are you hungry?" I ask.

"Yeah, let's get something to eat."

We walk inside to the visiting room and make our way to the vending machines. I catch sight of Cherry Red at a table with her husband. They are holding hands and smiling at each other. I am distracted from this sight by an odd feeling from behind me. I glance over my shoulder and uncover the reason: the entire visiting room is examining Cameron's back as he decides between a sandwich and a candy bar. I watch several inmates conspicuously lean over to their visitors to whisper something and then point Cameron's way.

I had sort of forgotten that Cameron is famous here.

I look at Cameron to see if he notices his audience. He seems enthralled with his vending machine choices and oblivious to the dozens of eyes staring at him.

"What are you going to get?" he asks me.

I glance over the possibilities. "Maybe just a diet Coke for now. What about you?"

He is transfixed by the vending machine that offers submarine sandwiches. This seems a questionable choice to me, sweaty cold cuts wrapped in plastic and then shoved into a rotating shelf, but Cameron so rarely displays any appetite that I think he must really want it.

In consultation with the visitor's manual, I have brought a clear plastic bag with dollar bills for the vending machine. I push the bag toward him. "Here," I say. "Just get what you want."

Out of the corner of my eye, I see a corrections officer closely watching.

Cameron sees him, too, and pushes the bag back at me. "I can't."

"Why not?"

"I can't handle any money. You have to get it for me."

He watches as I insert the bills and retrieve a sub sandwich. Like all Bureau of Prisons refreshments, the sandwich is starkly overpriced. It's also very small. I decide to get him two.

When we get to the picnic table, I put the sandwiches down in front of him. "I got you two," I say, "because they looked pretty small."

"Aren't you going to have one?"

I take a look at the nuclear pink lunch meat and involuntarily scrunch my face. "No, I'm good," I say. My tone might bear a twinge of disgust.

He opens a packet of mayonnaise. "Yeah, everyone here gets so excited for the vending machines because it's so much better than the food we normally get, but it's still stuff that regular people would never eat."

Though he appears unfazed by my insensitivity, I feel terrible.

I watch as he spreads mayonnaise on one half of a processed bun. "I just don't like lunch meat," I lie. "But I'm hungry, I am going to get something for me, too."

"You don't have to, just because I said that."

"What?" I exclaim. He raises an eyebrow at my dramatic reaction. "No, I really do want to eat something."

I leave him at the picnic table and return to the vending machines. Cherry Red is standing by the microwave. I smile at her as I select an inoffensive chicken cutlet sandwich that resides in the same machine as the rubbery subs. When I retrieve it from the machine, Cherry Red waves me over.

"You're going to want to heat that up," she says, pointing to my sandwich.

I look down at the sandwich and decide that this could do no further harm.

She shows me how to work the microwave, an early model that appears to have been manufactured in the late 1980s. I delicately remove the plastic, though some of the bun manages to stick to the wrapping, and place the sandwich on a small paper plate that is offered next to the microwave.

We stand side by side, watching my sandwich rotate.

Cherry Red playfully nudges my hip with her own. "Hey," she says. "You didn't say that you were visiting *that* inmate."

I'm not sure what to say. "I guess you didn't ask."

"My husband says he's a great guy, really polite and friendly. He told me that on Cameron's first day the entire facility stood outside waiting for his prison bus to arrive. Everyone was staring at him, my husband said, but he was really unassuming, just went to the library to get a book and then went to his bunk to read it."

Cameron has never described to me the circumstances of his arrival, but this sounds like how it might be. "I don't know how he takes all of that attention in a place like this," I say. "It would drive me crazy."

"Me, too," she says. "When his dad came earlier this month, everyone was all over him. He was so nice, shaking everyone's hands. But I always try to keep a respectful space. I am really here to see my husband." She points over to him, and he waves.

It's jarring to me that she knows so much about Cameron and his visits. I'm already acquainted with Cameron Douglas's father's handshaking abilities, so I change the subject. "You guys seem really happy," I say as I look over at her husband. "He's really lucky to have you."

"Aww, that's sweet. You guys are a really cute couple, too."

Though we aren't really a couple, I don't feel like correcting her. As kind as she is, she already knows too much. "Thanks," I say.

The microwave announces the arrival of my heated sandwich, and so I tell Cherry Red I will see her later. I stop by the condiments table and decide that mayonnaise could serve as an important buffer. I grab two packets.

When I make my way back to the picnic table, Cameron asks me, "What were you two talking about?"

"Nothing," I say. "Just my sandwich."

Cameron has made his way through the first sub and has started on the second. After applying liberal amounts of mayonnaise to both sides of the cutlet, I'm pleasantly surprised that my sandwich is not just edible, but actually kind of good. I'm enjoying it enough that Cameron notices and requests a bite.

As he leans over to take a bite of my sandwich, it occurs to me that this presents the first time that he and I have ever eaten a meal together. The fact that we are breaking bread in a federal correctional facility, that our supper has come from a Bureau of Prisons–owned-and-operated vending machine, somehow seems fitting. Criminal justice is the glue that holds us together.

Cameron notices me thinking to myself. "What?" he says. He brushes my hair away from my face.

"Nothing," I say.

He takes another bite of my sandwich.

Once we are sated, we sit and talk, mostly confessing all of the things we thought of each other during the case but did not say. I admit to him that on the day we met I first thought his tattoos referred to male sex organs. He sighs in a way that indicates I am not the first person to make this mistake. I laugh.

He tells me that when I brought him the Sharpie to fix his hems, he was certain that in doing so I was professing my feelings. I laugh even harder at this. "Because of a marker?"

"Because of how intent you were about fixing my problem."

We look at each other for a moment.

"Well," I say, breaking the silence. "You looked so ridiculous in that jumpsuit, I had to do *something*."

This makes us both laugh.

At a break in our laughter, my mind flashes back to the attorney room. "Just so you know," I say carefully. "I never told anyone else about that other problem I fixed for you."

He can tell that I'm trying to confirm that he's kept our secret, too. His eyes square with mine. "Neither did I," he says. "You don't have to worry, Jen."

The look of conviction on his face makes me feel silly for saying anything. "I know," I say. "I don't know why I brought it up."

I shake my head as though to throw away the thought, and the conversation moves on to lighter fare. At some point, Cameron grabs my hand, holds it to his face, examines each finger, gently rubs each pink-polished nail.

"What are you doing?" I ask teasingly.

He doesn't look up from what he's doing. "I always liked looking at your hands," he says. "I want to see what I was looking at."

"Please don't tell me you have some weird hand fetish."

He laughs. "No," he says. He looks up at me, flashes me a sheepish grin. "I'm just biding my time until I get the rest."

We haven't really discussed what any of this would look like in the absence of corrections officers. "You mean *if* you get the rest," I tell him with a smile.

"Oh, I'm going to get it," he says. "As soon as I get out of here, I'm coming for you, Jen."

"We'll just have to see," I say, not a little coy. "A lot can happen between now and then."

When visiting time is over, I get up to leave. We hug.

"Thank you for coming," he says as though I am a dinner guest.

"Thank you for having me," I say as though he is a dinner host.

He gives me the best kind of kiss, the kind that lasts long after it's over. I can confirm that it is conducted in good taste.

And so this is how it goes, on this visit and five others, the final of which will fall less than twenty-four hours before the feds arrive at my door. On that visit, in the final half hour, we will rush inside the visiting room from the picnic tables in order to escape a sudden downpour, finding seats near Cherry Red and her husband.

"It's amazing how it just came on so quickly, out of nowhere," Cherry Red says of the rainstorm. She leaves early so as to get home before the weather gets any worse.

We say good-bye. I never see her again.

As I prepare to go out into the rain, we wrap up our conversation. We've created a code word for the Escalera brothers and, using this word, I tell him I will keep close watch for any developments.

"Don't worry," I say. "I'm on it."

As we say good-bye, I tell him, "I'm going to miss you."

"You're going to see me in two weeks," he says.

"Still," I say.

"I love you," he says.

"I love you, too," I say.

As I make my way to the door, he takes his place in the inmate line. Before I grab the handle, I look over at him. He is looking at the ground, but I catch his eye. He smiles and places his hand, its thumb and pinky extended, to his ear.

"I'll call you," he mouths.

But when he does, everything is different. By that time, there is nothing that will ever be the same.

Months later, with my own case staring me in the face, I've long forgotten about the Escalera brothers. In early September, still months away from hearing from the government about my case, I receive an e-mail from a Google Alert that I had created for Cameron during his case and never bothered deleting.

The alert links to an article entitled "Deals Could Keep Cameron Douglas Off the Stand." It reports that the Escalera brothers have been offered plea deals and that they will likely plead guilty within a month.

The article doesn't say much more, other than the fact that the trial judge, the same one as in Cameron's case, granted Eduardo Escalera's request for a new court-appointed attorney. The article doesn't explain why a new attorney was requested, other than to say there was "a dispute over the details" between lawyer and client.

I don't give the article much thought, other than to briefly note that Cameron's long-held fear will not be realized.

The next day, however, I'm on the subway home when the thought occurs to me: If the brothers are pleading in a month, why would Eduardo Escalera feel the need to request a new attorney?

I shake my head at myself for even thinking about this. I have my own case to worry about. When I return to my apartment, I delete the Google Alert and put the thought out of my mind.

I don't return to the thought until several months later, a few weeks before my court date. My attorney calls me. Though my fate has already been decided, it still unnerves me to see his number on my caller ID.

"Just want to give you a heads-up. Though it might change, right now it is looking like the Escaleras may be going to trial and Cameron will have to testify."

That's obviously bad news for Cameron, but I don't represent him anymore. "Why does that matter to me?" I ask.

"Because of *Giglio*."

Giglio. Of course.

Giglio—not to be confused with the word "gigolo"—refers to the 1972 U.S. Supreme Court case *Giglio v. United States.*

In *Giglio*, the Supreme Court considered the appeal of John Giglio, who had been convicted of bank fraud. The key evidence at trial was the testimony of a cooperating witness. The government had at one point offered the cooperator immunity in exchange for his testimony; however, the prosecutor who made this offer left the case and did not share the fact that he made this offer with his successor. As a result, the government inadvertently withheld the offer of immunity from the defense. And at trial, when cross-examined about whether he had ever received any offer of immunity, the cooperator lied and said that he hadn't.

The Supreme Court granted Giglio a new trial. It held that the government is constitutionally required to provide the defense with any evidence that reflects upon the cooperator's propensity to tell the truth. This can include promises of immunity, past crimes, or any other prior bad act by the cooperator.

Such as, for example, receiving contraband from his attorney.

The defense is then entitled to cross-examine the cooperator about these so-called *Giglio* disclosures. Thus, should the Escaleras go to trial, testimony about what I've done will certainly be presented to the jury. On the record. In open court.

That line of questioning is never short-lived, I think to myself.

My attorney finishes my thought: "Given who is involved, there will obviously be some press attention."

I now have two cases to follow: one in federal court and one in the court of public opinion.

I want to hang on to any possibility that this is not going to happen. I remember the news article from September. "There was an article a few months ago that said they had plea deals on the table," I tell him. "Do you think it's still possible for them to plead?"

"That's not something the government would ever share with us. But I imagine it's possible."

"Do you think they will plead?"

I hear him thinking. "You know, if they've been offered a plea, it's possible. But it's also a real possibility that they won't."

I thank him and hang up. I still have the receiver in my hand when I dial Best Friend.

"So, there's a new development," I tell her.

"What do they want now?" she asks in exasperation.

"Actually, nothing. But it turns out that even if my case goes away quietly, if Cameron ends up testifying, then it will be all over the news."

"What? Why?"

Best Friend is a lawyer but has had the good sense to stay away from criminal law. "Because of *Giglio*," I say.

"Wait . . . did you just say gigolo?" She says this with such seriousness that it indicates she believes my case somehow involves prostitution.

This makes me laugh uncontrollably. Perhaps that is all there is to do as the situation develops.

"Not gigolo, *Giglio*," I sputter. And then, because I can't help myself, I add, "Either way, there is a decent likelihood that someone is going to get fucked."

And so, due to the requirements of our Constitution, my fate becomes wrapped up in the impending trial of people I've never met. Perhaps fittingly, Cameron's fear about taking the stand has now become mine, too.

As I await my own court date, I check the docket sheets for David and Eduardo Escalera on a regular basis to see if there are any developments. A few days before Christmas, two weeks before I am set to go to court, the trial judge sets a trial date for the Escalera brothers for February 14, 2011.

But trial dates often change. It's not uncommon for a case to have a trial date even though the parties plan to plead guilty. I remind myself of this when I learn of this development.

Still, the discovery prompts me to visit the Bureau of Prisons' inmate locator, which provides the whereabouts of every federal inmate. Because the government will seek Cameron's transfer only if he will need to testify, I'm checking to make sure he is still in Pennsylvania.

When I enter Cameron's name into the website database, it lists the name of his facility in Pennsylvania. I breathe a sigh of relief.

My fear of complete ruin does not alter the fact that Christmas is coming. Because of travel restrictions related to my pending case, I'm unable to visit my parents as I normally would. My mother and I have shamefully continued the ruse with my father and have devised an excuse to explain my absence.

"But you didn't make it last year either," my father says over the phone with disappointment.

This is true. Although I had plans to take vacation days around Christmas, because of the demands of Cameron's case I decided it would make more sense to stay home.

"I know, I'm sorry," I say. And then, I institute the agreed-upon plan. "It's just, I have to work on my research paper for my job talk next fall, and I can't lug all of the sources with me."

I am supposed to be working on a research paper, this is the truth. But it's not true that I have pulled a single source, much less any that could not fit into a standard carry-on bag.

But I know that my father will adhere to logic and agree that any obligations I have toward my job would trump a personal visit. This is why my mother and I hatched this excuse in the first place.

"Okay," he says. "I'm disappointed, but I understand." He sounds sad.

"Dad, I just can't make it," I say.

A few days later, I receive a Christmas card from my parents, penned in my father's hand. *Though your mother and I will miss you*, it reads, *we are so proud of you for all that you are doing in your new profession, and we wish you all of the best with it. Love, your dad.*

When I consider the card against the events of the past few months, I impulsively crumple it up and throw it in the garbage. His praise is so vastly misplaced on me that I don't even want to look at it.

I linger by the trash can as though the card might come out when I am not looking. I can see it sitting on top of all of the other refuse, my father's familiar script peeking out from inside. I reach down to grab it, and then rip the card into pieces. I chuck these into the trash can and walk away.

Moments later, I think better of what I've just done. I'm back at the trash can, observing the pieces I've made of my father's card. Strewn together, they remind me of the makeshift puzzles that my brother and I used to make when we were kids. We'd draw a picture and then rip it into pieces. The disparity in size between the drawing paper and our small hands resulted in scraps that more or less approximated the size of puzzle pieces. Using some illicitly obtained Scotch tape from my dad's desk drawer and working with the precision of art historians, we would reconstruct our drawings, adhering each piece to the last until our artwork would be fully restored. These were then presented to our mother, who declared them a waste of tape.

I reach down in the garbage again, carefully extracting each piece of the card. I place these on the counter and consider whether they could be taped back together like a homemade puzzle. Deciding that they can, that my father's card can be made whole again, I act quickly and with purpose. I gather the pieces in my hand, walk out my apartment door, and place them in the garbage chute down the hall.

My family observes Christmas as a secular holiday, my parents thinking it cruel for us to believe that Santa brought gifts for other children, but not for us. With all of my distractions, I'm having to complete the entirety of my shopping and baking and wrapping in a single day. I could probably have gotten away with not doing any of it—"I have a criminal case pending" is a universally accepted excuse—but my case has pushed me toward last-minute holiday distraction.

I remain tied to inmate locator. I check it on my phone while I stand in line to purchase a snoring toy pig for my friend's daughter. I check it again after I put various batters in the oven to bake. Just for good measure, as I frantically knit a scarf for an otherwise forgotten recipient, I check it each time I take breaks to keep my hands from seizing.

Cameron is still at his facility.

The next day, Christmas Eve, after very little sleep, I make the three-hour drive to my brother's house upstate. I check inmate locator on the road. When I arrive, much later than I had promised my very punctual brother, I ignore the annoyed look on his face and go to the bathroom. While I am there, I check inmate locator again.

Cameron is still at his facility.

Owing both to my late arrival and my brother's cupboards being bare, we had hoped in vain to find a restaurant open on Christmas Eve. Then we hoped to find a grocery store. Ultimately, we settle on the only place within twenty miles of his home that is open—Walgreens—and use the opportunity to concoct a Christmas Eve dinner consisting entirely of the processed food we were forbidden to eat as children.

As the cashier tallies our frozen pizza and chips and macaroni and cheese, I catch sight of a marshmallow Hello Kitty poised on a stick. My eyes widen: she is reminiscent of marshmallow figurines of Christmases past. Though my brother and sister would scarf these down, I found them far too precious to eat. I would display them on my dresser, until my brother would inevitably walk by and punch in their faces through the plastic.

Christmas Hello Kitty is as exquisite as the figurines from my childhood. She is gently dusted in colored sugar and is decked out for the holiday in a Santa hat and dress. I add her to the pile.

"What the hell is that?" my brother says with incredulousness as the cashier swipes Hello Kitty against the electronic scanner.

"I don't know, I wanted it."

"Are you actually going to eat it?"

"No."

He rolls his eyes.

Once we return to his home and consume our fat- and sodium-laden feast—one that ends up being among our better Christmas Eve dinners—I check inmate locator one more time. I have propped up Hello Kitty next to my iPad, and she waits in anticipation of what I find.

Cameron is still at his facility.

On Christmas Day, I vow not to check inmate locator. This is not because I have a variety of social obligations (though I do) or because it is Christmas (though it is), but because I doubt the BOP would transfer an inmate on a federal holiday, and even if they did, they probably would not bother updating inmate locator.

(When we return from Christmas dinner, however, I do take a quick peek at inmate locator. Cameron is still at his facility.)

The day after Christmas, I check inmate locator on my brother's laptop. I forget to close the browser after I do, and so when my brother goes to use the computer he is welcomed by the Bureau of Prisons home page.

"What's this?" he asks.

I explain to him about the Escalera brothers and *Giglio*.

"Jesus, Jennie, how much shit did you step in?"

"A lot," I say.

Cameron is still at his facility.

The next day, with my need to check inmate locator out in the open, I check it on a regular basis from my place on the sofa. Hello Kitty looks on from the kitchen counter in support. For the entire day, Cameron is still at his facility.

I begrudgingly head home, if for no other reason than I have to prepare for court the following week. It takes me some time to pack up all of my things and load them into the car. By the time I get on the road, I realize that I have not checked inmate locator. I stop at the next exit and retrieve my iPad for this purpose.

Cameron is listed as being "In Transit."

I sit in the car for several minutes, deciding what I should do, whom I should call. It does not take long for reality to set in: this trial is happening, and there isn't a thing I can do about it.

I push the iPad back into my purse and happen upon Hello Kitty's backside. I had thrown her in with my other belongings as I was packing. When I turn her over, I see that her marshmallow face has been punched in through the plastic.

I roll my eyes and observe the damage. Her smooshed face expresses bewilderment, and she looks like a crossed-eyed baseball mitt. Once a beautiful delicacy, her fall from grace has been swift and complete.

I look her over and decide there is nothing to salvage. I unwrap her plastic covering and take a large, satisfying bite out of her head. I throw her remains into my purse. Then I drive home.

Cameron stays at a transit facility for a full week. He is transferred to MCC two days before I appear in court.

I know that when Cameron arrives at MCC, he will be placed in the

SHU until he is assigned to a unit. He is thus sitting in the SHU when I arrive at the U.S. Marshals Service for processing. He has also very likely encountered the newly incarcerated defendants who are being processed at the same time as me.

I watch the defendant ahead of me in line, the Russian guy charged with a drug crime, as he is being processed. His young face makes me think he is close to Cameron in age. He will almost certainly see Cameron later in the day. For a moment, I think to myself, If you want to relay a message to Cameron to ask about the Escaleras' trial, this is your opportunity.

But I have no message for Cameron. There is no information he can provide that will improve this situation. And though it's only been a few months since we've seen each other, and I've essentially thought of him in one way or another every day since, to communicate with him now somehow seems socially out of bounds. The thought crosses my mind as the Marshal presses my hands onto the fingerprinting machine: it did not take long for him to become someone I once knew.

Once my court date is over, the countdown to the Escalera trial begins.

I am in regular contact with my attorney. Each time we speak, he tells me what I wouldn't like to hear.

"Looks like it's still happening," he says.

"You don't think they're going to plead?" I am stubbornly holding on to hope.

He always says the only thing there is to say. "I would think if the government is still offering them a plea deal, it's possible they would plead."

"They'd be crazy not to plead, right? And I can't imagine the government is thrilled about taking this case to trial. Maybe the brothers are just posturing?"

My attorney has infinite patience, but I can tell that all of my speculative questions are wearing on him.

The days of January quickly pass, and there is no news of a plea. Just to be safe, I have resurrected my Google Alert for Cameron so that if there is any update, I'm among the first to have it.

By the start of February, with no new updates, I have resolved myself to the reality that this trial will happen. I sink into despondency, unable to reconcile how I have managed to escape my own court date unscathed, only to be undone mere weeks later. My career is standing on its last legs. Sleeplessness returns. I spend long hours in front of the television set and my computer. I wish I could simply abscond to a distant country. Unfortunately, I am hemmed in by the terms of my deferred prosecution agreement, and so I must eke out an existence during one of the coldest winters ever in New York.

I'm fiddling on my computer late one Monday night when an e-mail comes through. It's a Google Alert for Cameron that links to an article in the *New York Post*.

The Escalera trial has been postponed.

The reason for the adjournment is so odd that for a moment I wonder if the article is a spoof. Eduardo Escalera's attorney has asked the court for a psychological evaluation of his client based on the fact that his "decision making is irrational." According to his attorney, Eduardo Escalera "does not understand the nature and consequences of the current proceedings against him."

The article explains: the government has offered to drop the drug charges against both Escaleras and only bring charges for illegal reentry, an immigration crime that carries a sentence that is a mere fraction of that for the drug crimes. In taking the plea, the brothers would serve a sentence approximately half as long as Cameron's.

But Eduardo Escalera doesn't want to take the deal. And, just as I had posited earlier, his lawyer believes he would be crazy not to.

The trial judge orders a psychological evaluation and postpones the trial until early summer.

I am so happy with this development that I jump for joy.

But the best news of all, the news that makes me hope again that all of this might go away forever, arrives a couple of weeks later. I'm curious as to whether the government has determined to keep Cameron at MCC until the summer or if they've allowed him to return to his facility in Pennsylvania in the belief that a trial is unlikely. I pull up the Bureau of Prisons' website and enter his name into inmate locator.

Cameron is listed as being "In Transit."

The Escaleras' insanity has granted me reprieve. But I do not celebrate for long. Instead, I soon begin to feel as though what I dread is simply delayed.

The situation on its own does not lend itself to this conclusion. After all, the person who carries my fate, Cameron, has left New York City. He is the only one who can reveal my crimes to the public and will only do so if he is forced by the brunt of the law.

My problems could be far away. But I hold them close.

I fixate on the progress of the Escaleras' case. I regularly check their court dockets to see if there is any movement toward trial. I scan the Internet for any news articles. I obsess so frequently about whether or not they will opt for their attractive plea deals that I believe I can picture them in their respective prison cells, going through the possibilities in their mind.

"Let's take the plea," Imaginary David Escalera says.

"But we'll get deported," Imaginary Eduardo Escalera replies.

"We'll get deported no matter what," Imaginary David points out. "Even if we're found not guilty."

"I don't want to cave," Imaginary Eduardo says.

"But it will be far worse if we don't," Imaginary David says.

"But the worse it is, the more that Cameron owes us," Imaginary Eduardo says.

This last line, based on pure conjecture and uttered only in my mind, always gives me chills. It's a preposterous proposition, that someone would purposely take a more arduous path simply because they believed they could later leverage it into something lucrative. And yet, when Imaginary Eduardo says it, there is something about it that seems to ring true.

I'm otherwise finding it difficult to move forward. I'm experiencing an odd paradox: while I do want to avoid the repercussions of my case becoming public, in personal interactions I feel uncomfortable holding it in. This might be because with the Escalera trial looming in the distance, my secret stands on shaky ground. But it might also be that the secret is too significant not to share, that what I've done is now a part of who I am, and to allow others to presume that I am an upstanding member of society is possibly dishonest, and certainly incomplete.

I limit my interactions to those that are absolutely necessary. I spin a cocoon of familiarity around myself, spending my time only with those who are acquainted with my case, and thus really know me, or by myself.

And so, when winter turns into spring, when actual cocoons are opened and butterflies emerge, I remain right where I am. I complain to anyone who will listen that I wish the Escalera saga would just be over already, that they would just decide. But deep down I know there is a comfort to being ensconced in this familiar fear. That beyond this purgatory, there is something much more formidable to confront. That by obsessing about the decisions of others, I do not yet have to think about my own.

CHAPTER 8

To Baghdad, with Angst

As spring yields to summer, my obsessive search for updates in the Escaleras' case does not yield very much. In May, Eduardo Escalera is declared as being of sound mind. He requests and is granted yet another new attorney—his third since his arrest, if anyone is keeping track—though the trial judge tells him this is the very last time and schedules a trial date for early October 2011.

There is thus more waiting. I'm given little choice but to try to proceed with my life.

Early July marks the time when the period of my deferred prosecution comes to an end. On July 7, six months to the day after my court date, the charges are dismissed. I expect to wake up the next day feeling different, but find I'm the exact same person I was the day before. It turns out that the dropping of charges does not, as I'd hoped, result in the erasing of history.

I begrudgingly turn my attention to work. I am required to produce a piece of groundbreaking scholarship for presentation to the faculty in the fall. I am to use this piece of research to dazzle law schools at the annual job fair, held one week after this faculty presentation, in the hopes of securing a tenure-track teaching position.

Most candidates spend anywhere between twelve to eighteen months preparing their piece. Because I decide my time is better spent fixating on my case, I end up according myself exactly four.

In order to write this academic article, I must first complete my research. With the deadline looming and my travel restrictions lifted, I cannot waste time. I am going to Baghdad.

Baghdad's earliest inhabitants can be traced back to a time in history when the rest of the globe consisted of little more than tectonic plates. Fifty thousand years later, the area comprising Baghdad and its environs was known as Mesopotamia. Four thousand years after that, for reasons both geographical and political, the region became known as the Republic of Iraq.

One of the oldest places on earth, Baghdad is in many ways where society was born. Here is where man first decided to read, to write, to do math. Here is where he first decided he ought to keep track of time. Put on shoes. Sit in a chair. Sleep in a bed. Eat from a bowl. Chop with an axe. Plant crops. Irrigate land. Construct homes. Create schools. Make cities. Enact laws.

Baghdad is where the world begins.

It is axiomatic that in a place of abundant creation, destruction is never far behind. As the region's earliest peoples grew into villages and those villages into communities and those communities into civilizations and those civilizations into empires, each considered Baghdad a crown jewel, an eyed prize.

And so, almost as soon as Baghdad was civilized, it was invaded and occupied. Gilgamesh had his turn in 2700 BC, and a thousand years later Hammurabi followed. The Akkadians, the Kassites, the Assyrians, the Greeks, and the Persians all laid claim as well. Baghdad was later considered a grand conquest among the Islamic caliphates, and so both the Umayyad and Abbasid empires included it among their holdings.

The Abbasids, their empire stretching from modern-day Morocco to Iran, were so enamored of Baghdad that they made it their capital. But even this came to an end several hundred years later, when the Mongols—led by Hulagu Khan, grandson of Genghis—came to conquer. In addition to the standard slaughter, Khan took the extra step of destroying Baghdad's most precious possession, its four-hundred-year-old grand library, at that time one of the foremost in existence. Tens of thousands of manuscripts of science and mathematics and literature were unceremoniously chucked into the Tigris, notoriously turning its waters black with ink.

And so on and so forth. Even now. The only constant in Baghdad is Baghdad itself, which despite millennia of external invasion still stands. Thus, there is only one rule in Baghdad, containing two interrelated parts. First, that there will always be empire. And second, that notwithstanding the first, Baghdad will always be.

I am headed to Iraq to examine its criminal justice system. For the past several years, long before my criminal exploits, I became interested in how criminal justice has developed in a new democratic Iraq. When I decided upon this research, I was aware that changes to Iraq's criminal justice system had been promulgated by the United States through a $300 million initiative. I knew that this initiative was supported by the expertise and manpower of a federal agency that typically concerns itself with the workings of criminal justice in the United States.

I did not know, however, that agents affiliated with this entity, the Department of Justice, would one day show up at my door in an unrelated matter.

The focus of this research project is the use of secret evidence. Under Baathist rule, secret evidence was critical in the regime's ability to control dissent. Men and women would be rounded up on the street without apparent reason. Once detained and tortured, they would be brought before a judge, where charges would be read and a verdict announced based on evidence that the defendants were not permitted to see. Guilt was a foregone conclusion, a sentence of death an assured eventuality.

In my research, I discover that secret evidence has been banned in legal traditions dating back thousands of years. Even the ancients saw the injustice in convicting someone without allowing him to confront the evidence against him. The use of secret evidence violates Talmudic law; it violates Islamic law; it violates the law of the Canon. And though the Romans would happily throw a defendant to the lions, they agreed that he had the right to cross-examine his accuser first.

But with its multimillion-dollar makeover, the U.S. government does not see fit to change Iraq's laws allowing secret evidence. And in the years that follow the U.S. construction of a new criminal court, several human rights organizations report that its use is common and accepted.

The deliberate denial of the right to confront is an interesting decision in creating a new democracy, especially given that this same right is part of America's legal foundation. The right to confrontation was among the first rights demanded of England by the First Continental Congress; the denial of the right was among the reasons cited for going to war against the Crown. When independence was won, the right became one of the very first enshrined in our Constitution.

The right to confront is what requires the government to present evidence in open court, what establishes a defendant's ability to cross-examine witnesses. It can be said to be one of several rights underlying the decision of the United States Supreme Court in *Giglio v. United States.*

It is the right that the Escalera brothers will exercise should they decide to go to trial.

And so this is how I find myself here, examining a criminal justice system that is devoid of a right I suspect might be necessary to the proper administration of justice, a right that in my own life could be the very cause of my downfall.

I first traveled to Baghdad in 2004, a year after the U.S. invasion began. At that time, Baghdad was an active war zone, replete with tanks in constant prowl, helicopters overhead, and ubiquitous gunfire. On the way to the hair salon, I walked past a small park. On the way back, the whole park was on fire.

Now, seven years later, here is the aftermath. Entering Baghdad's city limits feels like walking into a hospital room moments after the patient has died. The air is dense with loss. Baghdad's landscape is littered with bombed-out buildings and rubble. Her sidewalks are blanketed in refuse. Her streets are clogged with traffic, the perpetual honking of horns providing a dreary melody. People seem to move at a slower pace, as though every exertion must be made with considerable effort.

On the way from the airport to my aunt's home, the heat smothers my cousin's car, presses on my throat. Although the air-conditioning is on full blast, each time I inhale I feel my lungs become warm. We seem to be perpetually stopped at government checkpoints, which while established for public safety seem only to construct an ideal civilian target. Each checkpoint is crowded with cars, crowded with passengers, crowded with the desire for forward momentum. And yet, every encounter with these is eerily calm. It is as though the entire city holds its breath in anticipation of what might happen next.

At one such checkpoint, I look into the car next to ours. There is a woman sitting in the backseat on the driver's side, her head wrapped in a scarf, a baby in her lap. I politely smile. Her baby boy, his fat face a perfect circle, smiles so wide that his cheeks obscure his eyes. His mother looks down at him, then back at me. He doesn't know any better, her expression seems to say. And then she looks away.

There is an Iraqi saying, reserved for the giving of condolences in the wake of tragedy, that roughly translates to *I cover myself in black for you.* As my cousin drives over the Tigris, I look down at its blue-brown waters. I imagine them as they were in the time of Hulagu Khan, brimming with blackness in mourning for what life in Baghdad has come to be.

I can smell my aunt's cooking from the driveway. She emerges from the house with flushed face, her arms extended. When she hugs me, I note that her pink sweat suit smells of cardamom and lemon. I squeeze her five-foot frame and tell her that she herself is an Iraqi delicacy.

My aunt is a slightly older, substantially saner version of my mother. The eldest daughter, she is invariably the voice of reason, always expressed diplomatically, usually with a loving smile.

But while she is warm and nurturing, my aunt is very much a woman with whom one should not trifle. I once saw her dress down a man on the street who gratuitously admonished me for wearing a skirt that exposed the bottom half of my calves. The look of terror in his eyes as she gave him the what-for was so intense that I actually felt bad for him.

Inside the house I greet my uncle, one of the funniest men I know.

His smile is broad as he directs me to the dining table, which is so stuffed with platters that it looks as though it might break. At the table are place settings for me, my aunt and uncle, my cousin and his wife, and their two young sons, whose cheeks I can't help but squeeze with delight.

As I look over the table, I see that one place setting is different from the others. Placed to the right of six plates are spoons. Placed to the right of the seventh is a fork.

"Here is your seat," my uncle tells me, directing me to the place setting bearing a fork.

I feel a little embarrassed, as though my family thinks me to be someone foreign, ill at ease. "I really don't mind eating with a spoon," I say.

"No, please," my aunt says. She makes me a plate. "Eat," she orders.

I don't need to be coaxed. My aunt is an ob-gyn by training but bears the talents of an elite chef. Every dish is delicately prepared and flavored to perfection.

As I make my way through the plate, my aunt piles on more food. Between the jet lag and the carbohydrate consumption I feel precariously close to food coma. But I keep eating.

As we eat we exchange our respective troves of family gossip, which marriage appears to be teetering on the precipice of divorce, which cousin has gotten too fat. The boys tell me excitedly about their new school, their squash lessons, their obsession with WWE wrestling.

As expected, but nonetheless dreaded, the conversation turns to me.

"How is everything, how is your life?" my aunt asks me.

I swallow. "I'm fine."

She looks at me as though I should elaborate. I don't want to elaborate. And on my mother's strict instruction, I'm not going to.

"I'm guess I'm busy."

I try to change the subject to my research. My uncle has been kind enough to set up some interviews with members of the Iraqi Bar Association, and I tell him I think it will prove to be helpful. He is politely unconvinced. The barbarity of the Iraqi criminal justice system in the previous regime was hardly complex. The new court, my uncle hypothesizes, is probably like everything else in the new Iraq: the same or only marginally better.

"That's it," he says with a wink. "Your research is done."

I smile. I know that my interest in the new criminal court, and in criminal law, is puzzling to my family. They are all scientists by training, and for me to consider the rights of criminals strikes them as pedestrian. When they ask why this interests me, I explain in an ineloquent mixture of English and Arabic that examining changes in criminal justice is useful beyond criminals, that because criminal courts serve as tools of government constraint, they provide a unique prism with which to understand the government itself.

My answer goes over reasonably well. The boys are getting antsy; they want to play with the presents that I've brought from afar. My aunt gets up to clear the table. I manage to stand up, but my aunt refuses my help. She points me in the direction of my room, which is neatly made up for my stay.

I lie on the bed, almost too tired to sleep. It is still daylight outside. I hear the hum of air-conditioning abruptly stop: the electricity is out. Though I know the generator will soon kick in, in the intervening minutes it feels as though my room is being preheated for baking.

While I await salvation, I think about how my family considers the criminal law an odd area of study. I'm used to this. I've noted from a young age that my fascination with crime is possibly not normal. Most people seem to consider the criminal process as something that exists on a need-to-know basis, observed at a distance, either in snippets of news or in *Law & Order* franchises. No one wants to get too close.

But for some reason, I do. Perhaps a by-product of my rule-infused upbringing, as a child I was fascinated by anything having to do with crime and punishment. I obsessively followed criminal trials and, in a pre-Internet age, clipped and collected articles about these and pasted them into my journal. Crime was my preferred topic of conversation, the inevitable thesis of school term papers, the prevailing subject of the books I chose to read.

When I was in college, I finally got to see the criminal process up close. My freshman year, I located and then visited the municipal court located a few blocks from campus. When I saw that a rape trial was in progress, I took a seat in the front row of the gallery just as the victim was taking the stand. I was so transfixed that in my memory I didn't even take a breath. As she described the heinous details of her ordeal—her ex-boyfriend storming into her home, him locking her into the bedroom while her small children sat at the door, her placing her own hand over her mouth so that her children would not hear what transpired—my chest tightened as though it were happening now, happening to all of us.

I so misappropriated my relevance to this woman's testimony that when she stepped down from the stand sobbing and burst out of the courtroom, I found myself walking behind her, following her to the ladies' room. I had no concept of what she had been through, not a thing to say that might sound right. But I still stood next to her as she cried over the sink, mostly saying nothing, occasionally handing her a rough paper towel from the dispenser against the wall.

Now, as I lie in bed waiting for air-conditioning to arrive, I remember this woman, her damaged blond hair, her long flowered dress. At the time, I told myself that I ran to her out of concern, out of empathy for her suffering, respect for her courage. But I see now that this was only partially true. What also led me there was the promise of proximity.

It's possibly not a healthy thing, to want so badly to see crime and punishment up close, to watch its underbelly rise and fall. The compulsion likely renders me an oddity, a fork in a drawer full of spoons. All things considered, I suppose it was only a matter of time before I found myself exactly where I stand.

"Secrecy" is a common theme in Iraq's criminal court system. The court is located in a secured purgatory between the fortress of the Green Zone and the rest of Baghdad, closed to public viewing. Access is permitted only with advance government clearance. I receive such clearance by virtue of my U.S. passport and the helpful assistance of a member of the U.S. Embassy who vouches for the legitimacy of my research. Without similar clearance, Iraqi citizens are not allowed.

This level of restriction is not surprising. As a security measure against insurgent attacks, Iraq's entire political apparatus is located inside the Green Zone, outside of the access of the citizenry. The result is that Baghdad is reduced to two separate and unrelated spheres. The general populace has no oversight over its representatives, and the government regulates people and places it cannot see.

To everyday Iraqis, the Green Zone's impermeability is absolute: no one ever goes in, and no one ever comes out. It is the premise of *Charlie and the Chocolate Factory*, except with grave violations of the Geneva Conventions.

In traversing both spheres, I can confirm that they bear no resemblance to each other. The Green Zone boasts newly constructed homes on pristine streets. The happy hum of air-conditioning is constant. But while the Green Zone is clean and cool, there is something disconcertingly sterile in its construction. The entire setup looks as though everything has been unpacked out of a box, the contents of which could just as easily exist in Boise as they do in Baghdad.

My family asks me what the Green Zone is like. My cousin's wife, a notorious neat freak, asks me if its streets are cleaner than those in Baghdad proper.

"Maybe just a little," I lie. It's not as though she will ever know.

When we reach the area containing the court, my driver/translator directs me to security. Although I am accorded clearance in advance, I'm nonetheless at the whim of the Iraqi military officials who stand guard. It has thus been suggested to me that in order to ensure entry I should "try not to act Iraqi."

I therefore engage in the following exchange:

IRAQI SOLDIER (IN ARABIC): Passport, please.

ME (IN ENGLISH): I'm sorry, I don't understand.

IRAQI SOLDIER (IN ARABIC): You don't understand the word "passport"? [He is dubious because the word for passport is "bassbort."]

ME (STEADFAST, IN ENGLISH): No, I don't.

IRAQI SOLDIER (IN ARABIC): But you understood what I just said.

ME (SILENTLY CURSING, IN ENGLISH): I'm sorry, I don't understand.

He ultimately lets me through and directs me to a series of build-ings. Except they are not buildings, they are trailers, arranged in a man-ner that suggests that there is a film being shot nearby, or FEMA has recently stepped in.

"What is this?" I ask my driver.

"It's the criminal court," he says.

The series of FEMA-like trailers that I encounter actually house individual proceedings of both chambers of Iraq's criminal court, the investigatory and trial chambers, with defendants sporting nacho cheese–colored jumpsuits shuttled in between. It seems rather odd, the hundreds of millions of dollars spent to establish this trailer park. Perhaps since the public can't observe the proceedings, appearance is not considered a top priority.

I'm hoping to take a look at the court dockets. But I soon learn that in keeping with the theme of secrecy, court documents and records are not readily made available to the public.

"Why would they even want to see them?" a judge asks me when I inquire.

"But if they did want to see it, would you show it to them?" I ask.

"I suppose. Yes, if they came here and requested it, we would prob-ably show it," he says.

"But how could they come here to request it without special clear-ance?"

He shrugs. "I don't know," he says.

I think about my own legal troubles. In this system of criminal jus-tice, I think to myself, no one would ever know my criminal case existed.

In most of the proceedings I see—all of them terrorism cases—the entirety of the evidence consists of an anonymous witness statement claiming the defendant is guilty. When I inquire about the obvious drawbacks of this procedure, and the unfortunate history associated with its prior use, the judges insist that the use of secret evidence is necessary. The security concerns surrounding terrorism cases are very real, and without allowing witnesses the ability to keep their identity secret, they say, the cases could not be brought at all.

But the issue is not apolitical, I am told. In many instances the witnesses are American and Iraqi soldiers, and because their supervisors do not allow them to testify, the system allows them to accuse without consequence.

"Does it bother you," I ask a trial judge, "that in a criminal trial in the United States these witnesses would be required to testify, and here they are not?"

He thinks about this for several moments. "Not really," he finally says. He seems ready to say more, but doesn't.

Taking it all in, I am struck by the malleability of criminal justice, how this system manages to be so different from the one that produced the American lawyers who birthed it. Justice is apparently not carved in stone, but made of something pliable, something that can be shaped and stretched to fit whatever shape man prefers.

It's not difficult to see in this system that the absence of the right to confront is problematic. I privately conclude that while I don't want the Escaleras to exercise this right, I don't doubt it is a right they should have.

The principled part of me thinks what has been accomplished in this court system is a profound disappointment, a missed opportunity. But another part of me recognizes the impulse behind its construction. I know all about breaking rules to achieve what I believe to be a better outcome, choosing lawlessness for what I personally believe to be an overriding good. I can sympathize with the urge to game the system to achieve a self-interested result. It's not right, but the criminal in me understands.

Although I manage to remain somewhat focused on my research, my personal travails remain close. Every day before I go to court and after I return, I check online to search for any updates in the Escaleras' case.

At first, there are few. At some point late in the summer, inmate locator indicates that Cameron has been transferred from Pennsylvania back to New York City. This does not give me great pause, given that he was moved there once already and nothing came to pass.

A few days later, I receive a Google Alert leading me to an article in the *New York Post* reporting that Cameron is no longer on the government's witness list. Unfortunately, the story doesn't make enough sense for me to be excited. I can't imagine the government would go to the trouble of moving Cameron to New York City and not place him on the stand. But I have no way of obtaining the transcript in Baghdad without undergoing significant inconvenience, and so I forward the article to my lawyer, who writes back the next day to say that Cameron will still be testifying and that the trial seems to be moving forward.

And then one morning I check my e-mail and find a link to an article in the *New York Post*:

MORE DOUGLAS TROUBLE

I swallow hard and start to read:

> The feds won't let anything block Cameron Douglas' role as the star witness against his alleged drug suppliers—not even additional lawbreaking.
> The troubled Hollywood scion—currently serving five years in the slammer for dealing meth—has been caught in "additional criminal activity," according to court papers filed yesterday.

I take from this that the government has provided information of my crimes to the court. I read ahead to see if any details of what I've done have been disclosed to the press.

> Lawyer Lloyd Epstein, who represents Eduardo Escalera, said he had no idea what trouble Douglas had gotten into, or if it had occurred during the time he has been locked up.

I read the article again in the hopes that the second time around it will say something different. It doesn't.

My head somehow feels heavier than it was. I look at my watch.

With the eight-hour time difference, every possible person with whom I would like to discuss this development—my lawyer, my mother, Best Friend—is fast asleep.

I rub my eyes. I stand up and pace. I go back to my laptop. I sit on the bed. I lie down. I pull the blanket over my head.

I don't know how long I am lying there when I hear a soft knock on the door.

"Jennie?" It's my aunt.

"Yes?" I don't bother moving, so I suspect my voice is muffled.

"Don't you want to have breakfast?" I hear her open the door.

"I'm not really hungry."

In keeping with Iraqi tradition, she is equal parts galled and worried. "How can you not be hungry?"

"I'm not feeling too well," I announce through the blanket.

"Why, sweetheart?" From the sway of the mattress, I can tell she has sat down next to me.

"I—"

She pulls back the blanket and places her hand against my forehead. I'm hoping that the heat underneath the covers has caused my forehead to feel warm.

"You don't have a fever." She looks me over for a moment with my mother's same trademark precision. "Are you upset?"

"No," I lie.

"Then what?"

I'm not sure what I could possibly say about this to her. I can't really tell her that it seems increasingly likely that I'm about to lose everything that seems worth having. So I say something technically true but very incomplete. "I just miss my mom." I feel myself tear up.

As soon as I say it, I fear she might take this as a veiled criticism about my stay. And for a moment, I think I can see this thought pass across her face. But she looks at me with sympathetic eyes and wipes my cheek with her hand.

"I know," she says. "I miss her, too."

I sometimes forget that my mother had a life before she was my mother. That she and my aunt spent the first two decades of their lives at each other's sides, two peas in a pod, two halves of a whole.

But they then spent the next four decades on opposite—and opposing—sides of the world, visiting each other only in e-mails and phone calls.

The last eight years of this time apart have been very difficult on my aunt. The war has forced her into early retirement from a medical practice she loved. On two separate occasions, kidnapping threats from insurgents have required her and my uncle to pick up everything and leave the country. Her friends have suffered unspeakable losses. Her immediate family lives in a shroud of uncertainty, not knowing if they will stay here or try to find a new home somewhere else.

In remembering all of this, I recognize that I am being a self-centered asshole, thinking my problems to be worthy of such melodrama. I sit up and wipe my eyes.

"Come on," she says. "At least have tea with me while I make lunch."

I nod and get up. We descend the stairs to the kitchen. The table evidences that she is preparing stuffed vegetables in pomegranate-infused water. I see that several eggplants have already been gutted and that next to her ashtray many others await evisceration.

My aunt does not heed my declaration of not being hungry and places before me a plate of leavened pita bread, clotted cream, and date syrup. My appetite miraculously returns, and while she works her way through the eggplants, I smother the bread with the cream and drizzle it with syrup. It tastes so good that my horror over the *Post* article begins to fade.

My aunt is a multitasker, and so while she whittles vegetables and smokes a cigarette, she is also watching the kitchen television set. This is always set to a Dubai-based television station called Fatafeat, a food channel that carries popular cooking programs from every continent. My aunt watches this channel so much that my uncle often remarks that he is not sure if my aunt is married to him or to Fatafeat.

My aunt gestures toward the television show with her eggplant. "See, Jennie, this is an American show."

I look over at the set and see Emeril Lagasse's *Emeril Live.* "Do you like Emeril?" I ask my aunt.

She shakes her head. "I don't like his food. It just too *too* much."

This doesn't surprise me. I have learned the hard way that Iraqi cooking requires a delicate touch. On the television screen, Emeril is dousing sautéed pineapple in thick whole cream with reckless abandon and yelling *"BAM!"* while the audience cheers. I look over at my aunt, who takes a drag of her cigarette and shakes her head again.

"See?" she says.

I've finished my plate, but my aunt has already brought me another. At some point, *Emeril Live* goes to commercial, and my aunt is assessing upcoming programming.

She nods toward the screen. "Now her," she says with admiration, "I like. Everything she does is so nice."

I turn my head toward the television set, but I already know who I will see. It is Martha. She is in a commercial promoting her television program *Martha Bakes*, standing against a robin's egg blue background, an exquisitely decorated cake before her. My aunt is rapt with her description of what the next thirteen episodes of the program will bring.

I watch my aunt for a moment. "You know," I say, "that woman Martha went to prison."

She turns her attention away from Martha to me. She waits for me to explain.

"She sold stock based on a secret tip," I divulge. I don't even know why I am telling the story as though it's salacious. Martha's crimes obviously do not bother me one whit. But I nonetheless continue: "Then when the police asked her about it, she lied about it. And that's against the law. So she had to go to jail. Can you believe that?"

I'm begging her to be disgusted with Martha. Terrible Martha. You think you like her, but wait until you hear. She should have known better, done better, but she didn't. She had everything going for her, and then she threw it all away.

I'm leaned over the kitchen table waiting for her response. My aunt lights another cigarette and then shrugs her shoulders. "Eh," she says. "So many people like to say the bad things other people do. We all make mistakes, do bad things. She did a bad thing. So what?"

I get up to take my plate to the sink. Then I walk over to my aunt and put my arms around her small frame, hugging her tight.

She is not expecting this. "What's wrong?" she asks.

At first I say nothing, but then I notice she is trying to wriggle the hand with her cigarette free.

"You are just such a good person," I say.

My aunt takes a drag from her cigarette and looks at me intently. "Jennie," she admonishes me. "It is only for God to judge." She adds, in Arabic, "Isn't that true?"

"It's true," I tell her. She eyes me suspiciously for a moment. She knows something is up with me but does not press. Instead, she gives my cheek a big Iraqi kiss, picks up her cigarette, and resumes stuffing eggplants.

After we feast on the fruits of her labor; after my mother calls and tells me that she is certain that everything is going to work out; after I receive an e-mail from my lawyer explaining that the *Giglio* information will be made public only if there is a trial, I do feel better. But when I go to sleep, I realize that it isn't my lawyer or my mother or even the delicious lunch that has put my mind at ease. It is my aunt's mercy toward Martha, a woman whom she does not and will not know, that makes me believe that I can return to New York and face what awaits me.

My departure from Iraq is bittersweet. I'm relieved to return to a country that enjoys uninterrupted air-conditioning and political stability. But I will miss my family, and for all of its blown-out buildings and beat-up streets, Baghdad, too.

Access at the airport is restricted, so my family can't accompany me. My aunt is worried about whether I can make it on my own. I laugh and tell her I have been to dozens of foreign airports by myself, that I will be fine.

When I arrive, the protocol appears to be more or less what it is at every other airport. I hurl my two suitcases on a luggage cart and make my way to airport security.

A security officer is scrutinizing one of my suitcases. He places it back through the X-ray machine and gestures to another official to take a look. Together they appear to be studying something they see in the bag. They decide to place it through the X-ray machine once more. They look at the screen again and nod their heads. Then they look at me.

"Open the suitcase, please."

Mildly annoyed, I unlock the suitcase and pull the zipper. From the way they are looking at my bag, I can't discern the offending item. Soon, however, one of the guards points to a copper jug that I purchased at an outdoor market, reminiscent of the one that resides in my childhood home, which in turn was brought by my mother from Baghdad on a trip she took three decades earlier. The man says something that I am unable to fully decipher, and I ask if he would please tell me in English.

"You cannot have this," he says, referring to the jug. "You cannot take anything out of the country that is more than fifty years old. No. You cannot have it."

I'm aware of this rule, enacted to stop the bleeding of Iraqi antiquities out of the country in the wake of the looting of the Museum of Iraq. But while my jug is vintage, given the provenance of my mother's jug, it can't possibly be more than fifty years old.

"But how do you know this is more than fifty years old?" I ask.

He doesn't address my question. "You cannot have this."

"But how do you know it's fifty years old? There is nothing that makes that clear."

He shakes his head. "No. You cannot have this."

He still will not look me in the eye and this, combined with his staunch refusal to even discuss the matter, makes me angry. I move my head so that my eyes are in his line of sight. "Hello?" I say with not a little obnoxiousness. "Can you please explain to me how you are certain that this is more than fifty years old?"

Two other security guards appear from nowhere and join the chorus. "You cannot have this. It is more than fifty years old."

"Yes, I understand the rule," I say. I can hear the volume of my voice rising. "But how do you know this is more than fifty years old?"

He shrugs his shoulders. "You cannot have it."

This entire exchange has drawn a bit of an audience. While there is another security line that is moving, a fair number of passengers seem content to stop and watch.

I hear my cell phone ring. It is my aunt, thank goodness. I pick up the phone. "Auntie," I tell her with dramatic desperation. "They are saying I can't take the copper jug with me."

"What? Let me talk to them."

I hand my cell phone to one of the guards. The guard is telling her to come back to the airport to retrieve the jug. I can hear my aunt on the other end of the line saying she will do no such thing.

The audience grows in size. The guard with my phone moves a few feet away from the security station and I walk with him so I can continue to follow what is being discussed.

After a few moments, I think to look over at my suitcase, which is lying open at the security station. A security guard, his hands ungloved, begins lifting various of my belongings in order to remove the jug from the suitcase. I'm watching it in slow motion, his bare hands wading through T-shirts and pajamas and underpants in order to root out the jug from its home.

I don't believe what I am seeing. I run over to the suitcase and bellow, *"Do not touch my things!"*

Up to his elbows in my unmentionables, the man looks at me with genuine confusion.

"Put that down," I say, pointing to his hands.

He ignores me. The audience is now the size of an off-Broadway show. As he pulls the jug from its secure place in my bag, various pieces of clothing spill onto the floor. He does not make any attempt to clean up the mess that he has made, he only walks away, my sentimental souvenir in hand.

The guard who has been speaking to my aunt hands my phone back to me. "Jennie," my aunt says with angry resignation. "I am so sorry, but you have to give them the jug."

"But why?"

"You just have to."

I say nothing.

"Please, Jennie. You have to do what they say. They can really hurt you."

"They can't hurt me," I say, based on nothing.

"Please, I will never forgive myself if something bad happens." She sounds scared. It's unclear if she is afraid of them or of me.

"But—"

"Please!"

"Okay," I say begrudgingly. "This is such bullshit."

I walk back over to pull my belongings together. I crouch down on the ground and pick them up off of the floor. Then I bunch these together and shove them into the gap in my suitcase where the jug once was. Just observing its absence makes me seethe.

As I am still on the floor, trying to rearrange my toiletries, a man in a suit accompanied by a member of airport security approaches me.

"I need to see your passport, please." He holds out his hand.

"Why?"

"We need to return the jug to an address in Baghdad."

"What?"

"You can't just leave it at the airport. It is against policy."

I am incredulous at the stupidity of what this man is saying. I look up from my luggage and glare at both men. "Well, it sounds like you should send the jug to the Museum of Iraq, since it's such a precious relic."

At first they don't understand. When they realize that I am being sarcastic, they say, "Please, miss, your passport."

I zip up the suitcase and place it on the luggage cart. "No," I hear myself say.

"What do you mean?" The look of shock on the men's faces gives me a sick sense of satisfaction that only eggs me on further.

"I mean no, I will not show you my passport."

"You have to."

"No. I don't."

"Please, miss. I need it for the paperwork."

"Sorry," I say. I relish parroting his words back to him. "You cannot have it."

I expect that in the face of such open belligerence the men will be angry. Instead, their faces display confusion. I suspect they are not used to encountering someone so obstinate, so uncouth. I don't care. I grip the handles of my luggage cart and then make my way toward airport check-in.

When I'm standing in line, I feel a tap on my shoulder. I turn to see approximately twelve men in suits surrounding me. They don't appear to be particularly pleased.

One of the men at the front of the procession believes that my refusal to provide my passport must be based on some confusion. "Miss, we need to see your passport only to complete the paperwork. It will just take a moment."

"No," I say.

"You cannot say no," he says.

"I'm not going to show you my passport."

Various passengers who are standing in the line are pleading with me to just do what the man says. I ignore all of them. A now-familiar indignation washes over me, and reasonableness is beyond my reach. I can only see the stupidity of the rule that is being imposed and my unfettered need to break it.

The man takes out his cell phone. "If you are not going to show us your passport, we will have to take action."

"Fine," I say. I'm going to go to Abu Ghraib over this stupid copper jug, but I still can't bring myself to acquiesce.

He's still on the phone when I call over to him. "Make sure you call the U.S. Embassy as well," I say. "You are required to advise them of any U.S. citizens that you detain." I make this up, but it sounds like it could be real.

While I assert this with confidence, I do internally consider the possibility that he will actually follow my directive, that the U.S. Embassy will determine my criminal background and fly in Some Prosecutor to personally prosecute me.

But it doesn't come to this. After a moment, the sea of suits disperses. There is no explanation, but the matter appears to be dropped, and I am left to proceed with check-in.

I should be relieved that my obnoxious behavior did not culminate in further action. But I am overcome with anger, incensed that I have been forced to leave behind my cultural heirloom, livid that my only memento of this city is a series of senseless dictatorial directives, irate that my family is forced to endure such nonsense every day. The fury courses through my veins, causing my whole body to shake. As I rifle through my carry-on for my antianxiety medication, as I pretend to ignore the looks of disbelief from my fellow passengers, as I consider what I've observed on this trip in the way of justice, I want only to personally bring down this corrupt excuse for a democracy and the overpaid hacks who service it. I long to storm the walls of the Green Zone and oust this regime in favor of one that actually respects its citizenry. I am consumed with the desire to illicitly provide the people of Iraq with the sociopolitical equivalent of Xanax.

It isn't until later that I will look back on this incident and reflect on the fact that I have not learned anything from what I've done. That mere weeks after my charges are dropped, I can't keep myself from defying rules that do not meet my personal standards. That I cannot seem to fall in line. That there may very well be something profoundly wrong with me.

CHAPTER 9

Persona Non Bra-ta

Upon my return to New York, I have reached a point in my work obligations where I must pull myself away from the Escaleras' case as much as I can. It's now early fall 2011. Woefully behind on my article, I frantically attempt to throw something together that will look decent enough to prospective law schools. With my impending participation in the law school job fair, I must also pull together materials for eleven tenure-track interviews I have scheduled two weeks from now.

I have not done myself any favors by pushing everything to the last minute. The week before the job fair, I am slated to present a draft of my paper to the full faculty. My intention is to compensate for its dismal state with a dynamic presentation of my findings.

I am preparing for this presentation at home when I receive a call from my lawyer. He tells me that the Escaleras have made a successful motion to sever their trials into two. David Escalera's trial is slated to begin on Monday, the day of my presentation. Eduardo Escalera's trial is to start two weeks later.

My lawyer confirms that Cameron will serve as the key witness in both trials. There are now two opportunities for my crimes to be made public.

"But the cases could still plead out, right?" I ask.

"I would have to think so, yes," my lawyer says.

This is all I need to hear to get back to work. "Okay," I say. "Thank you for letting me know."

"But there's one more thing," my lawyer says.

There is always one more thing.

"David Escalera's lawyer called me."

"You? Why?"

"He says that he plans on subpoenaing you as a witness for the defense and wanted to know if you would appear voluntarily."

"You mean take the stand? In open court?"

"Yes."

"You've got to be fucking kidding me."

My lawyer indicates that he is not, in fact, fucking kidding me. Apparently, David Escalera's lawyer, presumably wanting to cast doubt on Cameron's testimony about his client, would like me to testify about what I did on Cameron's behalf. I suspect the thought is that this would make Cameron look like shit. It, of course, would make me look like shit, too.

This is probably not a valid basis to subpoena my testimony. If they file the subpoena, my attorney says, we will move the court to ask that it be quashed.

This plan gives me little comfort. Getting into a paper war with David Escalera will only increase the likelihood of press attention. I wish I had remained in Baghdad, outside the subpoena power of the court.

I think for a moment. "Please call him back," I say. "Tell him that if I take the stand, I will tell the jury that I think his client is guilty."

My lawyer is silent. Usually his silence indicates to me that I have said something that possibly reflects a relative level of mental instability.

I don't really care. I'm not getting on that stand. "I'm telling you right now," I say. "If I get on that stand, I will answer every question by telling the jury that I believe David Escalera is guilty of drug conspiracy."

I don't know if my lawyer ever relays my manifesto. A few days later, he does call me to say that David Escalera no longer wishes to call me as a witness. Relieved, I turn back to my presentation. I'm pleased with myself, pleased with the outcome. It does not strike me that there seems to be every indication that the trial is moving forward.

MONDAY

Monday is a big day. I am driving to school. I am mentally repeating my academic presentation in my head. I am nervous. I am excited.

Today is the day of my presentation. It's also the day that David Escalera is scheduled to go to trial. As of close of business on Friday, no plea agreement has been reached.

"Prepare yourself," my attorney tells me on Friday. "This looks like it might be happening."

But a wave of calm has come over me. I know I have logic on my side. For all of the posturing by the Escaleras over the past year, nothing can change the fact that (1) the vast majority of cases plead out, (2) many plead out on the eve of trial, and (3) no rational human being would risk years of his life behind bars when he can guarantee release in a matter of months.

They can't go to trial, I decide. They simply can't.

I look out the window. The sun so permeates my car that I must squint to see what's ahead. I feel as though I am driving into the light.

And so, today is very important. It proclaims both the end of the Escalera saga and the beginning of my academic career. I'm standing on the precipice of a whole new life.

I look out the window and smile. It is a crisp October day. A Monday. A big day.

I'm in my office, putting some final touches on my presentation. It's close to lunchtime. My cell phone rings, displaying the office phone number of my attorney. This is already a good sign. He is at the office, not at the courthouse, where he said he might be in order to observe testimony.

"Are you busy?" he asks.

"I have a few minutes," I say. "I have my presentation in a little bit." I don't take my eyes off my written remarks on the computer screen.

"That's okay. I just wanted to let you know that they have completed jury selection."

I look away from the computer screen. "What do you mean, they 'completed' it?"

"They've selected a jury."

"For the trial?" It's an inane question, but I hold out hope that I don't understand.

"Yes, for the trial."

I swallow hard. "This is really happening."

"This is really happening. I'll call you later when I know more. Good luck with your presentation."

When we hang up, I remain frozen in my seat. After a few moments, I try to drag myself back to my presentation. But when I turn to the computer, something is wrong. The screen is blurry, the words seem to bleed into one another. I try to adjust the monitor and then realize that the problem is me, that I am looking at the screen through thick tears. My presentation is reduced to garble. I have otherwise forgotten what I was going to say.

I remember little about my faculty presentation except this: it was an unmitigated disaster.

I will later describe it without exaggeration or embellishment as "the worst thing I've ever attempted in my life." This is a competitive category. It includes a failed keg stand during college that culminated in a bruised butt bone, a misguided effort to win an argument with a DMV employee that ended with me being escorted out of the building, and an ill-fated attempt on an airplane to practice my fledgling Moroccan Arabic that resulted in an inadvertent promise to marry my seatmate's son.

But those failures are fleeting. My presentation is almost certainly recorded somewhere as the worst in history.

In an act of self-preservation, my memory has erased most of the details, leaving me only with bits and pieces. I remember being in my office, wiping my tears. I remember walking down to the faculty library. I remember taking my place at the podium. I remember sounding out sentences, taking long pauses, trying to come to a point. I remember looks of disappointment, confusion, and sympathy.

I know it is awful even as it is happening. But it's the comment of one of my colleagues afterward that confirms to me that I have failed.

"Try not to fidget next time," she says. "It was a little distracting the way you kept playing with your bra strap."

When it's over, I go to my office, grab my purse, and run out of the building. As I drive home, I can barely hold my head up. The sun glares at me with disappointment.

But I don't know that the worst is yet to arrive. That all of it: the disapproval, the humiliation, even the exposure of my bra strap, are all harbingers of what's about to come.

Shortly after I return home, my attorney calls me. Luckily, there is too much at issue for him to ask me how my presentation went. I listen in silent despair.

"Opening arguments were this afternoon," he tells me. David Escalera's attorney has told the jury that the government's case should not be believed because Cameron Douglas cannot be believed and this is because he convinced a female attorney to bring him contraband.

I say nothing.

"Cameron will be sworn in as a witness tomorrow."

My lawyer has convinced the parties not to use my name in open court. While this is helpful, the comfort that it offers is still cold. A person of even mild intelligence could figure out my name in approximately three minutes by searching the court docket.

He offers other glimmers of hope. Cameron is going to have to explain other incidents that reflect on his credibility, and so my crimes may not get much play. The press will likely be more interested in what he has to say about his drug-dealing activities and anything having to do with his father than it will about me. It is possible, my lawyer says, that though the incident is mentioned in open court, it will never be reported.

I thank him, hang up, and promptly crawl into bed. Not to sleep—although if that were within the realm of choices, it would be my first—but because the physical exertion required of sitting seems too much.

It is still daylight out, and the sun is now smirking at me through my bedroom window. I pull down the shade.

I lie in bed, stare at the ceiling. I think of Cameron, probably doing the same. Here is the moment he has always dreaded. Now it is my moment, too.

And so things are as they always were: his suffering my suffering, his fears my fears. Separated only by space, there is nothing we can do but wait to see what happens next.

LATE MONDAY, EARLY TUESDAY

Overnight, an article appears on the *New York Post*'s website.

> The drug-dealing son of actor Michael Douglas got caught with "contraband" in the slammer. . . .
>
> But "most shocking of all," Douglas also got an unidentified female lawyer to smuggle him forbidden goodies while he was awaiting sentencing, defense lawyer Louis Aidala said.
>
> Aidala didn't identify the woman or specify any of the contraband.

TUESDAY*

MR. ANDERSON: Your Honor, the government calls Cameron Douglas.

CAMERON MORRELL DOUGLAS, called as a witness by the Government, having been duly sworn, testified as follows:

DIRECT EXAMINATION BY MR. ANDERSON:

Q. Good afternoon, Mr. Douglas. How old are you?
A. I'm 32 years old.

---

* Portions of this transcript have been reordered.

Q. Where did you grow up?

A. I grew up between New York and California.

Q. Where do you live now?

A. Right now I'm housed in the MCC prison.

Q. The MCC is a prison?

A. Yes.

Q. How long have you been in prison?

A. Two years, three months, something like that.

Q. What did you do that caused you to end up in prison?

A. I was involved in a conspiracy, drug conspiracy.

*

Q. After you were sentenced, did you engage in any additional misconduct?

A. Yes.

Q. What did you do?

A. I—I got into a relationship with a—my defense—one of the defense attorneys on my case, and she—she was bringing me Xanax because it's something that we'd been trying to do through the court and BOP, but it was just—was proving to be really difficult, so she was bringing that for me.

Q. What is the Xanax for?

A. For anxiety.

Q. How many times did your attorney bring you Xanax?

A. I would say maybe three times.

Q. How many pills in total approximately?

A. I'd say 30 or so.

Q. Did you use them all yourself?

A. No.

Q. Did you share them with other people?

A. Yes.

Q. Who? With other inmates?

A. With other inmates, yup.

*

Q. You also mentioned you had a romantic relation-
   ship with this attorney?
A. Yes.
Q. Did you kiss?
A. Yes.
Q. Did you do anything more than that?
A. No.

*

MR. ANDERSON: Your Honor, may I have just one moment?
THE COURT: Sure.
MR. ANDERSON: No further questions, Your Honor.

*

CROSS-EXAMINATION BY MR. AIDALA:

Q. Good afternoon. My name is Mr. Aidala. We have
   never met, have we?
A. No.
Q. We have never seen each other, have we?
A. No.
Q. We have never spoken to each other, have we?
A. No.

*

Q. Isn't it a fact that you were able to convince a
   young lady who was an attorney to smuggle drugs
   into a federal prison?
A. I asked her to.
Q. It was your idea, not hers, isn't that correct?
A. That's correct.
Q. You knew at the time it was a crime, didn't you?
A. Yes, sir.

Q. And you knew she was a lawyer, correct?

A. Yes, sir.

Q. You knew she had to go to high school, college, law school, take the bar exam, sweat out the possible results, get admitted, go through the character committee, you knew all that, didn't you?

A. If I sat down and thought about it, yes.

*

Q. You didn't give a damn about her, did you?

A. I don't think that's accurate.

Q. You cared about her to get her to smuggle in drugs to a federal prison to commit a crime and to risk her attorney's license?

A. I didn't—you know, I didn't look that far. I didn't look that far ahead when I asked her to do that for me.

Q. All you cared about was yourself, right?

A. I guess so. When I was asking her to do that, yes.

Q. You know so, don't you? You know so, don't you?

A. I don't really know what my state of mind was back then. I was a little out of it.

*

Q. Had you regaled her with alleged feelings of affection for her?

A. I don't believe so. I—

Q. Well, had you kissed and were you able to not be seen?

A. Yes, sir.

Q. As a matter of fact, after you were sent to Pennsylvania, didn't she continue to visit you there?

A. Yes, sir.

*

Q. You were able to manipulate her, isn't that right?

A. I just, I asked her. I didn't, I didn't convince her.

Q. Well, she just, it was like, Oh, that would be a great idea, I'll do it? Is that what you're trying to tell us?

MR. ANDERSON: Objection.

THE COURT: Sustained.

Q. You manipulated her in such a way that she did something that was a crime?

MR. ANDERSON: Objection.

THE COURT: Overruled.

A. No, I just asked her.

Q. And she just agreed, right? Right away?

A. I certainly didn't press her to do it.

*

Q. As a matter of fact, sometimes you don't know what's truth and what's fantasy, correct?

A. No, I think I know the difference between truth and fantasy.

Q. But you do lie, correct?

A. I try not to.

Q. And you tell lies to accomplish something you want for your own selfish self, correct?

A. No, I wouldn't agree with that.

Q. So the incident with the lawyer, that isn't something that you did to help yourself, is that what you are saying?

A. There was no lying or dishonesty involved in that.

Q. So if you expressed feelings of affection towards her, that was the truth? You felt that way about her, is that correct?

A. That's correct.

*

Q. Tell us what you told her to do.
A. She was involved in trying to get the medication for me through—
Q. Did you hear my question? Listen to my question.
THE COURT: He's answering your question. You may not like the answer, but he's answering your question.
Q. I'm asking, tell us what you told her to do with respect to smuggling in drugs?
A. I asked her to put Xanax in a balloon and to give it to me during our lawyer visits. That is what I asked her to do.

*

Q. Where did you tell her to put the balloon with the drugs?
A. I didn't specify anything specific on that.
Q. Where did she put it?
A. I don't know, sir. I don't remember.

*

Q. Well, she gave it to you, didn't she?
A. Yes.
Q. You were in a room where attorneys meet with their clients?
A. Right.

*

Q. She took it out from some part of her body, didn't she?
A. Yes, sir.
Q. You know so, don't you?
A. Yes, sir.

*

Q. Did she take it out of one of her body orifices?
   Do you know what that means?
A. I do. No, I believe from what I can remember I
   believe she took it out of, I saw her take it
   out of her bra.

I hear a sound from the living room that is familiar and disquieting. I am in my bedroom, ignoring it. I have just hung up with my lawyer, whose associate has been sitting in the courtroom watching Cameron's testimony unfold. He has been using the courthouse pay phone to update my lawyer, who in turn has been updating me.

When my attorney relays to me Cameron's testimony I politely explain to him that his associate must not have been hearing Cameron right. There is no way Cameron would share the medication that he so badly needed, I say. How is it that his visible symptoms vanished? And what purpose could it serve him to disclose my identity? No, there is no way.

As to the mention of my undergarments, I am particularly incredulous. Why would he say this? I remind my attorney of how I placed the pills in a bag of pretzels before Cameron even arrived in the attorney room. I explain that nothing could possibly be served by my harboring something in my bra, that its underwire caused additional scrutiny, that I'm not even sure how one could remove something from a bra in an attorney room without partially undressing.

"There must be some misunderstanding," I say. "That just can't be Cameron's testimony."

My lawyer says nothing. I think I can hear him shrug.

It is a heavy slap to the face, learning that everything in Cameron's testimony is exactly as my lawyer has recounted it to be. I want to reconvene the jury and explain. Explain to them that today is the first time that I've learned that these pills were being distributed to others, that I was supplying currency to men whom I do not know but who somehow know me. That the pills that I brought for Cameron were prescribed for a condition that I personally observed him experience. That Cameron can't speak to how I brought in the pills. That the contortion involved in removing a balloon of pills from one's bra while seated in a room with a glass door is beyond my physical capability. That due to the circumstances of our acquaintance, Cameron could not possibly see me take anything out of my bra, that he has never seen my bra, he has never seen anything at all that resides below my neck or above my knees.

That this has all gone so terribly wrong.

But the jury has been dismissed for the day. As I craft my explanation, they are probably at home eating dinner with their families, possibly, against the judge's orders, mentioning in passing the events of the day, about the celebrity drug dealer, about his attorney accomplice, about said attorney's underthings.

It is too late.

But correcting my attorney, reconvening the jury, these are just sideshows. Underneath my disbelief and defensiveness is the crushing realization that I have been betrayed. Cameron did not only break his promises about keeping his mouth shut, taking the fall. He did not only lie and mislead. He actively, willingly, placed me directly in harm's way. But even this is not the worst part. No, the worst part is me. I had taken an inordinate risk on behalf of someone who clearly did not care what happened to me. No, wait, that isn't the worst part. The worst part is that I acted out of love for someone who could not possibly have loved me in return. Nope, there is something still worse. The absolute worst part of all of this is that the entirety of what transpired has been captured by a court reporter. My love-starved stupidity is recorded in history.

The sound from the living room has grown loud enough to shake me from my thoughts. As I make my way into the living room, I immediately place it: the doorbell is ringing. Over and over and over again, in a manner not unlike that employed by Burly Man so many months before, the rapid presses composing an uninterrupted siren.

This can mean only one thing. And so I freeze. I stop so abruptly that I grab onto a piece of furniture for balance, knocking over a pile of books and papers on a nearby end table. They crash to the ground.

As soon as they do, the ringing stops. I hear movement on the other side of the door, as though the person behind it is deciding her next move. She knows that I'm inside, and I know that she's outside, but neither of us says a word.

I remain completely still. I am breathing so loudly I think she might hear.

Suddenly, the stranger begins ringing the bells of all of my surrounding neighbors, all of them elderly, each of them easy to scare. I can hear the symphony of bells through my door. She seems to be making a ruckus in the hopes that it will rouse me from my apartment.

The stranger does not know me, does not know that I am fully capable of cowardice when it serves my own interests. And so, while I feel awful for their intrusion, I selfishly remain where I am. It continues for several moments. Finally, a door opens. I can hear her demanding of my neighbor Rosie where I might be.

"I don't think she's at home." Rosie trembles. "Otherwise she would open the door."

"Well, do you know when she'll be back?"

"I'm sure she'll be home later today," Rosie says obliquely. "Maybe you can leave her a note."

The stranger is silent for a moment. Then she thanks Rosie and says that she will.

I continue to remain within earshot of the door, careful not to make a sound. I see a small piece of paper slip under the door. I hear Rosie's door close.

I wait for a moment. It is silent.

I start to take a deep breath, thinking that this is over. But as soon as I start to relax, my body stiffens at a thought.

The elevator did not make a sound. The stranger must still be outside my door.

I don't wait to see how long she remains. I quietly tiptoe to my bedroom. I will not return to my living room for two days. And by that time, everything that is going to happen will have already happened.

Ms. Ridha:
    I am a reporter
with the New York
Post. I am working
on a story you're
involved with and I
thought you might
like to comment.
    You can reach me
at ██████████████

Many Thanks,
██████████████

The phone keeps ringing. I avoid answering it. Dizzy with the discoveries of the day, I feel that there is little else that I need to know.

When I finally call my attorney back, he reports that the *New York Post* has discovered who I am and has asked for his comment.

"I know," I tell him. "A reporter was at my door."

"Okay. Maybe don't leave the apartment tonight."

I feel a surprising rush of silent anger at his well-meaning but obvious advice. I sort of hate my attorney right now. He has been my hero for fifteen months, but in this moment I can't stand him. Although I can follow the course of events that have led me here, I feel he was somehow supposed to protect me from this. As comforting as it is to feel you have someone looking out for you, it's just as troubling when you realize that he is not invincible.

I wonder if my clients ever hated me in this way, too. If they did, they were right to hate me. The right to hate your lawyer should be set forth in the New York Statement of Client Rights, alongside the right to have your phone calls returned and your bills itemized.

"How did they get your address, do you think?" he asks.

"It's public because I gave money to Obama in 2008," I say. I sort of hate Obama right now, too.

"We are preparing a statement to give the *Post*," he says. "I will send it to you so you can—"

I cut him off. "Just say whatever you think is best."

"All right." I can tell that he wants to say something helpful, but there isn't anything helpful to say.

"Thanks," I say, because that's all I can think to say to get off the phone.

He takes a breath, as though there is something more, and then thinks better of it. "I'll call you tomorrow," he says helpfully.

"Yes, okay. Great," I say.

We say good-bye, knowing that there is nothing great about any of this.

I field a series of calls from friends and family, each of which makes me more agitated than the last. The words of comfort are sincere, but I don't want to be comforted. I want this to not have happened. Why is everyone telling me I'll get through this, as though all of this is reasonable or expected? And why is everyone acting as though they could possibly understand?

The only words that break through are from, of all people, my usually disapproving mother. I've warned her that what's coming is going to very possibly be an assault on her traditional sensibilities. But in this moment, perhaps because I'm already so upset, she does not display the expected concern.

Instead, she says, "Jennie, your father and I adore you. We always will."

And for some reason, these words are a cold compress on my sting-ing face. I let go of the anger and find that underneath there is sad resignation.

I start to cry. Not because I am moved by a proclamation of my parents' love or even overwhelmed at the reminder that I have it. I cry because I suspect that after tomorrow is over, it is all that will remain.

WEDNESDAY

I awake after a fitful night of sleep. It is still dark outside.

I find it a curious thing, anticipating publication of something terri-ble that you've done. When I committed my crimes, I always presumed they would remain in the place where one's darkest secrets are normally stored, revealed only under threat of torture or maybe on a deathbed. I did not think that my worst moments would be put in print.

I look out the window. The sky has now shifted to a deep blue, the sun is about to cast its light on a new day.

Whatever there is to be said about my crimes has already been writ-ten, is already available at the newsstand, already sitting on the doorsteps of the paper's half a million subscribers. I look at my laptop, still at the foot of my bed from the night before, knowing that the story is inside.

I look out at the sky one last time before I open my laptop. I am painfully aware that these are the last moments; this is the beautiful before that becomes the ugly after. And so I enjoy the sunrise for one more minute, knowing that by the time it returns, everything will be different.

Here is the headline: DRUGS IN BRA.

This is already not good. It does not get better.

Cameron is described as having taken the stand against his drug supplier, as looking like a "scruffy and tattooed version of his father," as having "romanced a defense lawyer who got busted for smuggling him pills in jail," as having gotten "into a relationship with the woman while she represented him following his 2009 arrest for narcotics trafficking.

"The two shared clandestine kisses behind bars," the article says. I am stated to have "repeatedly used a balloon to sneak dozens of Xanax anti-anxiety pills into the Metropolitan Correctional Center in downtown Manhattan at his request.

"'From what I remember, I saw her take it out of her bra,'" the article quotes Cameron as saying.

"Douglas, 32, said the relationship continued even after he was shipped off to prison in Pennsylvania, where he told her to lie on an official form so she could continue to visit him."

The article lists my name; my age; my employment history, including the name of the law school at which I teach. I am described as having confessed to my crimes, as having been arrested, as having had my charges dropped.

The article does not make mention of Cameron's medical condition, choosing instead to heavily imply that the Xanax was provided for his recreational use. The incident is described as one of many "drug-fueled transgressions" by someone with a "drug-addled memory" who "started smoking pot at age 15, and moved on to harder drugs within a year or two."

My attorney issued a statement stating that I am "an outstanding young attorney." When I read this, I laugh out loud.

According to the article, I declined to respond to the tabloid's request for comment.

I read the article only once. I carefully close my laptop and place it on the nightstand.

I get back into bed. I pull the covers over my head.

Sleep arrives quickly. It turns out that when the moment you dread arrives, there is nothing more to dread. There is nothing left to do at all.

The phone starts ringing at some point in the middle of the morning.

I pick it up only to make it stop ringing. I know that there is nothing on the other end that can portend good things.

The first wave of calls are from concerned friends. They say all the things that a good friend is supposed to say, that is, everything that minimizes the damage at hand and nothing that actually reflects reality. I later learn that while they are making these assurances, they are privately acknowledging to one another that this is a complete disaster.

The role of a friend is to make you feel good about yourself. The role of a brother is to give you the harsh truth. "This is terrible," he says when he reads the article. "You'd better call Mom and make sure she doesn't read it."

Have you ever had to call your mother to tell her that your underwear is in the newspaper? If so, you know that this is not an easy task. This is especially true of my mother, whose modest sensibilities are easily ignited. I dread this conversation.

It's clear she's been waiting for my call. "How bad is it?" she asks.

"Mom, it's bad."

"What does it say?"

"I don't want to tell you."

"But I need to know," she insists.

"Why?" I ask. "They totally twisted everything in the worst way possible."

She assumes her interrogator voice. "Jennifer, read it to me."

I take a deep breath. Then, for the second time that day, I start reading.

There is a sound unique to Iraqi women that I call the Iraqi gasp. It consists of an intake of air so intense and sudden that it results in a noise like that of a whooping crane. It is prominently featured in my mother's response to the article.

She does not focus on the fact that the article makes me out to be a drug smuggler or even that it mentions my underthings.

She fixates on the kissing.

Here is where my mother's traditionalism really shines. While I presume as a general matter Iraqis kiss no more or less than any other people, kissing is something that is confined to intimate spaces. Kisses between men and women otherwise cannot be found, not at weddings, not in suggestive music videos, not anywhere. Unmarried people are to remain unkissed until further notice.

My mother understands that she has raised her children in a society that embraces kissing of all kinds. But even with this being the case, I have always suspected that she has assured herself that this still does not occur with her children. Now that it is in print, there is no opportunity for denial.

"It talks about kisses????!!!"

"Um, yes."

"Did you kiss him?"

I don't have the energy for this. "Well, yes."

"With tongue????!!!"

She is giving me an out, and I can sink no lower than I already have on this day, and so I lie. "No. Not with tongue, Mom."

She is silent for a moment. "What does 'clandestine' mean?"

"It means hidden."

"Oh." She thinks about this. "But why are they saying the kisses are hidden?"

I close my eyes and rest my head on the wall. I supposed I've earned this exchange, but it is not making things easier.

"They're not saying the kisses were hidden on me," I say. "They're saying we kissed when no one was looking."

"What! Why would anyone be looking?"

I don't point out to her that now that this article has been published, everyone is looking. Instead, I say, "I don't know, Mom. I honestly don't know."

O ther calls and e-mails flood in, but after a while I tire of telling everyone I am fine. From my location in the bedroom, I sporadically hear the buzzer ring, and then a few minutes later, my doorbell. I answer neither, but make a mental note that attention from the press may not be completely over.

My lawyer calls at some point in the day. His words are supportive, but I don't have a specific recollection of them. He will later tell me that a complaint has been filed against me with the New York Bar, the proceedings of which will determine whether I will continue to be licensed to practice law. I will simply nod and say, "Okay."

Later in the day, I get a call from a number I don't recognize. When I answer, I discover that it's the dean of my law school. Before he speaks, he clears his throat. He is choosing the appropriate words, a thoughtful thing for him to do, consistent with the person I know him to be. But it is also entirely unnecessary. I already know what he is going to say. I know. I will never have to worry about giving a disastrous academic presentation ever again.

When everything is over, everything is gone, there isn't much else left to do. Without a career to worry about, I throw my shoddy article and research notes into the trash. I call off my eleven job interviews—"I am no longer interviewing," I write without saying any more—delete my electronic plane ticket and my hotel room confirmation. I complete these tasks with stoicism, as though I am canceling my dry cleaning, not my future.

I am utterly heartbroken at the destruction of my professional path. I allow myself to remember a ten-year-old me, who decided that she was interested in a career in law. A twelve-year-old me, who spent her free time obsessing over *L.A. Law* and began following criminal cases. An eighteen-year-old me, who carefully plotted a rigorous college trajectory that would allow her to get to law school in three years rather than four. A twenty-one-year-old me, who moved from the Midwest to New York City to begin study at said law school, touted as one of the best in the country. A twenty-four-year-old me, who studied and sat for the Bar Exam. A twenty-six-year-old me, who completed a federal appellate clerkship and began to practice law in New York. A thirty-two-year-old me, who began teaching as a law professor. Now, as thirty-five-year-old me, having thrown all of this away, I feel as though someone has repeatedly punched me in the head.

But my devastation is perhaps not what it could be. I know this because in the phone calls I make to report that my career has imploded, everyone seems to be more upset than me. My mother bursts into tears, pleads with me to find a job, any job as soon as I can. My brother implores me to beg for my old job back. My lawyer urgently offers to find me work as a contract attorney, suggests that this will allow me to cling to a spot still within the legal community. Friends provide desperate ideas for legal-based businesses, for jobs that will not require me to show my face too much.

Although these conversations occur separately, in my memory they happen all at once, an anxious cyclone of well-intentioned advice and expectation, a distraught deluge of urgency and instruction. As I quietly listen to everyone panic, it occurs to me that maybe the reason they are this distressed is because the things that have been lost are more important to them than they are to me. That it's entirely possible that I've spent a lifetime following a path dictated by other people's objectives. That what's gone was perhaps not really mine to begin with.

I don't mention this to any of my concerned callers, because at this point I am essentially dead inside. But the thought does cross my mind—naturally when it is far too late—that my defiance at MCC was possibly misplaced. It was in simply living my own life where I maybe should have been breaking the rules all along.

With nothing good to think about, I try to distract myself with other news. I head over to a UK-based gossip site, a guilty pleasure in which I regularly indulge. I scan the stories on the right-hand side of the page in order to pick one that will make me feel good by comparison.

I see a headline about an attorney. Perfect. Surely this person has done something worse than me. I click on it, and I realize that it *is* me. I close my web browser.

I consider an e-mail sent to me by a friend, which curiously contains the full text of a commencement address delivered by David Foster Wallace three years before he committed suicide.

It seems an odd selection, given that I have just humiliated myself in front of the whole world, not completed the requirements of an undergraduate degree. But my friend has underlined this particular passage: *The really important kind of freedom involves attention, and awareness, and discipline, and effort, and being able truly to care about other people and to sacrifice for them, over and over, in myriad petty little unsexy ways, every day.*

I suspect that my friend is referring to the care I showed Cameron, the sacrifice I decided to make on his behalf. But this hardly feels like freedom. And so, because I use humor as a defense mechanism, I write her in response, "I wouldn't exactly say *unsexy*."

Only when I get into bed do I take a real accounting of everything that's happened. Here is where I curl my knees up to my chest and start to sob uncontrollably. Where I want to push out everything I have inside so that I can be someone or something else.

I stop when I am no longer capable of continuing. As I fall asleep, my final thoughts of the day rest on David Foster Wallace's word "freedom." I strain to understand how it could possibly apply, how anyone who has failed so calamitously could ever feel free.

AFTER

Rejected by society, I embark upon a quest for complete numbness. The events of the last few days have left me emotionally gutted. I am in pain and would like not to be.

My pursuit of nonfeeling is made possible with an entity I call The Couch.

The Couch is more than just my couch, although that's where it begins. The morning after the article is printed, not having the wherewithal to do much more, I decide to spend the day sprawled out on it, a pile of magazines at my side, a remote control in my hand. I haven't eaten anything of note in two days and am starving. I decide that there is no purpose in being a disciplined eater today. I should order *exactly* what I want to eat. And so I do. I choose a grilled cheese sandwich, no, wait, *two* grilled cheese sandwiches. Oh, and a soda. And a bag of kettle-cooked potato chips, of course. And a slice of chocolate cake. That's plenty. Hold on, they have milkshakes?

I use a food-delivery website to order my food. I prepay the tip. Then, under "Special Delivery Instructions," I type: "Please leave it at the door." And because I can no longer stand the sound of it, I add, "Please do not ring doorbell."

When the buzzer announces the arrival of the delivery person, I remind him to "please remember to just leave it at the door." I wait. I hear the ring of the elevator, the heavy plod of his shoes against the hallway carpeting, the soft rustle of the plastic bag that is gently set in front of my door, I hear him wait for a moment, then his fading footsteps, and then the elevator taking him away.

I count to twenty. I open my door for the first time in days, snatch the bag, close the door, and lock it.

I place the bag on the coffee table, unwrap each item, and then proceed to eat the entire lunch in a matter of minutes.

While consuming this amount of food in such a short period of time would normally make me nauseous, this time I feel nothing of the sort. In fact, I feel nothing at all. I want for nothing, other than a nap, which I take right there on the couch.

When I wake, I still feel nothing.

Although I'm not hungry, I want to keep it going. I repeat the motions of my lunchtime order, only this time selecting cheeseburgers instead of grilled cheese—cheese features prominently in this period of my life—and gummy bears instead of cake.

"Please remember to just leave it at the door," I announce into the intercom when this meal arrives. When I feel my stomach fill, I push down the food anyway.

I'm once again in a carbohydrate coma. It isn't long before I am asleep again. I don't even bother getting up to go to my bedroom, but simply remain in the same supine position I've assumed all day.

The next day, I repeat the same sequence of events, except with Chinese food for lunch and Italian for dinner. The following day, I return to grilled cheese but have Tex-Mex in the evening.

And so on. And so forth. I continue in this manner for an untold number of days and weeks, mostly because I lose track.

At some point, I wonder to myself if I should do something other than sit in a sea of takeout containers. But I find that I can't, that whenever I try to get up from The Couch, I begin to remember why I am there and only want its comfort again.

One night, I am resolute in my desire to try. And so, while the television blares on, I decide to sit on the rug and attempt to begin a quilt that I had planned on making before this mess began. Maybe if I just cut out the pieces, I tell myself. That will be a decent-sized achievement.

But like everything as of late, it goes horribly wrong. Either because

I am not paying attention or because I am experiencing sloth-induced atrophy, I don't cut the fabric as much as I do the corner off my left index finger.

I stare at the gap in skin. It stares back at me. And then my hand is covered in blood.

I'm not sure what to do about this. The tally of consecutive days in which I have not left my apartment is in the double digits, and I have no interest in breaking this streak, least of all in pajamas that reek of french fries and are now bloodstained.

I decide to stuff my hand into a bath towel and then peruse the contents of my medicine cabinet for anything that might be of assistance. I uncover a small package of gauze and a roll of medical tape.

When I place my finger under the tap, the falling water turns crimson. For a moment I consider suturing the thing myself but suspect that this is better achieved with something other than sewing thread. I wash the wound as best as I can, tie and tape the gauze around it, and sit on the edge of my bathtub with my hand held high above my head.

This situation is not ideal, not only because I am losing prodigious amounts of blood, but also because I am left in a cold bathroom without the sustenance of The Couch. I can feel emotions creeping in.

Wanting more than anything The Couch's welcoming embrace, I continually bring my hand down and peek under the gauze to see if there is still blood. There is. I lift my hand for a few more moments. When I check it again, the blood oozes at such an alarming rate that I decide I should change the medical dressing altogether.

I rewrap and wait. I raise my hand over my head, as though I am waiting for someone to call on me. This has to stop, I tell myself. At some point, the bleeding has to stop.

I spend so much time on The Couch that it seems like everyone else is living in a parallel universe. Sometimes I am up on The Couch so late into the night that I witness the sunrise. When law-abiding people are getting dressed and packing lunches and fulfilling their purpose, I contemplate whether this is the day I should change pajamas and if I want fried chicken or macaroni and cheese.

I hold steady to not leaving the apartment. However, one day, when there is a ring at my door accompanied by the voice of my mailman, I am forced into a human interaction.

My mailman, Stanley, is holding a huge pile of mail that he shoves into my hands.

"It seemed like you were dead," he says. He looks me up and down, and quite possibly sees that he isn't too far off.

"I'm sorry," I say. My voice is groggy from nonuse. "I've . . . Things have been a little crazy."

I try to maneuver myself in front of the door so he can't see that my living room is blanketed with takeout containers. I am not sure if I'm successful.

"Well, all right. Make sure the box doesn't get full like that again."

"I will, I promise."

I watch him make his way to the elevator. Once he's gone, I walk to the garbage chute and throw all of the mail I am holding into it.

An exchange like this one is the exception rather than the rule. I'm otherwise ensconced in a fortress of fleece blankets and pajamas and junk food, impervious to the realities of the outside world. The only thing I'm diligent about is answering the buzzer for food delivery, each time reminding the delivery person to "Please remember to leave it at the door." Sometimes this is the only thing I say out loud all day.

But then one day the outside world breaks through. It happens when I least expect it, when I'm watching a rerun of the MTV reality program *Jersey Shore*.

On this season of *Jersey Shore*, the castmates have apparently left their natural habitat of New Jersey for Italy. In this particular episode, one of the house's more outgoing members, Snooki, is excited because her boyfriend Jionni is traveling from New Jersey to visit her. This itself is an interesting plot point for the viewer, because we have learned at the outset that Snooki may or may not have cheated on Jionni with another castmate, Mike. Jionni's visit will thus present the first opportunity in which all three sides of the love triangle will be together. It is a scene from *Anna Karenina*, except with hair gel and spray tans.

We the viewer are led to believe that the love triangle will consume the bulk of Jionni's visit. Snooki has already noticed that Mike might be plotting to spill the beans about their interlude, something that she vehemently denies having happened yet seems worried whenever Mike brings it up. Snooki plans to go on the offensive; she tells the audience at home that if Mike even alludes to the possibility of having slept with her, "I'm legit going to punch Mike in the face."

Jionni arrives. Snooki is over the moon. In honor of his arrival, she dons a hot pink leopard print mini-dress that leaves little to the imagination. Indeed, a castmate remarks to Snooki that her dress is so short that he can "basically see her kooka," and perhaps she should change. But Snooki is steadfast in her sartorial choices and the gang heads out for a night on the town.

Trouble soon strikes. Snooki consumes a considerable amount of alcohol, as she is wont to do, and takes to the dance floor with a little too much gusto. As she dances before Jionni, she pulls up her dress. Though the exposed area is blurred to the viewer, we are told that Snooki has declined to wear underpants and thus has displayed her vagina to the entire club.

Jionni is aghast. He storms out of the club, onto the street, and away from the various castmates who run after him, pleading for him to come back. Snooki is too distraught—and possibly too inebriated—to run after him. Instead, she crumples into a hot pink leopard print ball on the sidewalk, sobbing.

After holding a small debate about the merits of dancing with one's vagina in full view, the castmates decide to scrape Snooki off the sidewalk and take her home. Mike, especially, is quick to point out that Jionni's departure is unwarranted. But Snooki is too upset to listen. Utterly bereft, breathless from crying, she insists that she does not deserve any of this.

In the critical scene, Jionni returns to the house, but not to make amends. He marches past Snooki, locks himself in the bathroom, and retrieves his belongings. Unmoved by Snooki's pleas, his judgment is swift. As he leaves the house for good, he speaks to Snooki in a tone so icy that a chill reverberates from the television set. "See ya," he says. "You're single."

It is a devastating moment for Snooki, one in which she begins to cry uncontrollably, tears pouring over hot pink leopard print. She yells at Jionni as he prepares to make his exit: "What did I do?"

"What did I do?" At first it sounds like Snooki asks this in search of an answer, as though to say: What's the big deal?

"What did I do?" But when I hear it again, I wonder if she might be asking this of herself, as though to say: What on earth have I done?

It is a subtle shift in tone, perhaps even something that I've imagined. But the difference occurs to me all the same.

And so here is where Snooki's pain meets my own. As I watch her howl with regret, I suddenly find that I am sobbing, too. I sob because Snooki has done an awful thing, a thing that she regrets, a thing that she can never take back. I sob because she has lost everything that's important and has in the course of a day changed her life for the worse.

I sob for Snooki. I sob for me. I sob for us both, for all that's been lost, stopping only to ask my television set and myself: What did I do?

It isn't too long after this that I make the decision to come off The Couch altogether. This decision is not planned. I need to temporarily leave The Couch because my remote control is not working and requires new batteries.

(In fact, I later find out that the remote is not in need of batteries, but has broken altogether, presumably from overuse.)

Because watching television is integral to The Couch experience, I reason that it will not hurt too much to rejoin society for a few brief moments before returning to The Couch and its comforts.

The proposition seems easy enough, to get dressed and walk a block and a half to the drugstore and back. But I'm unprepared for the reality that meets me.

The first harsh encounter is in getting dressed. When I try to pull on a pair of jeans, I notice that these have stalled somewhere in my mid-thigh area and do not seem to be able to move farther without suffering calamity. Indeed, the pant legs are so tight against my lower thighs that I think I might be losing circulation. It takes considerable effort to peel them off.

For the first time in weeks I think to consider my reflection. When

I look in the mirror, I am hard pressed to find myself. My body is unrecognizable to me, its surface area so large that, as though by hating the skin I'm in, I've tried to make more that I might like better. It has not worked.

I consider my bloated face for a moment, press my cheeks to see if I can deflate their puff. My hair is misshapen from constantly being pressed against the armrest of The Couch. My eyebrows have joined forces into a single, unified brow. And though I have slept plenty over the past few weeks, there are deep dents underneath both eyes.

I grab a bath towel and throw it over my mirror. It's not that I cannot stand the sight of myself, I think. It's that I am sitting shiva for my old appearance.

I dig out a pair of oversized sweatpants and pull on a T-shirt and fleece jacket. When I exit my building, my eyes must adjust to the sunlight. As I walk, I can tell that my center of gravity has shifted. I can feel my excess weight with each step.

I slowly drag myself along the sidewalk. I am relieved to reach the crosswalk, the drugstore well within my sights, the first half of this journey almost over.

And then I hear this: "Excuse me?"

The words sound as though they might be directed at me, and so I instinctively move away from them.

"Excuse me?" I hear it again, a woman's voice.

I slowly turn and look. An elderly woman stands before me. Her long white hair is pulled back into a ponytail. Dark glasses consume most of her wizened face.

"Could you help me walk across the street?" she asks. "I am blind in one eye and the traffic comes so fast."

I feel bad for having tried to avoid her. "Yes, no problem," I say. I extend to her a chubby arm, and she eagerly latches on to it.

The light signals that it's time to walk. "Okay," I say. "Here we go."

I take small strides so that we can walk in sync. She is talking about the weather—it is a bright, crisp day outside—and I'm nodding along until I realize she may not see me, and so I say "Uh-huh" at every pause in conversation.

As we make our way across the street, I can see why she felt the need to ask for help. The traffic surrounding the crosswalk is a nightmare: cars pushing past the red light, cars making illegal turns, cars swerving to the curb. There is often a tap dance involved in negotiating New York sidewalks, one that is hard enough to master with an able body and two functioning eyes. I imagine it must be next to impossible for someone suffering from a disability. I notice that as the cars come closer, the woman's grasp on my arm becomes tighter, as though I am all that stands between her and tragedy.

I am struck by this woman's predicament, how she must confront this every day, having to depend on the generosity of self-involved citizens such as myself. I tell her as we approach the other side of the street, "It's remarkable that you are able to manage this each day."

Since we have made it across, she unhooks her arm from mine. Then, somewhat unexpectedly, she turns and faces me. Standing in the sunlight, I can see her eyes through her dark glasses, one that is fixed on me, the other that appears to have found something more interesting behind me to the right.

She pats my arm, the one that has provided assistance. "All you can do is keep going," she says. "You just have to move forward." She thanks me and walks away.

For the briefest of moments I wonder if she is somehow talking about me. That she is not a woman in need of my assistance, but quite the opposite, she is some blind seer sent by the gods to guide me off The Couch and back into life.

As soon as I form the thought, I have enough common sense to dismiss it. Still, after I return from the drugstore, I decide to throw out the takeout containers, launder my pajamas, clean my apartment, and pluck my eyebrows. Whether or not she is heaven-sent, the woman's advice is sound. And so that's what I do. As best as I can, I move forward.

CHAPTER 10

Jewel of Denial

My life after The Couch is really two: one of what I say I'm doing, and one of what I actually do. I claim that I'm putting everything behind me, that I'm moving forward. In reality, I spend most of my days in various states of lounge, avoiding reality and devising methods of dress that cloak the excess weight I'm now carrying.

"It's good that this has happened," I insist. "Now I can find my true purpose." But I don't even try.

For the first time in my life, I remark how often it is we are asked "What do you do?" What *do* I do? With the fate of my license pending before a disciplinary committee, to identify myself as a lawyer seems only to tempt fate. And now that my teaching career is over, there is no basis in fact for me to claim to be a law professor. I am left to mumble some answer containing the words "used to" or "did."

I try to avoid the question altogether, but this is impossible. Our society seems to operate on the principle—not unlike that espoused by my mother's archaic List—that what you do is who you are. I'm asked to account for an occupation at environs as varied as the doctor's office (on the admittance form, I enter "?"), upon disembarkation at JFK (on the customs form I enter "TBD"), and, incredibly, at the place where I get a facial (by this time, I am so fed up with being asked that I enter "Really?").

I devise a survival plan. It consists of two indispensable elements: denial and victimhood. Denial sprinkles each thought with the delusion that none of what seems to be happening is actually happening. Victimhood convinces me that I've been done wrong, a victim of entities and phenomena far more nefarious than myself.

I remain in denial that the article that has been published about me holds any real truth. I point out that of the hundreds of news articles that are published about Cameron's testimony, the *Post* is the only one that mentions what I've done. And while this article is in turn picked up by a plethora of online gossip sites, the story is ignored by reputable news agencies.

"I mean, the article is in the *Post*," I say to anyone who will listen. I draw out the "o" in "Post" such that it resembles a groan. "Who really cares what they have to say?"

When this does not evoke the enthusiastic responses I'd hoped for, I turn to victimhood. I note the evils of tabloid reporting, how it relishes the demise of others, how it encroaches on people's privacy, spreads the disease of celebrity obsession. I am its most unjustified victim.

No one seems to get too worked up about this either. Instead, I notice that the only thing anyone wants to talk about are the details of my crimes, how I was capable of doing what I did. While these queries are couched as questions, they come across as something much closer to statement:

"I just don't think I would have been able to get past the guard without losing it."

"You really told no one? I don't know if I could do something like that and keep it to myself."

"Just the thought that I could get caught . . . I don't think I would be able to sleep at night."

I do not much enjoy these conversations. They make me feel as though I am alone in my compulsions, unique in the evils of which I am capable, defective in my design. That I almost certainly stand apart.

This is where the twin forces of denial and victimhood swoop in to rescue me. Denial cuts the lights, turning off these disturbing thoughts. Victimhood convinces me that to ask such questions when I am going through so much—it draws out the "o" in "so" such that it resembles a groan—is insensitive. Victimhood tells me that even among the people who claim to care, I am a victim.

On the outside, I try to hold my head up high. But in discreet moments, I feel a creeping fear that normalcy cannot be had. That for all my proclamations that the *Post* article is tabloid malarkey, its publication creates a line of demarcation. On one side is my old life, a life in which all of my sins are hidden. On the other side is what is becoming my new life, a life in which the exposure of my crimes makes me someone who may not belong.

I don't notice it at first. I'm so preoccupied with maintaining the outward delusion that my life will return to normal that I don't acknowledge that it's happening.

It starts out small. A fleeting thought. A flash of remembrance.

The crossword puzzle demands a seven-letter word with the clue: "Own up to one's sins."

In a romantic comedy that my friend and I rent, the protagonist tells his love interest: "I am currently unemployed; I'll soon run out of money; and I am the target of a federal investigation."

A television doctor discusses the possible dangers of Xanax.

These are just dumb coincidences, I think. But in the weeks and months following my exodus from The Couch, I notice a pattern. The more I tell others that I'm standing on solid ground, the more events transpire to shake my foundation, and in turn the more I fear that my crimes have come to define my life.

I first begin to realize that these are not coincidences when a news article is brought to my attention about Mother Goose, Cameron's heroin house arrest accomplice and head of the gaggle. In addition to creating a drug-laden electronic toothbrush, Mother Goose also had some involvement in the underlying drug conspiracy and thus has appeared as a government witness against David Escalera. She testifies to falsifying a UPS account that allowed for cross-country shipment of drugs, picking up cash from drug sales, and packaging drugs for shipment. She also admits that when she was confronted with the toothbrush debacle, she lied to DEA agents about what she had done.

While none of this is particularly upstanding, it should be noted that all of this took place while Mother Goose was high in the sky. I meet her after she has cleaned herself up and have a difficult time picturing her doing any of it. She is smart and accomplished—she attended college on a basketball scholarship—and personable. After she is released from a seven-month stint in prison in March 2010, I interact with her frequently over the phone and find her to be engaging and kind.

When I peruse the article—replete with a photo of Mother Goose smiling as she enters the courthouse sporting a lime green shrug—I see that it does not discuss her testimony against David Escalera. The article is about her testimony regarding me.

The article, entitled "Douglas Girl Falls For 'Con,'" relates that Mother Goose is asked on cross-examination if she ever knew about my relationship with Cameron. This evidence has some relevance because in her testimony she has described herself as Cameron's girlfriend. She apparently avers that she did not know about the "admitted jail relationship" but that she remains committed to Cameron, writing him a letter for each day he is in prison.

When I first read the article, I scrunch my face in annoyance. I'm galled at the suggestion that I have disrupted some unassailable union. Mother Goose has always been a featured member of the gaggle, a fact confirmed not only by my repeated interactions with the other geese, but also by Mother Goose herself, who more than once during the case would call me to subtly inquire as to the identity of other women who have been asking after Cameron.

It's not my problem that Mother Goose has chosen to cast her connection to Cameron as something that it is not, I think angrily. I don't owe this woman anything. *She* should apologize to *me* for making me out to be a home wrecker when I most certainly am not. *I'm* the victim here.

But then, a few days after reading the article, I begin to sort of feel bad.

I at first attribute the small guilt I feel to what I suppose was a lack of candor. In all the times I speak to her during Cameron's case, I never mention my own developing feelings for Cameron or his invitations to me to visit him at his facility. I suppose these omissions are significant enough to constitute dishonesty. Actually, as I think about it more over the months that pass, I start to think it might have been fairly disgusting.

The feeling becomes strong enough that a few months after the article is published, in late 2011, I feel compelled to dig out her cell phone number and text her to say that I've been thinking about her and I hope she is well.

really, she texts back, **cuz u r a fuckin whore.**

I don't expect this. I expect to be called a fuckin [*sic*] liar, or perhaps a fuckin [*sic*] phony. I don't think of myself as a fuckin [*sic*] whore, but I suppose no one ever does. Either way, the message makes me feel relieved, as though in opening myself up to this response I don't have to feel bad about my dishonesty.

But even after this, something still feels out of place. It doesn't rankle me daily, but every time I encounter someone who looks like Mother Goose or, oddly enough, is wearing a shrug, I feel a twinge of mysterious discomfort. Each time, I cannot determine what sin of mine remains in need of atonement.

I don't fully realize the exact nature of my transgression until more than a year later. It presents itself in a vivid dream. I dream that Mother Goose approaches me, carrying a baby. She tells me that this is her son, that Cameron is his father. I look down at the baby. He looks exactly like Cameron but with Mother Goose's brunette coloring.

Mother Goose asks me if I could watch the baby for her. I say yes. She hands him to me, and he is an absolute delight. I feed him and change him and play with him, and he giggles and smiles at every turn. I am completely enamored.

Mother Goose comes back at some point to retrieve the baby. As I hand him back to her, the baby starts to wail. He does not want to go. He clings to me, grabbing my shirt with his small hands. He cries so much that I begin crying, too. I decide that I am not going to give back the baby. I am going to keep him for myself.

I inform Mother Goose that I will be keeping her baby. Her face is frozen, almost indifferent. She does not say or do anything.

But somehow my brother shows up. "Give back the baby," he tells me in no uncertain terms.

"No," I insist. "I want the baby," I tell him. "And the baby wants me."

My brother is unmoved. "That doesn't matter," he says. "That baby does not belong to you."

This realization causes me to sob, so much so that I actually wake up crying. But before I do, I place the baby into Mother Goose's arms. "I'm sorry," I tell her. Her face remains expressionless, and so I explain. "He isn't mine," I say. "He should not be with me."

I push past the Mother Goose drama only to encounter that of the Escaleras. I learn that a jury has found David Escalera guilty of drug conspiracy, holding him responsible for a drug weight that subjects him to a five-year mandatory minimum. His sentencing is scheduled for the following spring.

I am presented with this news of David Escalera's conviction as though it is grounds for celebration, or, at a minimum, vengeful relish. But any initial twinge of schadenfreude almost immediately dissolves. My own misfortune looms so large that there is little pleasure to be had in that of someone else. Victimhood is at Level Orange, and I lament becoming what I consider to be a casualty of David Escalera's poor decision making.

Of greater note to me is that Eduardo Escalera's trial remains in the distance. Cameron is once again the government's putative star witness, and I am to prepare myself for more testimony, more press. I feel as though I have already been punched in one eye and am now bracing for a blow to the other.

For a brief moment I consider writing to Cameron at MCC to remind him that his testimony about my bra makes no logical sense. But I quickly abandon the thought, fairly certain that this could be construed as witness tampering. The only thing that I would like less than further public discussion of my underwear is another criminal case, and so I let the matter go.

The trial date of October 24 arrives and nothing happens. The trial is postponed. Then it is postponed again. And then again. The trial judge grants Eduardo Escalera two additional requests for counsel, bringing the total number of court-appointed attorneys assigned to work on his case to five. Then, in February 2012, he is found guilty of drug conspiracy. Like his brother, his sentencing is scheduled for spring.

By the time of his guilty verdict, I have stopped paying attention to Eduardo Escalera. This is because the government has elected to drop Cameron as a cooperating witness. This in turn is because Cameron has violated the terms of his cooperation agreement. This in further turn is because Cameron has committed a new crime, subjecting him to a new charge in an entirely new criminal case.

My foundation is rocked once again when I learn that shortly after delivering his testimony against David Escalera, Cameron is discovered by an MCC corrections officer to be in possession of narcotics.

At least this is what is reported. Having failed to deactivate the Google Alert bearing his name, I find in my inbox dozens of e-mails announcing that Cameron has agreed to plead guilty to possessing "a user quantity" of "a heroin-like substance" while awaiting Eduardo Escalera's trial. He is reportedly discovered holding them in his hand. When confronted, he allegedly tells the corrections officer that he serendipitously found the drugs on the floor and picked them up. The corrections officer is (perhaps reasonably) unconvinced, and the matter is referred to the government.

The prosecutors in Cameron's first drug case announce that they will charge Cameron with contraband drug possession, a felony that will carry a recommended sentence of up to twenty-four months. Their decision to bring charges is somewhat notable because behavior of this kind is often handled internally by the prison. In Cameron's case, he is punished twice. He pleads guilty to the contraband charge in federal court and while he is awaiting sentencing, the Bureau of Prisons administers its own punishment: Cameron is placed in solitary confinement for twelve months, his personal visits are suspended, his commissary account is closed.

For all of my resentment of Cameron as of late, I feel real sympathy for him. I think back to his three-day stint in the SHU, how hard it was for him to cope. I think, too, about how the mere suggestion of his cooperation would make him sick. I imagine that taking the stand has left him resorting to whatever will help him forget. I also can't help but have the self-serving thought that had MCC actually treated his anxiety, he probably would not have felt the need to resort to drug use.

After I read about what's happened, I can't sleep. I am upset enough to e-mail Best Friend at five a.m. about the development.

I guess they are making an example of him, I type. I hypothesize that the drug use and his crazy bra testimony are somehow related. Maybe he said that because he was high. And then, before I sign off, I add: Why didn't I just say no?

After I hit send, I feel angry. Angry at my sympathy for Cameron. Angry at Cameron for not just going away quietly. Angry at the sinking feeling that despite my insistence to the contrary, I feel emotionally intertwined with Cameron, with his fate.

Over time, I try to focus on other things. And yet, when I read that Cameron will be sentenced a few days before Christmas, I find myself marking it on my calendar.

I try to distract myself from reminders of my crimes by trying to discover what is left of my virtuousness. Given my abundant free time and lack of professional direction, I decide to do some volunteer work.

On a recent visit to my parents', I encountered a stray cat wheezing with disease, the hind portion of its mangy coat covered in tumors. The sight was so upsetting that I decide to dedicate time to giving strays a quality of life more akin to that of my spoiled, crotch-loving cat. Also, by volunteering with animals, I needn't worry that they will pepper me with questions about what I plan to do with my life. Animals are wonderful in that way.

I sign up for a volunteer training session at an animal shelter not far from my apartment. When I arrive, I'm shown to a small conference room where a dozen other prospective volunteers are seated. Our volunteer coordinator is exceedingly organized. She stands before us in a perfect pantsuit and a perfect bob and delivers a perfect PowerPoint presentation. She runs the volunteer program with the detail and authority that a lawyer does a case, and for this reason I immediately take to her.

The training outlines the duties and responsibilities of the volunteer. Volunteers are required to come in the same time every week. Volunteers must balance out the animal interactive tasks—dog walking, cat playing—with those that are more feces-based. Volunteers must make a commitment to participate for six months.

At a break in the training, the volunteer coordinator and I make small talk. As per usual, she asks me what I do. I sort of shrug my shoulders.

"I'm a lawyer by training," I say. "But not really as of late."

"You are?" she says. "You know, you're more than welcome to help out with our legal work. It might be more interesting to you than cleaning out kennel cages."

"I appreciate that," I say. "But quite honestly, I'd rather spend my time with the animals."

As the training draws to a close, the volunteer coordinator asks us to sign up for an additional session during which we will take a tour of the premises and become acquainted with the shelter's procedures. I sign up for a session the following week and mark it on my otherwise empty calendar.

Before we disperse, the volunteer coordinator distributes forms for our signature. As these are passed around, she explains that we have to fill out a form providing our contact information. We also have to fill out an emergency contact form. Finally, we have to sign a form consenting to a criminal background check.

When she describes this last form, I swallow.

She explains that the shelter often does events with children—they take some of the particularly well-behaved cats and dogs to kindergarten classrooms and school libraries to promote the shelter's mission. The background check is to weed out anyone who might pose a threat to the children, sex offenders, or those with a history of violence.

This is a sound policy. Still, after I sign the consent form, I erase the second training date from my calendar.

As I leave, the volunteer coordinator says she will see me next week. I nod and force a smile. On the walk home to my apartment, my eyes well with tears.

In the days that follow, I want to forget that any of this has happened. I try not to think about the fact that my crimes possibly preclude me from even cleaning up cat shit. The day of the second training session comes and goes, and I pretend not to notice.

A few days later, I receive a voice mail from the volunteer coordinator. Her voice is kind, almost conciliatory. "We missed you at our session last Saturday," she says. I think I hear her hesitate. "I wanted to let you know that you passed our criminal background check and that there are other sessions next week and the week after."

She begins to recite dates and times, but I cut her off by deleting the message. I do not call back. I do not return to the shelter. Gracious as she is, the volunteer coordinator does not understand. I did not skip the training session because I thought I would necessarily fail the background check. I skip the training session, and abandon the idea of volunteering altogether, because I do not want anyone to know who I really am.

My crimes loom large even in the safety of my own home. I realize this when a hefty manila envelope arrives from my law school that is said to contain the contents of my old faculty inbox.

I am confused by the size and weight of the envelope. Even when I was teaching I barely used my inbox. Perhaps it's something other than mail. I curl my fingers over the envelope's bulge, but feel nothing other than paper.

I rip it open and approximately two dozen letter-sized envelopes fall to the floor. When I realize what they are, my eyes widen.

Prison mail.

I'm at first bewildered as to how I have been found. I remember after a moment that the *Post* article named my law school. Since its address is publicly available, it turns out that I am easily tracked down.

When I take a seat on the hardwood floor to open the envelopes, I am wondering why so many people I don't know would want to reach out to me. Predictably, many are interested in legal assistance. I am uninterested in giving any. I note a slight feeling of distaste whenever the writer proclaims his innocence. Though he may very well be a man wrongly accused, because I consider my circumstances to stem from someone's refusal to accept responsibility, I am unmoved.

One letter reads:

Please find it in your heart to allow me to demonstrate that I did not commit this crime. I hope you will wish to hear my whole story.

I throw this aside.

I'm also unmoved by letters, and there are a few, that malign Cameron as a rat. For all of the damage and unpleasantness his cooperation has served up, he has at least taken responsibility for what he has done. And so when I read a letter that says:

I am aware how you was abused by that ("creep rat") Cameron Douglas. But I ain't nothing like him.

I throw this aside, too.

For as many letters seeking something case-related, the same number appear to seek human connection. There are letters requesting life advice:

I am seeking to make an investment. I have some money saved. I need to know from you what you know about real estate?

Many, many letters proclaiming love:

I am also single and open to explore opportunities that correspond with my comfort zone.

One thing is for sure. I am a man who is not afraid or feel intimidated by a woman of prestigious influence.

I am seeking after being incarcerated for three decades a special friend (smile). "Someone Adventurous."

Oh, my.

One letter includes a photograph of the author with his adult niece, her smile so big that I find myself smiling back.

Some writers introduce themselves and say something along the lines of *Jennifer, please feel free to respond to me.* One even anticipates any fear I might have in receiving a letter from an inmate I have never met. *Essentially, so that you know,* it reads, *under no circumstances will I put you in jeopardy.*

That is certainly a relief.

I look over the envelopes for quite some time. I am struck by the sadness underlying each letter, the apparent isolation that has propelled these men to reach out to someone they do not know. It makes me uncomfortable that their isolation feels familiar. It makes me uncomfortable that these men are possibly writing to me with such familiarity because they consider our predicaments to be similar. It makes me uncomfortable that they are probably right.

I rifle through all of the letters until one piece of correspondence remains. Contained in a bright red envelope, I open it to find a holiday card bearing a palm tree adorned with Christmas lights. It is a generous gesture, an overpriced holiday card paid for with an inmate's meager resources. On the inside of the card, the oversized lettering of the author's note confirms what I have most feared. Still, I can't help but smile when I read his note, if only for its unabashed enthusiasm:

Jennifer, it reads. *You are my kind of woman!*

A few weeks later, another piece of prison mail arrives. Unlike the others, it is mailed to my home. The return address, written in familiar scrawl, bears the address of a maximum-security federal prison in New York City. The inmate number is one that I have memorized from entering it so many times in the attorney log.

Four pages in length and contrite in its tone, there is apparently a lot to say about what has happened. When I read it, which I do approximately half a dozen times, I am neither happy nor sad. I do nothing other than cry, over what I am not entirely sure.

I love you, it begins, *and I'm sorry.*

• • •

It is almost Christmas. At the start of December, I begin to count down the days until Christmas Day by placing an "X" on each day of my dry-erase calendar.

These "X"s do not only count off the days until Christmas; they also necessarily count down the days until Cameron's sentencing on December 21. I have circled that date in red marker, not once, but over and over again, until it looks like a precarious vortex into which I must not fall.

My reasons for taking note of Cameron's sentencing are mostly self-serving. I do not wish upon him additional jail time. But I especially do not wish upon myself further humiliation. This remains a distinct possibility given that a sentencing judge can take into account all of his prior misconduct. While Cameron has received immunity for his part in our crimes, what he did—what we did—can still be used to assess this sentence and any others.

I'm still making halfhearted efforts to pretend my life is normal. On the day of sentencing, I have a series of holiday-related plans downtown. I consider forgoing these in favor of waiting to hear of any news but then think better of it. I should not attribute so much importance to myself, I think.

I keep checking my phone for any updates. I am running errands when I see on my phone that for simple contraband drug possession, the trial judge has sentenced Cameron to four and a half additional years. His original sentence has essentially been doubled.

A sour feeling in the pit of my stomach indicates to me that there is more to this sentence than Cameron's possession of drugs. I excuse myself from the rest of my plans and head home to my computer to investigate.

When I ultimately look at the hearing transcript, my fears are confirmed. Our crime consumes much of the judge's decision. He is not pleased. And he is not restrained in his displeasure.

One would expect that the judge would mention me by name, spelling it into the record lest someone mistake me for someone else. One might also expect that he would mention my bra: by this time I have come to realize that when given the opportunity to reference a woman's undergarments, everyone, regardless of status or stature, will seize it.

I expected, too, that no one would bother to point out to the judge the circumstances surrounding my end of our crime—the diagnosed condition, the prescription made on the judge's own recommendation, MCC's refusal to provide a medication appearing on its own formulary. Because Cameron did not use the medication for its intended purpose, these facts have no relevance to him.

What is less expected is for the judge to state his disappointment that he did not get his hands on my case:

```
The government and the defense, although in my
view this was a serious matter, they agreed and
decided that it was in the public interest to
dismiss the complaint against Ms. Ridha[.]
    That case was never presented to me until it
was over which surprises me somewhat.
```

It being Cameron's sentencing, he does not single me out. He also feels as though he should have been able to weigh in on Cameron's punishment as well:

```
There is no record of Douglas having been cited
or sanctioned, as I say, by BOP for possessing
the Xanax pills.
    I am constrained to say, sorry to say that
this incident seems to me was swept under the
rug both by the government and the defense.
```

It is odd to hear a judge put in a request to hear a certain case, mostly because the process does not allow for judges to handpick their caseload. Each criminal case is randomly assigned to a judge by use of a wooden wheel that when spun generates a judge's name. The government, presumably wanting to demonstrate that nothing was swept under the rug, gently reminds the judge of this procedure:

> It also, Judge, would not be normal—in the nor-
> mal course her case wouldn't have been brought
> here anyway. [The judge in her case] might be
> Your Honor, it might be some other judge in the
> Court.
>
>   So, I do think it is unfair and I respectfully
> disagree that that matter was swept under the
> rug notwithstanding whether or not you disagree
> with the leniency of her disposition.

The judge does not discuss the issue further.

To the objective listener the exchange can likely be chalked up to the judge's slip of the mind about the criminal process, a judicial brain fart about the assignment of cases. But when I hear this man lament that he did not personally stand in judgment of me, I feel my heart rate quicken. I inexplicably get up from my desk and chain my door, as though the judge might stop by, take matters into his own hands.

I move on to read what Co-Counsel says in Cameron's defense. Here is where my anxiety quickly gives way to something far more potent: shame.

At first, I am not particularly affected by Co-Counsel's arguments. He counters the judge's criticisms exactly as any attorney would, by shifting the blame. I am thus unimpressed when he says of me,

> If anything she deserves, in my opinion, much
> more blame for this.

And though I involuntarily roll my eyes when I read it, I am not moved when he says of what I've done, "it wouldn't have happened with me," because while self-serving and unrelated to the arguments he should be making on behalf of his client, it is certainly true.

I also don't disagree—because I can't—when he says:

> And in terms of what he told her to do, she
> should have said no.

But where my facade crumbles, where denial and victimhood evaporate for good, is the point at which I misread Co-Counsel's statement to say the following:

```
I realize that he asked her to do it but the
reason you have lawyers is to protect him from
things like that happening.
```

In fact, Co-Counsel actually says something slightly different—"to prevent things like that from happening"—but it is the word I have imputed to his statement—"protect"—that presents a blow to my stomach. I suspect that my error in reading was less than serendipitous, that on some level below the excuse-making and justification-having, deeper than the denial and self-pity, there has been a level of awareness that I have not allowed to come forward.

When I see it in print—or think that I do—the ground beneath me falls. I finally recognize the perversion in my insistence that by providing Cameron with what I believed he needed, I have done right by him, protected him from harm. Given this turn of events, I see now that I have done precisely the opposite.

The shame and regret I feel manifest as a physical mass at the bottom of my stomach. I sob uncontrollably to see if I might extract it. I find myself on my knees in front of my toilet, in the hopes it might come up. But even when my stomach is emptied, it is still there. It has never really gone away.

On the floor of my bathroom, wiping my mouth with my sleeve, I recall the afternoon on the courthouse steps, fearing that I had inadvertently hurt Cameron, praying that it would not come to pass. I remember my relief at the universe's benevolence that day, the lightness of heart that meant I could continue to go through life without carrying the damage of another on my conscience. Why I went on to ensure for myself the very result I wanted to avoid, I will never be able to fully answer.

What I feel I cannot unfeel. What I know I cannot unknow. I can no longer escape my culpability, the mess that I have made. My crime is all I see. My crime is all there is.

That it has taken this long to get here is probably itself a shameful fact. But I have arrived. In the harsh light of Cameron's punishment, everything becomes clear. For the first time in all of this, I feel like the criminal that I am.

At some point I manage to extricate myself from the bathroom floor. By this time, news of Cameron's sentencing has hit the major news wires. Press coverage of my crime spreads like an infectious disease, contaminating news outlets across the country and beyond. My bra is in the *Washington Post* and the *Wall Street Journal*. It is in Reuters and the Associated Press. It does not reprise its role in the *New York Post* but I think this is only because there it is old news.

At some point, keeping track of all of it seems as useful as trying to collect spilled wine. I can only watch the stain seep deeper.

It is possibly fitting that on the same day that the mainstream media reports my crimes, I finally see them for what they are. I can't imagine that I feel much different from those who are learning about my crimes for the first time. I share in the moral disgust, the disapproval, the virtual disbelief. Now that I see myself clearly, I ask alongside everyone else: How could she be so stupid? How could she do so wrong?

CHAPTER 11

Such a Shame

I'm surprised to find that facing reality is actually somewhat of a mixed bag. I expect to feel overwhelming shittiness, and I do. In opening my eyes to what I've done, I must now look at the totality of the damage: all of the people I have let down and embarrassed, all of the bonds I have broken, all of the hurt I have caused. The resulting shame is almost too much to take. It sifts in my stomach, racks my thoughts, takes up permanent residence in my chest.

But I do not expect that this terrible feeling will also come with the experience of relief. It turns out that self-pity is not just insufferable to those who witness it. Feeling sorry for yourself is an exhausting charade to maintain, and when I no longer do I find that I do breathe a little easier.

This being the only upside, I think it best to keep the feeling going. To anyone who will listen, I deliver a full confession of my sins. My congregation is mostly receptive, although I suspect that some are wondering what took me so long.

The only pushback I receive is in a phone call with my mother. She has called to tell me that she has told my father everything that has happened over the past eighteen months.

I feel badly that my father didn't hear it from me. But my mother insists time was of the essence. "I thought I should tell him before he sees it in the *Wall Street Journal*," she says.

This is a good point, but I still swallow. "What did he say?"

"You know your father. He just listened, and then sat thinking. He asked if you would be able to practice law anymore."

"What did you say?"

"I told him that you didn't know yet."

"Did he say anything else?"

"Not really. I can tell he's worried about you."

I'm not surprised when my mother says that my father's reaction is one of silence. This is his way. Unlike my mother, my father has no flair for the dramatic. Instead, he will silently think and worry and wonder. To comment on what has already happened would serve no logical purpose. He will keep his feelings to himself. If he is especially disturbed, he might blame himself.

I find his methods far less tolerable than my mother's. While at this point in adulthood I can endure my mother's histrionics, I have never been able to deal with my father's silences. Once, as a high school student, he caught me smoking a cigarette at a neighbor's party. He and my mother had already left, and so I assumed the coast was clear. I did not account for the possibility that he might return to the party to retrieve his jacket. When I happened to turn around mid-drag, he was standing there, a severe look on his face.

I didn't even bother with excuses, but silently joined him in the walk back home. It was a summer evening, and I batted away fireflies as I awaited my sentence. I glanced over at him and saw that he was taking swift, deliberate strides, his gaze fixed on the grass below.

Suddenly, he looked up. I braced myself for what I imagined was going to be an epic grounding.

"I am not going to punish you for this," he said. "Because it isn't your fault."

It did not seem right to agree, so I remained silent.

"It's mine," he said. "Obviously, if you think that is appropriate behavior, then I have failed as a parent."

I don't know if he said it because he knew the guilt it would cause was worse than any punishment, but that was its effect. I've sworn off smoking ever since.

And so it is the same when he discovers what I've done. When I call home a week later, he will answer the phone and ask how I am. And when I tell him I'm fine, he will simply say, "I really hope that you are."

He does not otherwise discuss it, at least not really. When I come to visit a few months later, he does not raise the issue but will listen when I do. As I speak, he has a look on his face as though he has just swallowed something bitter. Still, his concern is focused on how I plan to move forward. To this, I offer little answer, other than to say I plan to "figure it out."

Several months later, when it seems his worrying has gotten the better of him, I open my mailbox and find a card containing the following:

Dear Jennifer,

   I hope that all is well with you. First, I hope that you have been healthy and happy. Then, I hope that your plans for the profession and education are progressing at an excellent pace.

   If at any time you wish to have my opinion as I see things based on my life experience, I would be more than happy to provide my input. We can do this in-person or via Skype, email or phone.

   I have made a point of avoiding interference or preaching or giving the slightest impression of "know-it-all," leaving it up to you to decide if and when you might need my input.

   In the meantime, you have my love and best wishes. Love, Your father.

When I read the card, just as I do on the walk home from the neighbors' house, I vow never to commit a crime again.

On the phone with my mother, I try to change the subject. I decide this is a prime opportunity to share what I've learned in the wake of Cameron's second sentencing.

"Dad would be within his rights to be angry with me," I say. "I really should not have done what I did."

My mother dismisses this as though swatting away a fly. "You were trying to help," she says.

"Maybe, but look at all that I did in the name of helping," I say. "It was pretty dishonest."

"But you told everyone the truth about what you did." I hear her voice becoming high-pitched.

"I know, I mean what I actually did was dishonest, sneaking the pills to him," I say calmly.

"You are a good person!" she yells. "You were trying to help that boy! And look where it got you!"

Having expelled this line of thinking from my own brain, I feel compelled to expel it from hers, too. "Mom, it really was my fault, too. If I hadn't done what I did, none of this would have happened."

I think I can hear her throwing up her hands. "Why are you saying this to me, Jennifer? What are you doing to me?"

These two sentences usually mark the point at which we initiate verbal warfare. When I hear her say them now, my Pavlovian response is to open my mouth and begin to argue.

But I stop myself before I start. I'm being selfish by forcing my mother to agree with me. My crimes are not hers to own. And I suspect my trying to thrust them up on her is because I don't want to bear them all by myself. But if I claim to be someone who is accepting responsibility, I suppose this is exactly what I should be doing.

"Never mind," I say.

Our mother-daughter relationship has developed a funhouse quality where I insist on pointing out every one of my shortcomings, and she is being defensive for defensive's sake.

I take this as a sign from the cosmos that my world as it currently stands is upside down. I decide to make a concerted effort to forge my own path away from the chaos I've created for my family. I can sense their increasing discomfort with my predicament, and so for their sake much more than my own, I find myself inching away. Phone calls are fewer and shorter. Topics are avoided. Tone of voice is reassuring. Upsetting information is withheld.

My experience bears out a definitive truth that I come to learn in the course of my case: there is no such thing as a victimless crime. There may not be body bags or gunshot wounds, but in acts of consensual criminal conduct, in crimes that are not intended to cause harm, even in these crimes there are casualties. The victims of our crimes are the people who love us, the people we love.

• • •

I spend eighteen months denying I've done anything wrong. But once I begin to see my crime for what it is, I can't look away.

I'm reminded of it in unexpected places, in television story lines, songs on the radio, various nineteenth-century Russian novels. But I consider it in earnest when I decide to pick up Ronald Dworkin's philosophical tome *Justice for Hedgehogs*.

I'm not one for theoretical works. But *Hedgehogs* draws my attention because its subject matter extends beyond the meaning of law to the meaning of our collective existence. In an attempt to stave off an impending existential crisis, I decide it might be wise to explore in greater depth the meaning of life. Also, I like the little hedgehog on its cover.

Dworkin's main thesis is about the unity of value. In order to acknowledge the value in our own lives, he says, we have a duty to preserve that same value in others. There are therefore times when we are morally required to help those around us in need.

This idea is not particularly earth-shattering, but it is something that is not embraced by the law. The criminal law sees virtue only in *declining* to act. Crimes are usually defined by affirmative acts—pulling a trigger, picking a lock, placing Xanax pills in a bag of pretzels. Doing nothing is almost always the lawful thing to do.

This is true, by the way, even if doing nothing will certainly cause someone else harm. We know this from the notorious noncase of David Cash, an incident relayed in many criminal law textbooks, in which young Mr. Cash walked into a casino bathroom to find his best friend physically struggling with a seven-year-old girl. When he left without saying or doing anything, when he allowed his friend to rape and kill the girl without calling the police, when he told the press afterward that he was "not going to lose sleep over someone else's problem," he was not guilty of any crime. The law says that the hands that remain idle, even in the face of evil, are still considered clean.

I already know all too well that what I've done is a crime. But as I read these passages I find myself wondering—hoping—if in giving Cameron his medication there might be anything philosophically redeeming in what I've done.

But I don't turn up anything. Dworkin writes that our duty to help preserve another's value must never come at the cost of our own. He likens our relationship to one another as swimmers in an Olympic-sized pool, racing in separately demarcated lanes. If a swimmer is drowning in the next lane and you can help him without losing much ground in the race, Dworkin says, you have a duty to save him. But when the risk of loss to you is larger than the harm suffered, when the sacrifice would diminish your own value, the duty no longer exists.

When Cameron was struggling in the adjacent lane, I did not keep him from drowning. I did not preserve his value, and I certainly did not preserve mine. What I did was rush to his side, look him in the eye, and tie a brick to us both.

Not even an abstract theory of morality can relieve me. I have no grounds for mitigation, no asterisk for what I've done. My crime is what it has always been. I am left with nothing else, only slight solace when Dworkin points out: "Only a few people are fully satisfied with their own character and record, and they are fools."

I return to Dworkin's swimming metaphor several months later when I am actually swimming in the lane of a lap pool. I find myself observing the woman in the neighboring lane. We stroke in tandem, our heads bobbing underwater and above in synchronicity. Our movements become so closely timed that we seem to come up for air at the same moment. Our breaths are divided between us. She breathes my air, and I breathe hers.

It reminds me, somewhat strangely, of the weekend I spent locked in the attorney room when Cameron was sent to the SHU. How in the dry air of the sealed room, his cold became mine. How our breaths were divided between us, he breathed my air and I breathed his.

Con • spir • a • cy—*(n) from the Latin* conspīrarē, *"to breathe together."*

I did not save Cameron from drowning. I did not save myself either. But when I saw him suffering, I did not continue in pursuit of the finish line. I lifted the divide. I swam over. And while everything after was unmitigated disaster, a minuscule fact does remain: I did not keep swimming. I did not look away.

It is a triumph of the most intimate order, the tiniest of victories only in that my impulse was arguably the right one. And while this fact is but a grain of virtue in a desert of wrongdoing, I decide it portends something of note in my journey forward.

It is proof of promise. Reason for hope.

CHAPTER 12

Recognizance and Release

I t takes some time, but I eventually begin to discover some actual virtues of accepting responsibility. These are far from monumental; most of the damage remains done. I am still without direction. Having declined to make any real career moves, the drain on my bank account is unceasing. And I am mostly a criminal recluse, convinced that I remain unfit to rejoin society in earnest.

But owning up to what I've done does allow me to see my circumstances for the justified outcome that they are. I find that it is much easier to watch something slip through my fingers when I have only my own hand to blame.

Accepting responsibility also makes more bearable the public verdict about what I've done. I do not agree with what people say, but I can better understand why they are saying it. On the sole occasion that I bother to google my own name, the suggested search terms are "Cameron Douglas," "bra," and "arrested." The search results are not particularly complimentary. There are hundreds of news articles. Lots of blog entries. On one lawyer's message board, unable to discern how I have managed to escape prosecution, a group of lawyers posit that I must have performed sexual acts upon Some Prosecutor. This in turn inspires extensive speculation about my sexual skill set, which the commenters agree must be quite advanced. This seems a bit generous, but I do not chime in to say so.

Looking at the product of my google search, I see that criminal reprimand exists well beyond judges and courtrooms. It also becomes something entirely different when it is exposed to the public. I am right to have feared the arrival of the Escaleras' trials, not only because of the professional ramifications, but because it has placed my conduct before what appears to be a mostly unforgiving public.

Knowing this, I never bother googling myself again. But I do make peace with the awful things that are being said. And, more importantly, I reap their unexpected benefits. When the worst thing you've ever done is depicted in the most terrible way possible and broadcast across the globe for all to see, it stands to reason that there is really nothing left to hide. When you've disappointed and disgusted everyone you've ever known, there is really no one left to please. When the worst possible things have been said about you, there is really nothing more that can hurt you.

And so herein lies the greatest virtue of accepting my reality. Here, finally, is freedom. Even though I am at the bottom, even though I must crane my neck to see salvation, there isn't any further to fall. It is an underrated truism that comes to guide my journey forward: when the very worst has come to pass, there is really nothing left to fear.

Cameron is released from solitary confinement in the spring of 2012. I learn this one evening when my cell phone rings, the number listed as "Unknown," the caller on the other end a recording by the Federal Bureau of Prisons.

The shock of the phone call distracts me so much that I do not hear the number I must press to accept the call. After all the time that has passed, I have pushed this information from my mind. I know only that pressing one number accepts the call, and pressing another declines this and all future calls. I can't remember what either number is.

I look at the keypad and decide to start in the middle. When I press 5, I suddenly hear breathing on the other end.

"Hello?" I say.

"Hey. It took you a while."

I haven't heard Cameron speak in close to two years. He sounds different from what I remember. His voice is quiet and flat, almost despondent. The telltale bravado seems far away.

"I forgot which button to push," I say.

I suppose there is a moment that exists between all co-conspirators when they finally meet again. I have on many occasions pictured this moment, one in which I am finally able to confront Cameron about everything that's happened. On bad days, I fantasize about screaming at him and perhaps finally punching him in the face. On better days, I want to tell him that we owed each other better. But now that he is on the line, I draw a blank. I have no idea what to say.

He doesn't seem to know what to say either. The line is quiet for several moments. When the awkwardness becomes unbearable, I finally say, "How are you holding up?"

He begins to talk. Just as I did long ago in an attorney room, I silently listen as he tells me about the atrocious conditions of solitary, about his new lawyer, about his appeal. He tells me about his new correctional facility, that it is rougher than his old facility, that he is playing flag football.

As he talks, I feel a seeping unhappiness. Speaking with Cameron reminds me of everything that's happened, everything I've done.

At some point, a once-familiar female recording can be heard on the line. "This call is from a federal prison," she warns. In the time since I've last heard this recording, quite a lot has happened.

"I forgot about her," I say, referring to the recording. "How's she been?"

He laughs. "She's good," he says.

Perhaps because I have cracked a joke, he seems a little more at ease. His voice softens. "I was really worried about you," he says.

I feel tears forming, the kind that arrive when the moment is otherwise too overwhelming to endure.

"Oh" is all I manage to say.

"I miss you," he says.

"Oh," I say again.

There is silence. I swallow.

"So much has happened," I say.

"I know," he says. He does not elaborate.

"I'm glad you're doing better," I say.

More silence.

"And it's nice to hear your voice," I say.

"Yeah, you, too," he says.

He pauses. "Jen?" he asks.

"Yes?" I say.

"Do you think that when I come out I could come live with you?"

At first I think he is making a joke. But then I remember reading an article about long-term solitary confinement, how it can cause inmates to develop delusionary thoughts. I remember, too, the psychiatrist's recommendation that Cameron never be placed in solitary. I proceed with diplomacy.

"Cameron, I don't know if that's such a good idea," I say.

"Why not?" he asks.

"Well, don't you think you should focus on getting out first?" Though he is challenging his sentence, his release is otherwise set for 2017.

"I guess."

The recording chimes in again. There is not much time left on the call.

"Hey," he says. "I love you."

By this time, I have long come to terms with the fact that this can't possibly be true, at least not in any conventional meaning of this phrase. But Cameron often uses "I love you" as a proxy for words he does not want to say. Being on the receiving end of Cameron's proclamations of love is like being in an Albee play: tones bear more meaning than words. In the brief romantic time we spent together, I learned to decipher the difference between an "I love you" that means "I am sorry," an "I love you" that means "you are going to hate what I am about to say," and an "I love you" that means, to a certain degree, "I love you." When I hear the expectant tone in his voice, I know that Cameron is asking more than telling, and what he is probably asking is whether or not I forgive.

It is finally my chance to say my piece. As I search my thoughts, however, I discover I have no piece to say. I know by now that our collusion is necessarily equal parts of him and me. I know that I am not a wronged party as much as I am a party in the wrong. I know that the forgiveness he seeks is not really mine to withhold.

My answer is thus preordained. "I know that," I say. And then, before the phone cuts out, I add: "I love you, too."

This is not the last time we communicate. We will intermittently exchange letters and e-mails. I will write him to let him know that a tabloid reporter showed up at my apartment door asking about his dad. He will e-mail me to let me know that he has moved facilities. He will write to me when he is placed in solitary confinement a second time, for drug possession. He will write to me when he is placed in solitary confinement a third time, for reasons he does not explain. Each time, I will write him back to tell him to hang in there, that I wish that all of this had ended differently.

At one point, he will write to say that he has "sustained" a broken femur and hand. He doesn't explain how or why, only that he has had two rods placed in his leg so that he can walk again. Being ignorant of human anatomy, I do an Internet search for "broken femur" and learn that the impact needed to break a bone of its size and density is akin to that from a car crash or a huge fall.

A few months later, it will be reported in the papers that he was attacked after an inmate put a bounty on his head for cooperating with the government. Reading the article, and imagining what may have happened, will cause me to shudder. I will remember my naïve belief that I could somehow protect him from harm. I will be overwhelmed by the seeming inevitability of it coming to pass.

Our correspondence is far from regular. We drift in different seas. Months of silence will pass before one of us sends a Christmas e-mail or a letter remarking on the arrival of summer.

On the rare occasions we interact, we don't much address what has happened. I never bring myself to ask Cameron about why he did the things he did or said the things he said. At first this is because I decide there is no possible answer that would make things better, that there isn't enough between Cameron and me for this to matter. Over time, however, I begin to wonder if my epic self-implosion was something separate from Cameron, if by colluding with someone who I knew was everything I was not supposed to want, if by doing the things I knew I was never supposed to do, I unconsciously saw an escape out of a perfectly acceptable life that I nonetheless could no longer bring myself to live. As awful as this selfish thought is, I find enough truth in it that I don't bother holding Cameron responsible for bringing about what on some level I wanted to bring upon myself.

There are some relationships that stand the test of time. But Cameron and I are not family. We are not ex-lovers in any real sense. We aren't former roommates or college friends. We are not much more than parties to a relationship between a misguided attorney and her former client, two people who did terrible things.

And yet, due to the realities of the Internet age, I suspect that to one degree or another the connection will always remain. Bound by our wrongdoing, our agreement to stray from a virtuous path is etched in stone. For better or worse, and no matter what happens next, we will forever be known as partners in crime.

The Escalera brothers are sentenced in early summer 2012. David Escalera arrives at sentencing subject to a five-year mandatory minimum. Eduardo Escalera is better positioned: a jury has found him responsible for a drug weight without any mandatory minimum.

Their sentencing falls two years after their arrest. Had they accepted the deal that was offered to them by the government, they would be weeks away from release.

Both men are sentenced to ten years. They are currently scheduled for release in 2019.

Shortly after he is sentenced, I decide to pull David Escalera's sentencing papers from the court docket. I realize that I have no idea who he is. I would like to read a little more about this person who once unknowingly held my fate in his hand.

According to his papers, David Escalera is in his late thirties. At the time of his arrest, he was living in southern California. He is skilled at handiwork. He was married, but divorced his wife when he learned that the younger of their two small sons was not biologically his. His ex-wife was later deported to Mexico, and for reasons not explained took with her only her younger son, leaving the other boy behind. Because his father is incarcerated and his mother lives outside of the country, Little David is placed in the custody of a family member's ex-girlfriend.

Little David is ten years old. He writes a letter to the judge that is appended to his father's sentencing papers.

> Judge please bring my dad y I need him and my dad need my dad so much and I need to see him as. he need to see him to Please I am sad Please give me him.

When I read Little David's letter, when I realize that he will now spend the rest of his childhood without his family, I feel profound embarrassment that I ever considered myself a casualty in this case. Having done nothing to find himself where he is, Little David has a future that is far from assured. I sometimes find myself thinking about him, hoping he is managing, asking what will become of him, wondering if he ever comes to know the sad circumstances through which he inadvertently became his father's greatest victim.

Summer turns to fall. To the outside observer, my life could be described as "aimless." It is a matter of fact that I have still not embarked on any discernible plans to move forward professionally. I halfheartedly search job listings. I do not put together a résumé. I do not contemplate any conceivable explanation I could make to a prospective employer about everything that has happened.

These all seem like exercises in futility, a waste of time better spent wasting time. Divested of the trappings of my professional existence and having failed to secure a meaningful income, time is all I have, and I soon begin to relish it.

Each day, I savor every section of the newspaper, even the boring business section. Magazines no longer accumulate into a looming tower on my coffee table; these are now read and recycled the same day they arrive. I make my way through my bookshelf, the unread contents of which are stuffed three books deep.

My home is in impeccable order. My diet root beer–stained rug is a thing of the past. I dust and scrub and mop and spray. I shelve away every item I own in a clear container with a label specifying its class and species.

I take on minor fix-it projects. I nail and hammer and twist. When my toilet inexplicably stops flushing, with the help of an Internet printout and latex gloves, I repair it myself. When I make it function, I experience a feeling of accomplishment no different from when I passed the Bar exam. My toilet did not flush. Now, because of me, it flushes with ease.

Like many reformed criminals, I rediscover religion. A series of spiritual writings leads me to the practice of meditation. For a half hour each day, I find a space where my failures are reduced to illusion, where I can see the part of myself that is still capable of virtue.

I take to heart this passage in a book called *The Art of Dreaming*: "Most of our energy goes into upholding our importance. If we were capable of losing some of that importance, two extraordinary things would happen to us. One, we would free our energy from trying to maintain the illusory idea of our grandeur; and two, we would provide ourselves with enough energy to catch a glimpse of the actual grandeur of the universe."

I have shown that I am quite capable of losing my own importance. I am void of grandeur, illusory or otherwise. I am thus primed to take in all the magnificence the universe has to offer. I take long bike rides into the uppermost part of the island, surrounded by lush trees and quiet. But for a nearby parking lot that appears to be a hub for anonymous sex, I am in the world of Walden. I sit in the grass and spend hours watching birds fly and ducks swim. I savor the sunset. I watch a squirrel eat a candy bar.

My days are of my own choosing; I answer only to myself. I take walks along the river. I sit in cafés consuming books. I scrounge together enough money to go to movies and sometimes even a play.

In passing the time this way, the vestiges of my criminal case have no relevance. Stripped down to my essence, the only person I have to be is exactly who I am. I wake up every morning and go to sleep every evening feeling at peace. On some days, I think I might even feel joy.

My sense of contentment is invariably interrupted by some well-meaning interloper, usually a family member, who will inquire as to when I will be getting up off my ass and start doing something with my life. When I politely dismiss these inquiries with promises of "soon" or "someday," there is a part of me that feels sorry that others cannot see the pleasures there are to be had in simple things. Another part of me knows this is bullshit, that my inertia is not because I have discovered the bliss of doing nothing but because deep down I'm scared to try again. I am my broken toilet: I await someone or something to repair me, to make me right. Until then, I am only good for doing nothing.

A repairman does not arrive. But something else does. There is something quickly approaching, something that demands my undivided attention, something that will bring unexpected change.

Her name is Sandy. And she's on her way.

The imminent arrival of Hurricane Sandy has caused an unprecedented pause in the city's normal course of business. Public transportation is shut down. Regular television programming is interrupted with City Hall press conferences about evacuation protocols and the importance of having a battery-operated flashlight. Supermarkets are mobbed with customers.

The city distributes maps that designate different zones according to the possibility of flooding. The city issues a mandatory evacuation order for the most precarious neighborhoods, designated Zone A. The city suggests evacuation only for the next most precarious neighborhood, designated Zone B.

I don't want to evacuate my apartment. The problem with my desire to remain is that my building abuts the East River. I consider several different maps of Zones A and B. On one version of the map, my building is contained within the outermost perimeter of Zone A. On another, the line of demarcation is across the street, rendering my building just inside Zone B. I decide that it is safe to consider myself in Zone B, outside the purview of the city's evacuation order.

The day that Sandy is slated to arrive, the city is shut down. Businesses, schools, government buildings are all closed. When Sandy visits, it does not matter whether you have put your life back together. She's coming either way.

I am in bed the morning of October 29, 2012, fast asleep. I am jolted awake by the sound of an intercom that is so loud that I at first believe it to be coming from inside my bedroom.

It is the sound of a police loudspeaker, presumably from a police car outside my building.

"FOR YOUR OWN SAFETY YOU ARE REQUIRED TO EVACUATE!!!" the voice exclaims.

I roll over and place my pillow over my head.

"YOU MUST EVACUATE!!!"

I close my eyes tighter, hoping that I can beckon sleep quicker by wanting it more.

"YOUR EVACUATION IS MANDATORY!!!"

I groan.

"YOUR FAILURE TO EVACUATE IN COMPLIANCE WITH THIS DIRECTIVE COULD RESULT IN YOUR BEING CHARGED WITH A CLASS B MISDEMEANOR!!!"

I jump out of bed. My next movements are foregone, as though programmed in advance. I first reach, of course, for proper clothing. Then I shove my bare feet into my running shoes and throw on a jacket. I have a printout of the evacuation map sitting on my dining room table. I grab it, and run to the elevator.

The weather outside is wet and dreary. I fix my eyes on a police cruiser just outside the building. There are several officers milling about.

"Excuse me," I say to an officer. He is facing away from my building.

He looks at me.

I point to my building. "I live in that building there."

He does not look where I am pointing. "And?"

I pull out the evacuation map. "Well, according to this map, I am in Zone B, but I can see you are asking people to evacuate—"

"So?"

"Well, I just don't want to be—" I can't bring myself to say the words "charged" or "misdemeanor," so I say, "I don't know if I am supposed to evacuate or not."

He points at the other officers, all of whom have their attention directed at a building on the other side of the street.

"Does it look like we are evacuating your building?"

"Well, no, but—"

"Does it look like anyone else is evacuating your building?"

"No, but I just wanted to be sure—"

"Look, if you have to evacuate, you'll know about it."

The lawyer in me wants to get this in writing. I want this man to certify that my decision to go back into my apartment and get under the covers will not have any legal implications. I look at him for a moment, searching for ways to make this official.

"Okay, miss?" he says. He is visibly annoyed.

"Uh, yes. Okay. So, you're saying it's fine if I go back upstairs."

"Yes. Please do me a favor and go back upstairs."

"Oh. Okay, yes. Sorry. I'm going."

As I turn toward my building I see that he is shaking his head, as though to say, I am on duty during a national disaster and this idiot is showing me a map.

But he does not know. How could he? He could not know that I have struggled in the past with discerning the difference between what I want to do and what I am supposed to do. He could not know that I am trying so hard to be good.

Back in my apartment pulling together storm supplies, I note that my desire to avoid exposure, criminal or otherwise, has developed to the point of reflex. This seems like proof of something, although I am not entirely sure of what.

I charge my cell phone and iPad. I fill the tub with water. Using blue duct tape, I tape a big "X" on my living room window. When I step away to admire my handiwork, it looks as though I have checked off a gigantic box. I feel ready for whatever is coming my way.

Sandy arrives later that day in the evening hours. I harbor myself from the storm in my living room. While the most prudent thing would be to distract myself, Sandy is too alluring for me to look away. I tuck myself into the windowsill and wait to see her worst.

I look down onto the street. The elaborate law enforcement presence from earlier in the day has disbanded. The streets are empty other than a single police cruiser that sits at the intersection facing the East River. The colored lights seem lonely in the steadily pouring rain. Without anyone else around, the police car looks as though the NYPD is prepared to apprehend the storm itself.

The pounding of Sandy's rain becomes fast and heavy. It runs along the sides of the streets and pools in the gutters. Her wind has reached a level of speed that causes street signs to whip and then fall. I look down at the police car and wonder why it is still there.

And then, the river rises.

It happens almost in slow motion. The water from the river pours into the intersection. At first, the flooding is modest, a foot or so of water. But this moves quickly and soon there is much more. The sidewalks are no longer visible, and the water keeps coming.

Sitting in my window, I watch the inevitable standoff between Sandy and the police vehicle. As water gushes into the street, the police vehicle initially stands its ground. But the car is so poorly matched against the thrust of Sandy that as I see the water collecting under its tires, I hold my breath.

Suddenly, the police cruiser backs away from the intersection, far enough to turn in the other direction. I hear the tires screech as the vehicle flees the scene.

This happens not a moment too soon. Within minutes, the streets are completely underwater. Entire cars are submerged. Sandy's waters engulf the tops of street signs. The public pool across the street is overflowing. The river water gushes so quickly that its current sweeps up objects and carries them toward First Avenue. I watch as a garbage dumpster and a park bench float by together, as though on a date.

The hurricane is an incredible sight to behold. I am in awe of Sandy, struck by her sheer power, terrified by her indiscriminate destruction. Her might is so staggering that everything else—everyone else—is rendered insignificant.

I find myself opening my window, sticking my head out, inhaling her breath. Though it is almost November, her air is warm and sweet. I close my eyes. This is it, I think. This is the storm.

Sandy departs, but not without first leaving us in darkness. Just as the rain starts to slow and the wind becomes tempered, the lights go out. Having ravaged much of the tri-state area, Sandy's final act is to take our power away.

When I wake the morning after Sandy, I run to the window. The water is gone, the streets are mostly dry, and the weather is surprisingly clear. But the electricity is still out. In an e-mail that I draft to my parents from my cell phone, I tell them that I hope it will be back later in the day.

It is out for almost a week.

At first I try to embrace the lack of electricity. I still have gas for the stove, and so I commit to trying a new recipe each day using a single pan. Having gone through an unfortunate scented-candle phase years earlier, I dig these out so that when darkness falls my apartment is decently lit and delightfully fragrant. I assemble a pile of books along with some crossword puzzles.

This won't be that bad, I think.

But it does not take long for me to hate being alive. Every day is an inevitable countdown to darkness. My apartment reeks of a putrid mix of jasmine and freesia and musk. I have little appetite, and when I do, I alternatively eat oatmeal or fistfuls of popcorn from a king-sized bag purchased before the storm. I hold up the bag and speak to it out loud. "When I bought you," I tell the shiny red packaging, "there was light."

Without hot water, in order to bathe I must pull out every pot I own and heat enough water to fill the tub. The process takes hours. In the abstract it seems an exotic proposition, something from *Out of Africa*, to bathe in a tub with water heated by the stove, surrounded by candles. In reality it is a cold, wet mess. I emerge from the tub shaking, somehow less clean than when I started.

It turns out, too, that reading by candlelight is a myth. I can't see the page well enough without creating a fire hazard. I spend evenings using up precious cell phone power complaining to Best Friend, or else sitting on the couch sulking.

Because of damage caused by the storm, the residents of my building are advised not to leave the apartment unless absolutely necessary. A few days into the apocalypse, low on supplies and completely out of cell phone power, I decide to brave it. A single exit provides limited street access. I join the crowded sidewalks of unwashed masses heading to a neighborhood thirty blocks uptown that is rumored to have electricity.

This proves to be an unpleasant experience. The natives are not welcoming. They are alternatively miffed at the foreign intrusion or looking to make a quick buck. An asshole on Fifty-fourth Street sells me a flashlight and batteries for fifty dollars. When I am sitting on the floor of a Duane Reade charging my cell phone, I watch in empathy as a young woman, filthy just like me, is accosted by an old crone in a fur coat for purchasing too many items.

"Is there another storm coming?" she snipes. "Do you really need to buy all of that?"

The young woman is embarrassed, looks down at her basket, seems to contemplate placing her feminine hygiene products back on the shelf.

When the furry monstrosity makes her way to the next aisle—her presence in an aisle dedicated to menstruation is its own mystery—the defender in me emerges. I get up from the floor in solidarity with this young woman. "Don't listen to her," I insist. "You can buy as many tampons as you want."

She gives me an exhausted smile. "God, I hate it here," she says.

"Me, too," I say. I offer her the other socket in the wall outlet.

"This neighborhood is awful," she says as she sits down.

"I know," I say. "I don't understand why anyone would live here."

"Yeah, I'd rather be without electricity than live up here," she declares.

I don't know if I would take it that far. That's how badly I want the power to come back.

Without electricity to spare, I have no idea of the true horrors caused by Sandy. When I access news websites on my iPad, it is strictly to see if there are any updates about the return of power. I don't know that whole areas of New York and New Jersey have been flattened, that thousands of homes are destroyed, that people are found drowned in their own homes. I have not yet read the horrifying story of a Staten Island woman who lost her grip on her two small sons while trying to flee, the storm sweeping them out to sea. I don't know that people have lost everything they owned.

But I am embarrassed to admit that knowing any of this probably would not have provided much perspective. I have always had a peculiar relationship with electricity, one that makes it supreme to everything else. I first learned this in Iraq, where I somehow managed to inure myself to the constant sound of machine-gun fire but felt the lack of electricity in the sweltering heat warranted my emergency airlift elsewhere.

I try to explain this to Best Friend, who lives outside of Sandy's path. "I don't think I can make it much longer. I feel as though I might be coming unhinged," I tell her through tears.

"It'll be okay, Jen," she says. "Everything will be back to normal soon."

"But what if it isn't?" I say.

"What do you mean?"

As I say it, I hear my voice crack. "What if the lights never come back on?"

She laughs, not realizing I am serious.

"No, really," I say. "How do we really know that the electricity will work again? What if they can never fix it?"

Best Friend is unfazed by my meanderings. "Jen, it's going to be fine. You know what they say. It's always darkest before the dawn."

I am on Day Five of my post-Sandy hysteria. Feeling stir crazy, I decide to buck authority and go out for a run. This does not just contravene the directive of my landlord. Technically, all city parks are closed. Also, because I will need to bring a flashlight to navigate the unlit stairwell of my building, I will need to stow it away in my mailbox during my run. This is technically against the law.

I weigh the costs and benefits and decide that for the sake of my sanity, I am willing to take the risk. Perhaps I am not as reformed as I thought.

By the time I make it to the front door of my building, I can't contain my excitement to get outside. But as I walk out of the building, I remember that all of the regular exits out onto the running path are closed. The exit facing the park is flooded. Another gated exit is locked. I feel myself begin to panic.

I walk back to the lobby of my building. Because the lack of electricity has disabled the key card entry system, the landlord has hired a security guard to monitor the entrance. This specific security guard is an interesting choice. I would approximate her age to be late forties and her height to be around five feet. She seems happily ensconced in the magazine that is strewn across her stout legs.

I am not quite sure how she is qualified to protect hundreds of residents from looting or robbery, but she seems pleasant enough.

"Excuse me," I say.

She looks up distractedly from her magazine.

"How do I get out of here?"

"Whaddaya mean?" Her voice is low and boasts a heavy accent that is unmistakably Brooklyn.

"I mean, how do I get to the park? I want to go to the running path."

"Ya know, you're really not supposed to go outside."

"I do know that," I say. My voice takes a pleading tone. "But please, I just want to go for a run, just for a little while."

She opens her mouth as though she is going to object, but then thinks better of it. "Whadda I care?" she asks rhetorically. "Just go behind the other building, there's an exit over there."

"Thank you so much," I say.

"You'd better be careful. It's a mess out there."

"I will, I promise."

She shrugs and then goes back to her magazine.

On my way to the running path, I can see the full extent of Sandy's aftermath. On the service road outside my building, three cars are smashed into one another. A tree trunk has been uprooted from the ground. Thick branches and debris are everywhere. The river, usually calmly emitting a fragrant blend of fish, weed, and garbage, now bears menacing eddies. The waterline is so high that it seems to warn that Mother Nature is willing to do this all over again.

I start my run at the top of East River Park. I use the word "run" quite loosely. The pace at which I usually advance can be generously described as a "jog," and more accurately as a "putter." I only ever pass runners of the geriatric variety.

But today I feel a surge of energy. I find myself moving at a speed so unexpected that I look down at my feet to watch them work. I actually pass several able-bodied runners on a narrow path in order to make my way onto the wider thoroughfare.

The park looks as though its contents have been shaken in a snow globe. Trees are knocked on their sides. Park benches are ripped out. Heavy branches and trunks litter the running path.

The extent of the devastation causes me to think once again about Sandy, about the laws of nature. These laws are inalienable. When the rain pours, the river will flood. When the wind blows, trees will fall. When the storm is over, the sun will warm us with its rays. These rules do not bend. They do not vary by jurisdiction. They cannot be amended. We have no choice but to live within their lines.

Criminal law, on the other hand, is not natural. Our laws are man-made. They can be erased and rewritten and applied haphazardly. The law has no basis in science, it does not fully correspond to even the most basic moral code. All of man's worst evils—killing, torturing, pillaging—are crimes, except in the hundreds of thousands of instances where they are not. And though we are forced to conform ourselves to its mandate, the law sometimes creates the very wrongdoing it is designed to prevent.

The criminal law is not really of us. It is more likely upon us, covering us like an uneven coat of paint, applied too thick in some spots but barely touching others.

As I run, I find comfort in this thought. If the criminal law is something separate from who we are, then perhaps the urge to resist its directives is not necessarily unnatural. Maybe criminals stand apart from the human race only in our willingness to subject ourselves to painful consequences. Although it sounds like a platitude printed on the side panel of a box of maxi pads, I consider the possibility that compliance with the law does not come from some innate love and respect for authority as much as it does from an established love and respect for yourself.

I'm running faster. I've been so lost in thought that I don't know exactly where I am. Because of the many detours I've had to take around the damage, I am away from the promenade, a few blocks inland. I slow my pace so I can get my bearings. The Williamsburg and Manhattan Bridges are behind me. I'm outside of the island's numerical grid, and so I try to find a street sign in the hope it bears a name I recognize.

I jog down a little farther. Here, the environs begin to look familiar. It takes me a moment to place them. I am a few blocks from MCC.

I have no great desire to revisit the scene of my crime, the place where I broke the law and ended up breaking out of my life. I lurk cautiously around a nearby block in order to catch my breath, conscious not to go any farther.

As I stand in MCC's shadow, I think about all of the days I spent inside its walls. Memories return as though they have been stowed away in this neighborhood. I remember my first day on Cameron's case, its steady procession from criminal case to circus. I remember the Sharpie marker, the newspaper articles and transcripts, waiting for the count to clear.

And then another memory: it was early into the case, long before my criminal exploits began. In the attorney room, I am explaining to Cameron how the sentencing guidelines correspond to drug weight. When I look up to see if he understands, his face is red and bears a look of concern.

"What's the matter?" I ask.

"Nothing," he says. "I'm listening."

"Are you sure?"

"Yes."

I pause, giving him an opportunity to speak.

"This is not the most straightforward thing, so you shouldn't feel embarrassed if you have questions," I say.

He takes a breath and asks, "Do you think I am a bad person for dealing drugs?"

I examine his face for a moment. Cameron is not a stranger to fish-

ing for answers to make himself feel better. But his expression is grave
enough that I think he is asking seriously.

"Cameron, it's not my job to judge you."

"I know, but still."

I think for a second. "Well, do I think it was the *best* idea to deal
drugs? I mean, no, probably not."

He laughs at my diplomacy. "Well, I know it wasn't the *best* idea."

"Look, you did a not-great thing," I say. "But it doesn't have to be
who you are."

He looks at me and says nothing.

I keep talking. "We can always be someone different from who
we used to be. There's this quote my ex-boyfriend told me, I forget
where it's from. 'The past is a foreign country: they do things differently
there.'"

The quote—I later look it up—is from *The Go-Between* by L. P.
Hartley. It is somewhat misplaced, given the fact that the protagonist
wishes he could return to the past. But perhaps the longing for innocence is all the same.

Cameron thinks about this. "Yeah, I guess so," he says.

As I say it out loud, I become more convinced. "I'm not just trying
to make you feel better, I do really believe that," I tell him. "I wouldn't
work in the law if I didn't."

"But you know what, Jen?"

"What?"

"I think your ex-boyfriend had it wrong. I don't think the past is a
foreign country. I think the future is a foreign country. Because we don't
know what's going to happen. It's totally new."

His one-upmanship makes me smile. I don't bother explaining to
him that the quote did not belong to my ex-boyfriend.

I think about this. "I guess that's true, too," I finally say. "Maybe the
future could be a new country that you are moving to. And all of this
can just be what you leave behind."

He is satisfied by this answer. He nods in agreement, and we return
to discussing the sentencing guidelines.

My walk down memory lane is over. I have caught my breath. As I
ready myself to run home, I turn around for a moment. For good mea-

sure, I walk to the end of the block. And then, with MCC at my back, I begin running.

W hen I reach the end of my run, daylight is disappearing. Wanting to savor every moment before darkness falls, I stand along the river's edge. I observe the surrounding wreckage with renewed optimism. The damage is extensive, the park grounds will have to be completely cleared. But once the fallen trees and orphaned branches have been removed, once the broken benches and trash cans are replaced, there will be an opportunity to build something new. Maybe even something better.

I walk back to my apartment and find the same security guard sitting in the lobby, still reading her magazine. She glances up at me for a split second and returns to its contents.

"You made it," she says with disinterest.

"I did," I say.

I wait for a moment to see if she might look up. She doesn't. I retrieve the flashlight from my mailbox. Then I begin the long climb home.

ACKNOWLEDGMENTS

For all of their talent and hard work in helping to bring this book together, I give great thanks to Kathy Anderson, Brian Belfiglio, Ilsa Brink, Caitlin Dohrenwend, Diana Jiminez, Mark Melnick, Emily Reimer, Mike Ricca, Lisa Rivlin, Katie Rizzo, Isabelle Selby, Elizabeth Serrano, Gwyneth Stansfield, Kate Watson, and Shannon Welch. I am particularly grateful to Katrina Diaz at Scribner for such careful and considered editorial assistance, to Terra Chalberg for gracious support and guidance, and to my amazing agent, Rachel Sussman, for absolutely everything.

I am profoundly thankful to Shaina Oliphant for unwavering loyalty and support, both in the creation of this project and in the unfortunate events underlying it. Her good humor and spirit have gotten me through many a difficult day, and her love has taught me what friendship truly means. Special thanks, too, to Sebastian Moultrie for all-around goodness and sweetness to his aunt Jen.

I will forever be grateful to my parents, who somehow managed to provide their love and support even when the things I've done have been mostly incomprehensible to them, including, I should add, writing it all down here. ("If anyone asks," my mother recently told me, "I am just going to tell them that I didn't even know you wrote a book.") I can't help but love them terribly, and I have come to see that it was only by abandoning the lessons they spent a lifetime teaching me that I was able to stray so far, and it has only been by adhering to the values that they instilled in me that I have been able to bring myself back.

In this book and in life, I am always thankful for the works of Michel

Foucault, a self-described "delinquent" whose books have greatly enriched my thinking on matters of crime and punishment. Most of the philosophical meanderings contained in this book can be traced to one extent or another to his writings, in particular *Discipline and Punish* (1977), "Governmentality" (in *The Foucault Effect*, 1991), and *Wrong-Doing, Truth-Telling* (2014).

Finally, my deepest gratitude goes to my editor, Colin Harrison. Working with him on this project has been one of the most meaningful experiences of my life, and I feel blessed every day to have had this opportunity. By never settling for the surface, by always pushing me toward the truth with a capital "T," Colin has made this a better book and me a better writer and, quite possibly, a better person. It isn't a moment too soon.

ABOUT THE AUTHOR

A graduate of Columbia Law School, Jennifer Ridha has at various times in her life been a lawyer, a law professor, and a criminal defendant in the United States District Court for the Southern District of New York. She is pursuing a doctoral degree in legal anthropology, urban studies, and criminal justice. *Criminal That I Am* is her first book. Visit her website at www.jenniferridha.com.